PREAMBLE

This White Paper sets out to foster debate and to assist decision-making — at decentralized, national or Community level — so as to lay the foundations for sustainable development of the European economies, thereby enabling them to withstand international competition while creating the millions of jobs that are needed.

We are convinced that the European economies have a future. Looking at the traditional bases of prosperity and competitiveness, Europe has preserved its chances. It possesses assets which it has only to exploit — assets such as its abundant non-physical capital (education, skills, capacity for innovation, traditions), the availability of financial capital and highly efficient banking institutions, the soundness of its social model, and the virtues of cooperation between the two sides of industry.

Given the scale of the needs that have to be met, both in the European Union and elsewhere in the world, recovery must be achieved by developing work and employment and not by endorsing basically Malthusian solutions. Yes, we can create jobs, and we must do so if we want to safeguard the future — the future of our children, who must be able to find hope and motivation in the prospect of participating in economic and social activity and of being involved in the society in which they live, and the future of our social protection systems, which are threatened in the short term by inadequate growth and in the long term by the deterioration in the ratio of the people in jobs to those not in employment.

In other words, we are faced with the immense responsibility, while remaining faithful to the ideals which have come to characterize and represent Europe, of finding a new synthesis of the aims pursued by society (work as a factor of social integration, equality of opportunity) and the requirements of the economy (competitiveness and job creation).

This major challenge confronts us all. That is why we are arguing, first and foremost, the need to press on with building a unified Europe which will increase our strength through cooperation and through the benefits of a large area without frontiers of any kind. That is why we are calling on everyone — and not only political decision-makers and business leaders — to contribute to the combined effort by seeking to understand the new world and by participating in the joint endeavour.

Nothing would be more dangerous than for Europe to maintain structures and customs which foster resignation, refusal of commitment and passivity. Revival requires a society driven by citizens who are aware of their own responsibilites and imbued with a spirit of solidarity towards those with whom they form local and national communities — communities that are so rich in history and in their common feeling of belonging.

The contribution which the European Union can make is therefore to assist this movement, which reconciles our historical loyalties with our wish to take our place in this new world that is now emerging.

3

CONTENTS

PART A

White Paper

The challenges and ways forward into the 21st century

Why this White Paper?

The one and only reason is unemployment. We are aware of its scale, and of its consequences too. The difficult thing, as experience has taught us, is knowing how to tackle it.

The Copenhagen European Council in June invited the European Commission to present a White Paper on a medium-term strategy for growth, competitiveness and employment. That decision followed an in-depth discussion between the Heads of State or Government based on an analysis by the President of the Commission of the weaknesses of the European economies.

The White Paper draws in large part on the contributions from the Member States. It has also been guided by the discussions — often beset by conflict — under way in our countries between governments and social partners (employers' and trade union organizations).

The European Commission is aware of the difficulty of the task. For if the solutions already existed, our countries would surely have applied them; if there were a miracle cure, it would not have gone unnoticed. With national situations being so different, any proposal has to be presented with sensitivity and caution. That being so, the Commission does share the view, expressed by many Member States, that joint responses would strengthen the hand of each player, and therefore of the European Union.

There is no miracle cure

- **Neither protectionism,** which would be suicidal for the European Union, the world's largest trading power, and would run counter to its proclaimed objectives, in particular that of encouraging the economies of the poorest countries to take off;

- **nor a dash for economic freedom:** turning on the tap of government spending and creating money can, like a narcotic, produce a short-lived illusion of well-being. But the return to reality would be all the more painful when we had to repair the damage wreaked by inflation and external imbalances. The worst damage would be higher unemployment;

- **nor a generalized reduction in working hours and job-sharing at national level:** this would result in a slowing-down of production due to the difficulty of striking the right balances between the demand for skilled workers, the optimum utilization of plant and the supply of labour;

- **nor a drastic cut in wages to align our costs on those of our competitors in the developing countries:** socially unacceptable and politically untenable, such an approach would only worsen the crisis by depressing domestic demand, which also contributes to growth and the maintenance of employment.

How has it come to this?

We will not dwell here on the analysis presented in Copenhagen. This has been confirmed and fleshed out by the national contributions and the Commission's research: competitiveness, growth and employment are closely interrelated, and have been for some time.

Over the last 20 years

- the European economy's potential rate of growth has shrunk (from around 4% to around 2.5% a year);

- unemployment has been steadily rising from cycle to cycle;

- the investment ratio has fallen by five percentage points;

- our competitive position in relation to the USA and Japan has worsened as regards:

  employment,
  our shares of export markets,
  R&D and innovation and its incorporation into goods brought to the market,
  the development of new products.

And yet the Community over the past few years enjoyed what all observers agree was a period of growth and restructuring prompted by the 1992 objective. That objective was not an illusion: it swiftly received broad support from all sections of society, and the structural changes it generated account for many of the nine million jobs created between 1986 and 1990.

The 1992 objective: A tangible reality

- Nine million jobs created between 1986 and 1990;
- One half of a percentage point extra growth each year;
- A 3% saving on the costs of international transport;
- Investment up by one third between 1985 and 1990;
- Three times more company mergers and acquisitions in the Community over the period in question;
- Twice the number of European companies involved in mergers and acquisitions in the rest of the world;
- A doubling of trade in the Community in sectors previously regarded as sheltered from competition;
- 70 million customs documents done away with.

This integration process is not yet complete since certain sectors are being only gradually opened up to competition; it does, however, amply demonstrate that Europe has been capable of anticipating developments, creating a stimulus and responding to it.

How, then, can we explain the fact that all these achievements have not made it possible at least to cushion the effects of the world recession? Was the single market process merely a flash in the pan?

The truth is that although we have changed, the rest of the world has changed even faster.

The present crisis can be understood only in the light of the universality of the trends which have been shaping the global economy and their acceleration since the end of the 1970s.

Changes in the décor

In geopolitical terms

- new competitors have emerged and have shown their ability to incorporate the latest technical progress;
- the end of communism has opened up new potential for economic growth: 120 million people in neighbouring countries with a standard of living well below our own. But we have not been able to harness this for a new dynamism;

In demographic terms

- the ageing of the population and the transformation of family structures;

In technological terms

- the new industrial revolution is well under way and is causing rapid and far-reaching changes in technologies, jobs and skills;
- the economy is becoming increasingly knowledge-based, manufacturing activities are being farmed out, services are taking the lion's share, and the possession and transmission of information is becoming crucial to success;

In financial terms

- the interdependence of markets resulting from the freedom of capital movements together with new technology is an inescapable fact of life for all economic and financial operators.

The heart of the problem: The three types of unemployment

Since the beginning of the 1970s, unemployment in the Community has risen steadily except during the second half of the 1980s. Today 17 million people are out of work. Over the last 20 years, 80% more wealth has been created but total employment has risen by only 9%. To explain this, a distinction must be drawn between the three different forms of unemployment:

Cyclical unemployment

In a context in which labour resources are increasing by some 0.50% a year, any slackening in growth immediately triggers a sharp rise in unemployment. This is particularly so at present when, for the first time since 1975, Europe has experienced a slowdown in economic activity.

Structural unemployment

At the end of the 1980s, when the economy was going strong, unemployment still stood at 12 million.

The explanations for this rigidity of unemployment are now clear:

- The role we have come to play in the new international division of labour has not been an optimum one because we have neglected future growth sectors in concentrating too much on the rents and positions established in traditional industries.

- The relatively high cost of unskilled labour is speeding up the rationalization of investment and holding back job creation in services. This has resulted in the loss of millions of jobs.

- Our employment environment has aged: by this term we mean the whole complex of issues made up nowadays by the labour market and employment policy, the possibilities of flexibility within or outside enterprises, the opportunities provided or not provided by the education and training systems, and social protection.

- Finally and more especially, the countries of the south are stirring and competing with us — even on our own markets — at cost levels which we simply cannot match.

Technological unemployment

This problem is as old as industrial society itself, which has continually changed — albeit not always smoothly — by incorporating technical progress. Nevertheless, the phenomenon now seems to be undergoing a change of scale. This is not to say that technological progress in enterprises is doing away with more jobs than it is creating: for example, the employment situation is on average more favourable in those firms that have introduced microelectronics than in those that have not done so.

It is nevertheless the case that we are once again passing through a period in which a gap is opening up between the speed of technical progress, which is concerned primarily with how to produce (manufacturing processes and work organization) and which therefore often destroys jobs, and our capacity to think up new individual or collective needs which would provide new job opportunities.

And yet technical progress is presenting opportunities for growth and employment, on condition that we alter our development model, meet the needs stemming from the upheavals in social life and urban civilization, preserve our rural areas, and improve the environment and the quality of our natural assets. In so doing, we will pave the ways for our entry into the 21st century.

Ways forward into the 21st century

In order to reverse the disastrous course which our societies, bedevilled by unemployment, are taking, the European Union should set itself the target of creating 15 million jobs by the end of the century.

It is the economy which can provide the necessary pointers to a reappraisal of principles inherited from an age in which manpower resources were scarce, technological innovation was made possible through imitation, and natural resources could be exploited at will. We are thus setting out a number of broad guidelines which have a predominantly economic basis, although it will be seen that they cannot be dissociated from the major trends which are affecting society itself: an economy that is healthy, open, decentralized, competitive and based on solidarity. However, these efforts would be in vain if we did not once again make employment policy the centre-piece of our overall strategy.

A healthy economy

The people of Europe need stability. The false prophets of inflation and of a return to exchange-rate variability represent special interests. Their bad money still threatens to oust the good.

The White Paper is, accordingly, consistent with the guidelines submitted to the European Council, in accordance with the new Treaty (Article 103), to mark the beginning of the second stage of European economic union, which must be successful if a single currency is to be achieved. We must therefore place our thinking within a **macroeconomic reference framework** for both economic and monetary convergence which will increase the opportunities available to our economies.

This strategy could be applied in two phases, the first consisting of pulling out of the current recession as quickly as possible and the second from the mid-1990s consisting of returning to a path of strong and healthy growth. The macroeconomic policies to be implemented for these two phases are set on similar courses but have different points of emphasis.

The gradual reduction in public deficits is necessary during the initial phase in order to bring indebtedness under control and to continue to increase public saving during the second phase. This will call for increased efforts to restructure spending — and in particular to curb operating expenditure — in favour of public resources allocated to tangible and intangible investment and to an active employment policy.

Stable monetary policies consistent with the aim of low inflation will be a constant benchmark throughout the period. They would lead to further interest-rate cuts that would make more attractive the **investment** essential to the modernization and competitiveness of our economies. Investment in infrastructures, housing and environmental improvement projects would thus be given a particular boost.

Finally, the **trends of all categories of income** should be made consistent with the objectives of monetary stability and cost moderation. During the first phase, the task would be to avert an acceleration which would frustrate the reduction of interest rates in

the long term; during the second, it would be necessary to guarantee an adequate rate of return to permit an increase in the investment ratio and hence in growth.

Growth Path compared
(average % change per year)

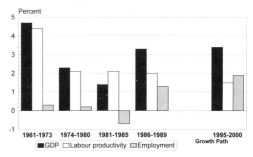

An open economy

Only properly managed interdependence can guarantee a positive outcome for everybody.

Each of the major bursts of growth in the European economies started with a qualitative leap in international trade. The most spectacular contribution probably came from the establishment of the multilateral trading system resulting from the Bretton Woods agreements after the Second World War.

Today we are perhaps seeing the beginnings of an equally important leap forward with the very rapid integration into world trade of developing countries and former communist countries.

Where is the Growth?
(Percentage of world output)

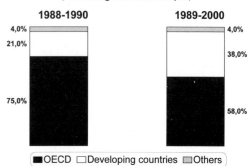

The Community must be open and prepare itself for this prospect. This is why the conclusion of the Uruguay Round negotiations is of such importance for it too. For the first time, these negotiations will produce a global agreement between industrialized and developing countries containing balanced concessions aimed at fair access to all markets.

Among the issues in these negotiations, the transformation of GATT into a fully fledged international institution designated a 'multilateral trade organization' would guarantee a sustainable and harmonious development of international trade. The Community is attached to this idea: it regards it as the means of ensuring that GATT has the authority to stand up to hegemony, and to address other issues where the existence of multilateral rules would be invaluable. There is indeed a need to ensure better consistency between the various bodies responsible for fostering healthy competition and between the international institutions responsible for monetary or other relations, to deal with the inequality of the conditions for **direct investment,** and to guarantee a fair sharing-out of burdens in the area of environmental protection.

The strengthening of the multilateral trading system, its effective application and the transparency of its rules are, for the Community, the best guarantee of success with its own effort to adjust. This is part and parcel of the goal of achieving coherent world management of the problems posed by development inequalities and the concentration of poverty in certain regions.

The European Union must first demonstrate this openness of mind and recognition of the unavoidable globalization of the economy to its eastern and southern neighbours. Enormous potential exists, but it requires us to invest massively, to transfer a considerable volume of know-how and to open up our markets more widely. If all of these countries manage to pursue reasonable policies of adjustment and modernization, they will fully benefit from our action and return those benefits to us in the form of new markets and, consequently, new jobs.

Decentralized economy

The market economy has a decentralizing effect. This was the reasoning behind the 'single market' project (Objective 92). Its aim was not only to achieve economies of scale but also to set free the dynamism and the creativity inherent in competition.

Decentralization now also reflects a radical change in the organization of our societies, which are all confronted with the growing complexity of economic and social phenomena and the legislative or regulatory framework.

Hence the growing importance of the local level at which all the ingredients of political action blend together most successfully.

The information society

● The dawning of a multimedia world (sound — text — image) represents a radical change comparable with the first industrial revolution;

● Tomorrow's world is already with us: by the end of the century there will be 10 times as many TV channels and three times the number of subscribers to cable networks. In the USA it is estimated that six million people are already involved in teleworking;

● The USA has already taken the lead: 200 of its biggest companies already use information highways;

● At the heart of the development model for the 21st century, this issue is a crucial aspect in the survival or decline of Europe;

● It can provide an answer to the new needs of European societies: communication networks within companies; widespread teleworking; widespread access to scientific and leisure databases; development of preventive health care and home medicine for the elderly.

Hence also the decentralization movement affecting the business world. SMEs are often cited as models because they embody operational flexibility and a capacity for integration which the units which make up the big companies are now trying to imitate. Hierarchical and linear empires are gradually giving way to interactive organizations.

This movement towards decentralization, supported by the new technologies, is taking us towards a veritable information society. The corollary to decentralization is information sharing and communication.

The European dimension would give the information society the best possible chances of taking off. The Commission is therefore proposing, in the context of a partnership between the public sector and the private sector, to accelerate the establishment of 'information highways' (broadband networks) and develop the corresponding services and applications (see Development theme I).

A more competitive economy

Drawing maximum benefit from the single market

While industrial policy continues to be controversial no one is in any doubt as to the responsibility of governments and of the Community to create as favourable an environment as possible for company competitiveness. Compliance with the competition rules is an important element. It helps to ensure that the single market is a living reality. However, where companies are concerned, progress is needed in three areas.

The first concerns the body of rules (laws, regulations, standards, certification processes) which assure the smooth functioning of the market. The rules have to be supplemented in line with the initial target (whether they concern intellectual property or company law, for example). It must also be simplified and alleviated. But, above all, how it then develops has to be guaranteed against the risk of inconsistency between national and Community laws. This means fresh cooperation between governments at the legislative drafting stage. Likewise, care should be taken to ensure that the Community legislation affecting companies is consistent, especially the environmental legislation.

The second condition revolves around **small and medium-sized enterprises.** While they are a model of flexibility for big companies, they are also increasingly a factor of competitiveness as a result of 'farming-out' and subcontracting. Hence the measures taken on the initiative of big companies to galvanize their suppliers and clients. How-

ever, the 'demography' of SMEs, i.e. their birth, growth and regeneration, is also a matter of national policy. In some countries it will be necessary to adapt their tax systems, rights of succession and access to equity and to simplify intercompany credit regulations and practices. While most of the work has to be done at national level, the Community, for its part, must help to fit SMEs into the dynamics of the single market. The immediate task, therefore, is to work towards simplification and information. An initiative will shortly be proposed in this connection.

The third condition concerns the accelerated establishment of trans-European infrastructure networks (see Development Theme II).

The trans-European infrastructure

Why?

● Better, safer travel at lower cost;

● Effective planning in Europe;

● Bridge-building towards Eastern Europe.

How?

● Remove regulatory and financial obstacles;

● Get private investors involved in projects of European interest (applying the provisions of the Treaty, 'declaration of European interest');

● Identify projects on the basis of the master plans adopted (transport) or in preparation (energy).

In order to establish these networks, promote the information society, and develop new environmental improvement projects, the Commission proposes to accelerate the administrative procedures, act as a catalyst, to use the existing financial instruments and to supplement them through recourse to saving as indicated in the Annex.

Stepping up the research effort and cooperation

Without eschewing competition, the ability to cooperate and share risks is increasingly becoming a sign of creativity. Our laws, our tax systems and our programmes have to be adapted as a result, both at national and at European level. Community competition policy has thus made broad allowance for these new forms of intercompany cooperation.

As part of an increase in the overall research effort, cooperation between the different countries' research policies and between companies will be encouraged. This cooperation will gradually become a basic principle and not just one 'aspect' of Community research and development policy. This principle will help to identify major priorities and to promote meetings between operators and especially between producers and users concerning important issues of common interest, this being the only guarantee that market potential is taken into account when defining **research priorities.**

The Commission will propose to the Member States that this new approach should be followed for a limited number of major joint projects geared to the following:

- **New information technologies,** the importance of which has already been emphasized.

- **Biotechnology,** where the early use of research resources will make for greater synergy between chemical companies and the big potential users in the health and agri-foodstuffs sectors.

- **Ecotechnologies,** meaning radical innovations targeting the causes of pollution and aiming at environmental efficiency throughout the production cycle. Ecotechnologies will soon provide a major competitive advantage.

An economy characterized by solidarity

These options show how the dynamism of the market can help boost growth.

Experience has also shown, however, that the market is not without its failings. it tends to underestimate what is at stake in the long term, the speed of the changes it creates affects the different social categories unequally, and it spontaneously promotes concentration, thereby creating inequality between the regions and the towns. Awareness of these insufficiencies has led our

countries to develop **collective solidarity mechanisms.** At Community level the Single European Act has helped to restore the balance in the development of the single market by way of joint flanking policies as part of economic and social cohesion.

However, the social welfare system is now being re-examined in many Member States to reduce costs through greater responsibility. The new model of European society calls for less passive and more active solidarity.

Solidarity, first of all, between those who have jobs and those who do not. This key concept has not figured at all in the collective discussions and negotiations of the last 10 years. That is why we are proposing a sort of European social pact, the principle of which is quite simple but whose detailed arrangements would be adapted to the specific circumstances of each country and each business; in the spirit of a decentralized economy and of subsidiarity, new gains in productivity would essentially be applied to forward-looking investments and to the creation of jobs.

Solidarity between men and women making it easier to reconcile family life and working life and ensuring that greater account is taken of the role of women in the development of human resources (social services, working hours, diversified training).

Solidarity also between generations, with an eye to the repercussions of a demographic trend which will see falling numbers of persons of adult working age. It is absolutely essential that all decisions taken today take account of this demographic dimension. That is why we must not only tackle unemployment, which is jeopardizing all our social security systems, but also expand, and not reduce, the volume of work which generates wealth and so finances solidarity.

Solidarity, once again, between the more prosperous regions and the poor or struggling regions. Hence the conformation of economic and social cohesion as an essential pillar of European construction.

Solidarity, lastly and most importantly, in the fight against social exclusion. If only one proof were needed that our economies have not yet reached maturity and that there are still needs to be met it would be the existence in Europe of some 50 million people below the poverty line. This is a matter for the Member States, but it is also the business of each citizen to practice 'neighbourly solidarity'. We need a comprehensive policy, preventive as well as remedial, to combat the poverty which so degrades men and women and splits society in two. The areas of action are familiar: renovation of stricken urban areas, construction of subsidized housing, adaptation of education systems with extra resources for children from disadvantaged backgrounds, and an active employment policy which attaches high priority to the search for an activity or training accessible to everyone rather than the registration of and payment to the unemployed, even though, in the last resort, this is still essential where all other means of social reinsertion seem, for the moment, to be exhausted.

Action on jobs

As we have seen, the Community has failed to match the substantial increase in generated wealth with parallel improvements in job opportunities. Looked at more closely, however, the performances of individual States differ quite considerably. For instance, Germany and Spain have enjoyed a comparable rate of growth over the last 15 years of around 2.3%, yet their average levels of unemployment are 6 and 16% respectively. Over the same period, meanwhile, the United Kingdom, France, Belgium and Italy have all had an unemployment rate of around 9% of the active population, but with growth rates ranging from 1.8 to 2.5% on average. These disparities tell us a lot.

In a general manner, they show that growth is not in itself the solution to unemployment, that vigorous action is needed to create jobs. However, such action must take account of national circumstances. More specifically, the inflexibility of the labour market, which is responsible for a large part of Europe's structural unemployment, can be traced back to specific institutional, legal and contractual circumstances in each country. **The educational system, labour laws, work contracts, contractual negotiation systems and the social security system form the pillars of the various 'national employ-**

ment environment' and combine to give each of them a distinctive appearance. In each case, the entire system must be mobilized to improve the functioning of the labour market. This goes to show, once again, that there is no miracle solution; nothing short of coordinated action by the various players responsible for the components of these systems can effect the necessary transformation. Moreover, in each country the methods of social dialogue will reflect national traditions.

Priorities for action on jobs

- lifelong education and training;
- greater flexibility in businesses, both internally and externally;
- greater expectations from decentralization and initiative;
- reduction in the relative cost of low-qualified work;
- thorough overhaul of employment policies;
- efforts to meet new needs.

Investment in education and training: Knowledge and know-how throughout life

Our countries' education systems are faced with major difficulties, and not only of a budgetary nature. These problems are rooted in social ills: the breakdown of the family and the demotivation bred by unemployment. They also reflect a change in the very nature of what is being taught. Preparation for life in tomorrow's world cannot be satisfied by a once-and-for-all acquisition of knowledge and know-how. Every bit as essential is the ability to learn, to communicate, to work in a group and to assess one's own situation. On the other hand, if tomorrow's trades require the ability to make diagnoses and propose improvements at all levels, the autonomy, independence of spirit and analytical ability which come of knowledge will once again be indispensable.

Lifelong education is therefore the overall objective to which the national educational communities can make their own contributions. Difficult choices will have to be made, between increasing university capacity or quality, between higher education and vocational paths. However, each country should be aiming towards universally accessible advanced vocational training.

As is shown by the Member States' contributions, principles and methods of financing may differ. In some cases, the emphasis is on equal opportunities for all individuals and the proposed response is the provision of training capital or cheques financed by the redistribution of public resources. In other cases, advanced vocational training is linked to businesses and so contractual mechanisms will be proposed for training investment or for co-investment with the participation of wage-earners. In any event, public and private efforts must be married to create the basis in each Member State for a **genuine right to ongoing training.** This should be a key area of social dialogue at European level. A start has in fact already been made. To enhance this right, the Community will have to facilitate cooperation between the Member States with a view to creating a genuine European area for vocational qualifications.

The need for double flexibility — both internal and external — in labour markets

Generally speaking, the flexibility of the labour market has deteriorated under the effects of an accretion of partial measures designed to reduce registered unemployment. All of these measures now need to be re-examined by all the players with a view to removing obstacles to employment.

The question of labour flexibility needs to be examined from two angles: that of the external labour market, where supply meets demand, and that of the market internal to each business, i.e. the human resources at its disposal which it adjusts according to its needs.

Improving **external flexibility** means making it possible for more unemployed persons to meet the identified requirements of businesses. The first step here is to improve geographical mobility. This could be encouraged by injecting new impetus into the accommodation market and, in particular, by removing obstacles to the construction of rented accommodation.

The provision of a framework for exercising the right to advanced vocational training has already been mentioned. This is a major pillar of flexibility, which also calls for initiatives, sometimes radical, from the two sides of industry in cooperation with the public authorities:

- In certain countries of the north of Europe the campaign against undeclared work involves reducing certain unemployment benefits and cutting direct taxation on low incomes. However, unemployment benefits can only be reduced so far before the poverty line is reached;

- In several southern countries, the laws on the conditions under which workers on unlimited contracts may be laid off need to be made more flexible, with greater assistance being given to the unemployed and with less recourse to precarious forms of employment;

- In many countries, in both north and south, labour compartmentalization is detrimental both to the mobility of the active population and to the retraining of the unemployed. Bridging access needs to be established through collective negotiation;

- In general, the adjustment of income guarantee mechanisms needs to be combined with active placement policies.

Internal flexibility is the result of optimum management of a company's human resources. The aim is to adjust the workforce without making people redundant wherever this can be avoided. Focusing on the continuity of the link between the company and the worker, it maximizes the investment in human resources and staff involvement. It is up to individual companies to improve internal flexibility by means of staff versatility, the integrated organization of work, flexible working hours, and performance-related pay. Tailored to the European company model, it should be central to negotiations within the company.

17

The virtues of decentralization and initiative

The optimum operation of the labour market calls for a large degree of decentralization within 'employment areas'. In return, the national authorities should focus on the quality of training and the homogeneity of qualifications. The successful experience of several Member States shows the importance of effective participation of the social partners in the decentralized management of employment areas.

Likewise, it is only by a decentralized approach, i.e. at company level, that adjustments to working hours can lead to improved competitiveness, and thereby encourage job creation and job retention.

Thus we can see how at Volkswagen imaginative negotiations based on a four-day week have led to a sensible, socially responsible form of part-time working. More flexible retirement schemes, more diversified working years, and greater provision for part-time working correspond in many situations to the wishes of salaried staff and the interest of undertakings which are concerned to make better use of their capital. Very often, such 'downward' adjustments in working hours are blocked by inflexible practices which standardize the working week in Europe at between 37 and 39 hours. To remove these obstacles, it is necessary, on the basis of the specific provisions of each country, to review labour legislation (role of legislation on working hours) and contractual practices (overtime pay), and in many cases simplify the way in which pension rights are calculated.

Reducing the relative cost of unskilled and semi-skilled labour

The problem of social security contributions has to be seen in the broader context described in Part B of this document (Chapter 9). In most countries of the Union, labour costs have to bear the heavy burden of statutory charges. It should be remembered that between 1970 and 1991 they rose from 34% to 40% of GDP whereas, for example, they remained stable in the United States, at below 30%. Are we not to see this as a cause of the economic slowdown and especially of the increase in unemployment?

To return to unskilled and semi-skilled labour, which is very closely linked to long-term unemployment, it should be noted that, in eight out of the twelve countries of the European Union, social security contributions are relatively more onerous on low incomes. These countries suffer the most from what is one of the most severe structural causes of unemployment and undeclared employment in the Community.

Studies have been carried out in several countries with very high levels of security contributions. These studies show that a reduction of 30 to 40% in social security contributions for low-paid workers would increase employment by 2%. In other countries, the possibility of replacing existing forms of income guarantee payments with a system of negative tax deserves close attention.

For most countries of the Union, it is essential to reduce the non-wage costs of unskilled and semi-skilled labour by an amount equivalent to 1 or 2 points of GNP by the year 2000. The improvement in tax revenue resulting from this measure would offset the cost by up to 30%. The remainder should be financed by savings or other revenue. Irrespective of its intrinsic merits, the CO_2/energy tax proposed by the Commission is one of the best ways of offsetting reductions in the cost of employment. Homogeneous taxation at source of investment income as proposed by the Commission since 1989 would be another possibility.

A full-scale overhaul of employment policy

Investing in human resources is not the task of business alone. It is also the task of government. It is no longer possible to leave masses of unemployed people in Europe unoccupied. Such is, however, the structure of government spending on unemployment: roughly two thirds of public expenditure on the unemployed goes on assistance and the remainder on 'active measures'.

Employers' Social Contributions
(Comparison at different wage levels)

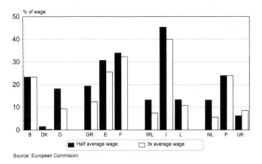

Source: European Commision.

A complete reversal of attitude is required, the aim being to prevent long-term unemployment. On the one hand, the unemployed should be offered, according to how long they have been unemployed, first training leading to meaningful qualifications, then the possibility of working, possibly in the public sector, for a number of months. In exchange, unemployed people who are thus given real assistance in returning to employment would make a personal investment in this training and employment. This, too, is a question of a social dialogue in which the unemployed should themselves be involved.

Such a substantial change would require a considerable increase in public employment services, the objective being for every unemployed person to be monitored personally by the same employment adviser. The job of the employment service would become more diversified but comprise three main tasks: provision of information, job placement and support.

Contrary to popular opinion, such an overhaul of employment policy would not be prohibitively expensive. For example, it has been calculated that the cost of tripling operational expenditure on the public employment services in the countries of the Union would mean an increase from 0.17 to 0.5% of GNP. Spread over a period of three years, the corresponding expenditure would be almost entirely offset by the fall in unemployment, estimated at 100 000 in the first year, 400 000 in the second year, and a million in the third year.

Bringing the long-term unemployed — those who have been unemployed for more than 12 months — back into employment is a difficult but not impossible task; this is demonstrated by the success of initiatives in several countries aimed at creating a real route back into employment for such people. These initiatives should be generalized, in cooperation with various associations and the local authorities.

Finally, active employment policy should cross a new threshold in promoting youth employment. Anyone who leaves the school system before the age of 18 without acquiring a meaningful vocational certificate should be guaranteed a 'Youthstart'. It is proposed that a scheme should be progressively established at national level which will give everyone access to a recognized form of training, whether or not accompanied by employment experience. Moreover, at Community level, 'European Union civilian voluntary service' could be introduced, comprising a training element and public utility work in another Member State of the Union, to be financed by European Social Fund pilot initiatives. This initiative could back up the 'Youthstart' arrangements.

Dealing with new needs

Many needs are still waiting to be satisfied. They correspond to changes in lifestyles, the transformation of family structures, the increase in the number of working women, and the new aspirations of the elderly and of very old people. They also stem from the need to repair damage to the environment and to renovate the most disadvantaged urban areas.

Sources of new jobs: Examples

The scope for job creation depends largely on the existing structures and services in each country, lifestyles, and tax rules.

However, several estimates agree that some three million new jobs could be created in the Community, covering local services, improvements in the quality of life and environmental protection.

Local services

- Home help for the elderly and handicapped, health care, meal preparation and housework;

- Minding pre-school-age children and schoolchildren before and after school, including taking them to and from school;

- Assistance to young people facing difficulties, comprising help with schoolwork, provision of leisure facilities, especially sports, and support for the most disadvantaged;

- Security in blocks of flats;

- Local shops kept in business in rural areas, and also in outlying suburban areas.

Audiovisual

Provision of leisure and cultural facilities

Improvements in the quality of life

- Renovation of rundown areas and old housing with a view to increasing comfort (installation of bathrooms and noise insulation) and safety;

- Development of local public transport services, which should be made more comfortable, more frequent, accessible (to the handicapped) and safe, and the provision of new services such as shared taxis in rural areas.

Environmental protection

- Maintenance of natural areas and public areas (local waste recycling);

- Water purification and the cleaning-up of polluted areas;

- Monitoring of quality standards;

- Energy-saving equipment, particularly in housing.

The objection will be voiced that if such needs exist, the market should rapidly provide for them. In fact, the development of both the supply of and demand for such new services comes up against barriers:

- on the demand side there is the problem of price, already referred to in connection with the costs of employment;

- on the supply side there is reticence to take jobs which are perceived as being degrading, because they are often synonymous with domestic service and unskilled or semi-skilled work.

As a result, the development of the services in question is either left to the undeclared employment market, or is publicly funded, which is expensive. A new initiative could stimulate both demand and supply, thus creating a 'continuum' of possibilities ranging from supply totally protected by public subsidies to totally competitive supply. Thus a new 'social economy' would be born, benefiting:

- on the demand side, from incentives such as income tax deductibility, or the local issuing of 'vouchers' along the lines of luncheon vouchers, issued instead of providing the social services normally provided by employers and local authorities, which can be exchanged for local services ('service vouchers');

- on the supply side, from traditional subsidies for the setting-up of undertakings, which could be increased in cases where a 'social employer' undertakes to employ formerly unemployed people. Specific training would be provided to develop the skills needed for these new professions.

In order to be compatible with budgetary constraints, this balance will have to take different forms in different countries.

Call for action

The analyses out in this document and the possible solutions identified should guide us towards a sustainable development model, both from the viewpoint of the effectiveness of the triangular relationship growth-competitiveness-employment and as regards the environment and the improvement in the quality of life.

The effort to be made calls for adaptations in behaviour and policies at all levels: the Community level, the national level, and the local level. Since we are aware of the differing situations in Member States, we deemed it preferable not to formulate the possible solutions in unduly concise terms. It will be for each Member State to take from the document the elements it regards as making a positive contribution to its own action.

Nevertheless, in the Commission's view, the individual chapters of Part B should provide the basis for work in the various specialized meetings of the Council of Ministers. If conclusion along these lines were reached at the forthcoming European Council meeting, this would facilitate and actually set in motion the mobilization of the Community institutions in the pursuit of the objectives set.

As for Community action proper, it is proposed to impart a new impetus or give a new form, but only in accordance with five priorities:

● Making the most of the single market;

● Supporting the development and adaptation of small and medium-sized enterprises;

● Pursuing the social dialogue that has, to date, made for fruitful cooperation and joint decision-making by the two sides of industry, thereby assisting the work of the Community;

● Creating the major European infrastructure networks;

● Preparing forthwith and laying the foundations for the information society.

These last two priorities hold the key to enhanced competitiveness and will enable us to exploit technical progress in the interests of employment and an improvement in living conditions.

It needs to be stressed that the implementation of these two priorities in no way calls into question the financial decisions taken as part of Package II by the Edinburgh European Council. There is, therefore, no need to review the ceilings on resources.

Recourse to saving is the only other source of financing. It would be modest in magnitude since the borrowings envisaged would account for less than 2% of total market issues.

For the rest, what we are advocating is not only economically indispensable but also financially viable and hence carries no risk of adding to national public deficits.

Through these forward-looking measures, the Community will lay the foundations for sound and lasting economic growth the benefits of which will far outweigh the cost of raising the funds required.

As a parallel development, and this is also one of the far-reaching changes made to our growth model, the new-found consistency between macroeconomic policy and an active employment policy will eliminate all the behavioural or structural rigidities that are partly to blame for the underemployment with which we are having to contend. It will then be possible to satisfy the numerous needs that have not yet been met as well as those to which the changes both in the organization of our societies and in the organization and sharing-out of work will give rise.

The Commission thus calls on everyone to conduct a lucid analysis of our strengths and weaknesses and to adapt behaviour to the rapid changes taking place in today's world, setting our sights and focusing our determination on what the future holds.

Development theme I

Information networks

1. Why?

> Throughout the world, production systems, methods of organizing work and consumption patterns are undergoing changes which will have long-term effects comparable with the first industrial revolution.

This is the result of the development of information and communications technologies. Digital technologies, in particular, have made it possible to combine transmission of information, sound text and images in a single high-performance system.

> The dawn of the 'multimedia' world

This will have far-reaching effects on production structures and methods. It will spell changes in the way companies are organized, in managers' responsibilities and in relations with workers. Small businesses will benefit most: the new communication services will enable them to make savings of, on average, 4% of their turnover; they will also be very much in evidence on the major markets opening up. Working conditions will be transformed by the greater flexibility possible with regard to working hours, the place of work itself (teleworking) and, inevitably, terms of contract and pay systems. According to some estimates, six million Americans already work at home. New data transmission systems will enable companies to globalize their activities and strategies, forging forms of partnership and cooperation on a scale never possible before.

> The change will also affect consumption patterns.

The need for physical mobility will be reduced by the availability of products and services combining the advantages of mass production with consumers' specific, and even individual, requirements. A new, far richer range of novel services in the form of information, access to databases, audiovisual, cultural and leisure facilities will be opened up to everyone. More specifically, it will be possible to gain access to general information directly, without any complicated technology, via a portable computer connected, if need be, to a television set or telephone.

> The same phenomenon will affect us as citizens.

It will be possible to make the services provided by the public authorities faster, more selective and less impersonal, provided measures are taken to safeguard privacy. Certain services in which the public authorities have traditionally played a leading role (health, education, social security, etc.) could be provided far more widely, rapidly and effectively. Market forces will be able to play a greater part. Doctors, teachers and students will have instant access to vast databases.

> This is not a technological dream for the next century.

Some aspects of this new society are already being put into place; many people are beginning to reap the benefit. Naturally, these changes will be led by the Triad powers first, but will gradually extend to the rest of the planet. They will be dictated, above all, by the needs of the users, both companies and consumers alike. Industry is already beginning to adapt to these new prospects. large-scale reorganizations are in train. They are making the traditional distinctions, for example between electronics, information technology, telecommunications and the audiovisual sectors, increasingly obsolete. They are blurring the borderlines between the secondary and tertiary sectors, between industry and services. They are transforming the balance of power in industry: the capitalization of Nintendo, the video game maker, is already one third of IBM's and its turnover is almost twice that of Microsoft, the leading software producer. This process has already started in the USA, where it is giving birth to unprecedented partnerships and mergers between companies.

It will gain ground in Europe. It is forcing the public authorities to review the regulatory framework.

> Concern has been expressed about employment, but it is difficult to assess this factor precisely.

Rapid dissemination of new information technologies can certainly speed up the transfer of certain manufacturing activities to countries with distinctly lower labour costs.

> However, the productivity improvements which these technologies will allow throughout industry will also save large numbers of jobs which would otherwise have been lost.

We are witnessing rationalization of the service sector. However, the enormous potential for new services relating to production, consumption, culture and leisure acitivities will create large numbers of new jobs.

For example, the services generated by Minitel in France have created more than 350 000 jobs. The foreseeable growth in the number of audiovisual services will considerably increase the demand for new programmes. By the turn of the century there should be 10 times as many television channels as now and three times the number of subscribers to cable networks.

In any event, it would be fruitless to become embroiled in a fresh dispute about the 'machine age', as was the case with the first industrial revolution. Worldwide dissemination of new technologies is inevitable.

> The aim must be not to slow down this change but, instead, to control it in order to avoid the dramas which marked the adjustments in the last century but would be unacceptable today.

Above all, these changes have been brought about by market pressure and companies' own initiative. The government decisions taken in the USA and Japan aim at organizing and speeding up the process, by supporting companies' efforts. The emphasis has been on establishment of the basic infrastructure and support for new applications and technological development. The US programme to establish the 'National Information Infrastructure' provides for a total investment of ECU 85 billion.

> It is in Europe's interests to meet this challenge since the first economies which successfully complete this change, in goods conditions, will hold significant competitive advantages.

Compared with its leading competitors, Europe holds comparative advantages from the cultural, social, technological and industrial points of view. Since 1 January 1993 its market has been largely integrated, although too many monopolies and too much overregulation persist. Interoperability has not yet been achieved.

Already, the States which have taken the lead with deregulation have the fastest growing markets and falling consumer prices.

> Europe's main handicaps are the fragmentation of the various markets and the lack of major interoperable links. To overcome them, it is necessary to moblize resources and channel endeavours at European level in a partnership between the public and private sectors.

2. How?

The action plan is based on five priorities:

Priority	Means
1. Promote the use of information technologies	— launch European projects on applications and public services (transport, health, training, education and civil protection) and strengthen cooperation between administrations (IDA programme)
	— promote teleworking
	— ensure closer involvement of users in the drafting and implementation of technology policies
2. Provide basic trans-European services	— develop the basic networks (ISDN and broadband)
	— ensure network interoperability
	— ensure closer coordination between telecommunications policies and aid from the Structural Funds
3. Create an appropriate regulatory framework	— end distortions of competition
	— guarantee a universal service
	— speed up standardization
	— protect privacy and ensure the security of information and communication systems
	— extend intellectual property law
4. Develop training on new technologies	— encourage acquisition of the basic knowledge required in order to use new technologies and exploit their potential
	— ensure widespread use of new technologies in teaching and training
	— adapt the training for engineers and researchers
5. Improve industrial and technological performance	— increase the RTD effort and adapt it to the new market conditions (fourth framework programme)
	— promote industry and technology watch
	— take up the results of RTD in industrial applications
	— negotiate equitable conditions of access to the competitive market at world level

The keys to the success of this plan are to define the measures clearly, to specify a timetable and to put in place the resources.

It is proposed that a task force on European information infrastructures be established with a direct mandate from the European Council. This task force will have the job of establishing priorities, deciding on procedures and defining the resources required. It should report to the President of the European Council by 31 March 1994 so that the plan can be put into action by mid-1994 after consultation with the parties concerned and the approval of the European Council.

3. Which networks?

The transport network has motorways with several lanes, and access roads and service areas allowing motorists to drive wherever they choose.

The communications network will also have:

- **highways** along which information will move: these will be the broadband optical fibre networks;

- **access roads and service areas:** these will be the services (disks, files, databases, electronic mail services and host computers);

- **highway users** who will choose applications for their work or private life.

Europe's telephone networks are already international, but the digital networks for carrying information in the form of text, data or images are mainly being developed on a purely national basis.

In order to provide greater access to a wide range of interactive services and create a common information area, action must be taken:

- to ensure coordinated project management;

- to interconnect the various networks and make them interoperable;

- to invest and innovate in order to provide a wide range of information in the shortest possible time.

Such an approach is essential to stimulate the creation of new markets. New projects must be undertaken rapidly and resolutely

in order to break the vicious circle perpetuated by the weaknesses on both the demand and supply sides.

To this end, the nine strategic projects listed in the attached list are proposed.

They cover infrastructure, services and applications alike.

Establishment of a high-speed communication network

This infrastructure is necessary for the development of multimedia services. It would use the most advanced data transmission technologies (optical fibre) and fully capitalize on the digitization and high-speed transfer of information (high definition, interactive and multifunction systems).

This would extend the integrated services digital networks to be established throughout the Community by the year 2000.

Initiation of three programmes to develop electronic services

These services are necessary for diversification of the applications on a given infrastructure network:

- **Electronic images:** interactive video services will revolutionize working methods, training and leisure activities. The objective is to ensure Europe-wide interoperability of these new *à la carte* services by 1997.

- **Electronic access to information:** this will entail bringing together information (administrative, scientific, cultural or other data) in databases to which all users in the Community should have access.

- **Electronic mail:** the various commercial electronic document transmission services must be made interoperable; development of this service is particularly important to make small firms more competitive.

> **Promotion of four priority applications: teleworking, teletraining, telemedicine and links between administrations.**

- **Teleworking:** Projects are already under way in the Member States. The Community would support pilot programmes on the establishment of a transfrontier network for the management of human resources.

- **Teletraining:** The objective is to establish a network linking more than 100 universities or colleges by 1996 and giving them all access to common training modules.

- **Telemedicine:** By the year 2000, multimedia links are to be established between the main cancer research centres, bone marrow banks and social security centres.

- **Links between administrations:** To ensure smooth operation of the internal market (taxation, customs, statistics), it is essential to improve the interchange of data between administrations and to provide companies and the public with easier access to this information.

4. What decisions?

At the moment, the Council of Ministers and the European Parliament are continuing their discussions on the development of data communications (IDA) networks. In the autumn the Commission submitted two proposals on telecommunications networks containing a series of guidelines (master plan) on the integrated services digital network (ISDN) and broadband networks.

5. Financing options?

The estimated funding needed over the next 10 years will be ECU 150 billion. Some ECU 67 billion will be needed between 1994 and 1999 for the priority projects selected. They will be covered mainly by private investors. Financial support from the national and Community authorities will play a marginal role to provide an icentive, as with other networks.

The Community could provide ECU 5 billion over the entire period from its budget for networks, from the Structural Funds and, in particular, from the research programme. This could be supplemented by EIB loans and European Investment Fund guarantees and the new financial mechanisms described in the Annex.

Trans-European telecommunications networks:

Information highways	Target area for Strategic Projects	Investment required 1994-1999 *(billion ecus)*
Interconnected advanced networks	— establishment of high-speed communication network	20
	— consolidation of integrated services digital network	15
General electronic services	— electronic acces to information	1
	— electronic mail	1
	— electronic images: interactive video services	10
Telematic applications	— teleworking	3
	— links between administrations	7
	— teletraining	3
	— telemedicine	7
Total		67

Development theme II

Trans-European transport and energy networks

1. Why?

Europe's ascendancy in the past was due to the quality of its communications networks, which gave its inhabitants easy access to natural and technical resources. By developing the movement of people and goods, Europe has been able to marry economic prosperity, quality of life and commercial efficiency; it has also been able to remain at the forefront of technology and to back highly successful industry, Airbus being a good example. Our transport, energy and telecommunications systems are clear evidence of this tradition.

We need to continue along this road, to enter a new phase and to visualize other frontiers in the light of the globalization of markets, the growing mobility of capital and technology and the investment needs which are becoming apparent in the East and the South. The development of trans-European transport, telecommunications and energy infrastructure neworks answers

Promoting new or better designed infrastructures, accessible to all citizens, will permit:

- better, safer travel at lower cost, and thus an increase in trade, while reducing costs and distances and creating scope for other activities;
- effective planning in Europe in order to stem the emergence of serious socio-economic disequilibria in all Member States;
- bridge-building towards Eastern Europe, which is essential in order to meet the immense investment requirement resulting from the state of decay of communications and to organize the necessary economic complementarities.

this need which all the Member States emphasized in their contributions.

This is also a chance to:

- give our industries the opportunity of engaging in promising medium- and long-term projects and of developing new products;
- seek the optimum combination of existing transport modes (multimodality), in order to enhance performance and at the same time reduce their environmental impact.

Making traffic faster, safer and more environmentally compatible, facilitating and boosting trade, and bringing Member States closer to their eastern and southern neighbours would herald the advent of the European Union.

These networks are the complement to the single market. After the huge collective effort made to eliminate frontiers between the Member States, it is now necessary to increase physical links, including those with the most distant countries. This is also a key factor in competitiveness, minimizing costs to businesses and private individuals, and optimizing existing capacities by improving their compatibility.

2. Why now?

Our investment in infrastructures has been slowing down over the last 10 years.

This is particularly true of transport; the result is rigidities, procedural slowness and malfunctions, which are blamed by economic circles as being one of the main causes of the current decline in competitiveness. This can now be remedied with the aid of the new provisions of the Treaty on European Union (Article 129).

> The fact that not enough attention has been paid to developing infrastructures is one of the reasons for the deterioration in the quality of life.

Time wasted because of traffic congestion, under-utilization of the new communications media, environmental damage owing to the failure to use the most efficient technology are all to some extent contributory factors in the present malaise of our cities and the resulting social discord. The same is true of the thinly-populated rural areas, whose isolation is a threat to their very existence.

The rapid progress made in data processing, environmental engineering, propulsion methods and new materials completely change the outlook. We are living with separate, compartmentalized networks, with means of transport which are often environmentally damaging. It will henceforth be possible to combine different transport modes, to use electronics to organize links and traffic better, to connect networks in all sectors for which different national authorities are responsible and to integrate stringent environmental standards in infrastructure projects. **A wholly new generation of projects is emerging, and a completely different development logic.**

Countries such as the USA and Japan are making significant, targeted efforts to renew their infrastructures. New industrial powers such as Singapore, Taiwan, certain parts of China and Argentina are creating networks which integrate the latest technological advances.

> By focusing the necessary resources on trans-European projects, we shall maintain our capacity to compete with the rest of the world and improve the quality of life in Europe.

Equally, it is inconceivable that we should develop an economic partnership with the countries of Central Europe and Russia as a preliminary to a deeper association without, at the same time, embarking on bold infrastructure projects. The two are complementary.

> Finally, potential investments by the end of the century, which are put at more than ECU 250 billion, are a key factor in the economic recovery of Europe.

3. How?

> Article 129 of the Treaty on European Union spells out the Community's tasks and instruments relating to the establishment of networks.

Within the framework of a system of open and competitive markets, action by the Community shall aim at promoting the interconnection and interoperability of networks as well as access to such networks. It shall take account in particular of the need to link island, landlocked and peripheral regions with the central regions of the Community (Article 129b).

It **shall establish a series of guidelines** covering the objectives, priorities and broad lines of measures (master plans); these guidelines shall identify **projects of common interest**; it shall support the **financial efforts** made by the Member States for the projects identified, particularly through feasibility studies, loan guarantees or interest rates subsidies; it may also **help coordinate** the policies pursued by the Member States and cooperate with third countries (Article 129c).

The European Parliament and the Council of Ministers decide on the guidelines and projects of common interest by qualified majority; Member States must approve the guidelines and projects that concern their territory.

The Community has two tasks:

- encourage private investors to take a greater part in projects of European interest;

29

- reduce, to this end, the financial or administrative risks involved.

It is therefore recommended that **priority** should be given to projects of Community interest, the financial and administrative arrangements for which have been well prepared, and for which environmental impact assessments have been carried out.

Project evaluation will concern the financial risks, the possible sources of financing, the legal status (duration of concessions), management and the environmental impact. This procedure is particularly important in the energy sector where the main implementation difficulties are not so much financial as related to the length and complexity of administrative procedures.

> An administrative and financal action plan will be drawn up for each project, in order to guarantee investors the necessary predictability and stability.

4. Where are we now?

(a) Transport

The plan for high-speed trains had already been accepted by the Council in 1990, and it will be updated in 1994 for integration in a multimodal perspective.

On 29 October 1993 the Council and the European Parliament approved three master plans on:

- **combined transport,** with work in two stages of 6 and 12 years;
- **roads,** with 55 000 km of trans-European links including 12 000 km of motorway to be built in 10 years;
- **inland waterways,** with the establishment of an interoperable network in 10 years.

Three other plans will be presented in 1994 on:

- the **conventional rail infrastructure,** with a view to integrating lines for passenger traffic (regional, urban) and freight in the intermodal network and to extending links towards Central and Eastern Europe;
- the **airport infrastructure,** with a view to improving the linking-in of the Community network internationally and of

advancing the opening-up of certain regions of the Community;

- **seaports,** with a view to promoting intra-Community trade and trade with the rest of the world and relieving congestion on certain inland links, with beneficial environmental effects.

(b) Energy

A master plan and projects of common interest for electricity and gas will be presented at the beginning of 1994. Their implementation will depend to a great extent on the establishment of a genuine internal energy market.

5. What are the priorities?

The projects will focus above all on the trans-European transport network. This is the sector which will require the most substantial investment, and where the gap between available financial resources and needs is biggest. The aim is to develop a truly multimodal strategy, which is essential in order to improve the efficiency of the economy and the quality of life.

> It is proposed that major priority projects of Community interest should be selected on the basis of the master plans already approved, in order to bring all the countries of the European continent closer together. These concern:
>
> - new strategic transfrontier links (Brenner rail link, Lyons-Turin rail link, Paris-Barcelona-Madrid rail link, Berlin-Warsaw-Moscow motorway link);
> - improving connections between the various transport modes (Heathrow-London-Channel Tunnel link);
> - improving interoperability and efficiency of networks by installing traffic management systems (air, sea, land) and thus significantly reducing nuisance factors.

The development of energy networks reflects two priorities: the reduction of costs by making better use of existing capacities, and enhancing security of supply. The first priority is more particularly concerned with electricity, while the second applies to gas.

This will permit more rational overall use of the available energy throughout the whole European continent.

As far as electricity is concerned, the objective is essentially to increase interconnection of networks and thus avoid their saturation in some cases and, in others, provide a better service to the more remote areas.

> Making better use of existing electricity capacities will help protect the environment.

With regard to gas, Europe must come to terms with growing consumption which will increasingly by covered by imports from the North Sea, Algeria or Russia.

> It is essential, in the interests of economic security, to speed up construction of trans-European gas pipelines capable of guaranteeing supplies and creating avenues for long-term cooperation with the producer countries.

Eight major programmes will shortly be proposed to the Council with this in mind. the success of all these projects is closely linked with the deepening of the internal market.

6. Financing options

The financial requirements for the next 15 year can be put at more than ECU 400 billion; by the end of the century alone, they will probably amount to ECU 250 billion (ECU 220 billion for transport and ECU 30 billion for energy).

The total investment involved for the proposed projects amounts to ECU 82 billion for transport and ECU 13 billion for energy.

The purpose of the above assessment is to create the best possible conditions for financing by the market in the framework of a public- and private-sector partnership.

> Financing is based on three principles:
>
> ● **financial equilibrium:** this can to a large extent be ensured by private investors;
>
> ● **compatibility with public finances:** any contributions from Member States will respect the guidelines relating to the public debt;
>
> ● **subsidiarity:** the Community will support feasibility studies, provide loan guarantiees or promote the closing of missing links in the framework of projects of common interest.

With regard to the 26 transport projects already examined in the framework of the master plans (23) or in other Council bodies (3), the Community has already financed feasibility studies and work to the tune of ECU 332 million.

It could provide almost ECU 15 billion over the period 1994-99 from its various instrument, which would be added to loans of an equivalent amount (growth initiative facilities).

The eight major energy programmes will require ECU 13 billion, of which 10 must be provided by the market.

The budgetary contribution of the Community could be significantly reinforced by loans from the European Investment Bank and by European Investment Fund guarantees, as well as by the new mechanisms specified in the Annex.

Annex

Investing in the competitiveness of Europe

The trans-European networks are an essential element for the competitiveness of the European economy and the smooth functioning of the single market.

1. Transport and energy networks — ECU 250 billion by the year 2000

These networks of transport infrastructures will enable our citizens to travel more quickly, more safely and more cheaply. They will also form a link to eastern Europe and to north Africa. In total some ECU 400 billion of investments in the transport and energy trans-European networks will be required in the next 15 years, of which some ECU 220 billion by 1999.

Article 129b of the Treaty makes clear how to proceed. The Community[1] establishes a set of guidelines that identify projects of common interest. It then supports the financial efforts of the Member States (feasibility studies, loan guarantees, or interest rate subsidies). It can also contribute to the coordination of the Member States' policies and cooperate with third countries.

The principal guideline networks *(schémas directeurs)* have been proposed by the Commission or adopted by the Council and the Parliament. The Commission has identified a series of priority projects for the next five years (25 transport projects amounting to ECU 83 billion and 10 energy projects costing ECU 13 billion) covering the Community, but also extending to central Europe and north Africa (energy).

2. Telecommunications — ECU 150 billion by the year 2000

A system of information highways for the Community will allow the best means to create, manage, access and transfer information. It involves:

- the creation of infrastructures (cable and land or satellite-based radio communication), including integrated digital networks;

- the development of services (electronic images, databases, electronic mail);

- promoting applications (teleworking, teletraining, telemedecine and linked administrations).

The amount of investments that could be put into effect by the end of the century has been estimated at ECU 150 billion.

3. Environment — ECU 174 billion on large environmental projects by the year 2000

The environment is an integral element of the trans-European networks, for example concerning combined transport networks designed to get traffic off the roads onto rail. The Commission has nevertheless environmental programmes of sufficient size to merit eligibility for financial support from the Community. These concern urban waste water treatment and renovation of water supply distribution systems at an estimated cost of ECU 314 billion in total over 12 years or ECU 174 billion by the end of the century. The Community could help finance some ECU 25 billion in this area of environmental concern over the period 1994-99.

4. Financing the trans-European networks and large environmental projects

The major portion of finance for these investments will be raised at the level of the Member State, either through private investors (especially in the telecoms sector) or via public enterprises. The Community can, however, play a role, as foreseen in the Treaty, by supporting the financial efforts

---

[1] The Council decides by qualified majority in co-decision with the European Parliament (Article 189b); guidelines and projects of common interest which relate to the territory of a Member State require the approval of the Member State concerned.

of the Member States and mobilizing private capital. [1] This requires a panoply of financial instruments, as set out in the table below, some of which exist already and two of which are new ('Union Bonds', 'Convertibles'). The new instruments are needed for projects specifically included in the Master Plans and complement the lending of the European Investment Bank, which is more general. The budgetary elements remain within the Edinburgh ceilings. National budgets would not be required to support additional financing. In the case of the new instruments, the capital and interest would be repaid by the promoters of the projects, with the Community budget available to back the repayment of the Union Bonds and the capital of the European Investment Fund available in the case of the Convertibles. There would be no risk of destabilizing the capital markets given that the amounts concerned represent less than 1 % of the Eurobond and bank credit markets.

---

[1] In addition the EIF can guarantee up to a total of ECU 6 billion of private loans for large infrastructure projects, averaging ECU 1 billion per year to 1999.

Community financing of the trans-European networks

(average financing per year 1994-99)

Source:		Amount in billion ecus	
Community budget:			**5.3**
of which: TENs		0.50	
Structural Funds:			
	(TENs):	1.35	
	(environment):	0.60	
Cohesion Fund:			
	(TENs):	1.15	
	(environment):	1.15	
R&D:			
	(telecommunications):	0.50	
	(transport):	0.05	
EIB (loans):			**6.7**
Union Bonds [1] (esp. transport and energy):			**7.0**
Convertibles [1] **guaranteed by EIF** (esp. telecoms):			**1.0**
	Total		**20.0**

---

[1] See box p. 34.

New facilities

Union Bonds

'Union Bonds' for growth would be issued on tap by the Union for long maturities to promote major infrastructure projects of strategic interest covering the trans-European networks plus cross-border projects with EFTA, Central and Eastern Europe and North Africa. The beneficiaries would be project promoters (public sector agencies, private companies) directly involved in TENs. The EIB would be invited to appraise and advise the Commission on the overall structure of the financial arrangement and act as agent for individual loan contracts.

'Convertibles' guaranteed by the European Investment Fund

Bonds issued for long maturities by the private or public company promoting the project, guaranteed by the European Investment Fund. These would be either:

- convertible wholly or partly into shares or investment certificates; or
- by accompanied by subscription warrants giving the holder a right to buy shares at a certain price; or
- performance-related through a share in the profits of the company or venture concerned.

The maturities of the bonds and of the exchange terms would be coherent between the expected returns of the project and the exercise period of the option. The EIF would create a special window for this type of guarantee, especially for major projects linked to telecommunications networks.

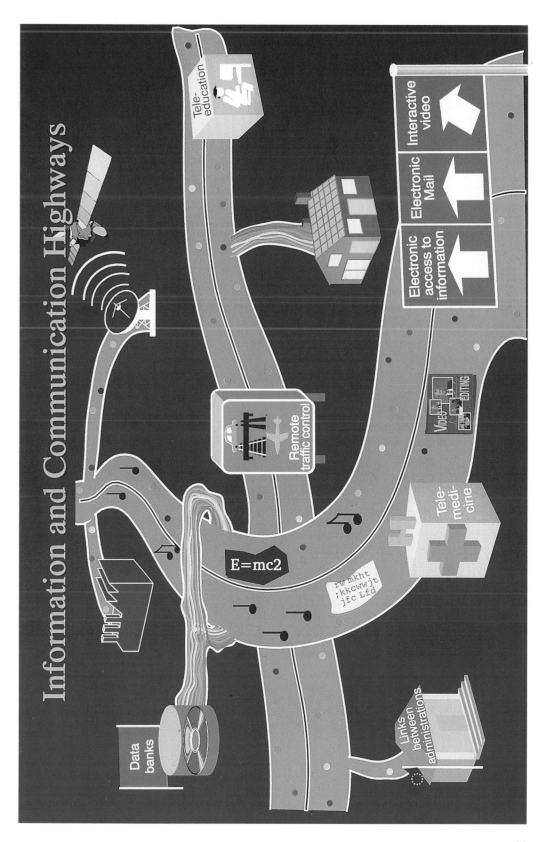

Information and Communication Highways

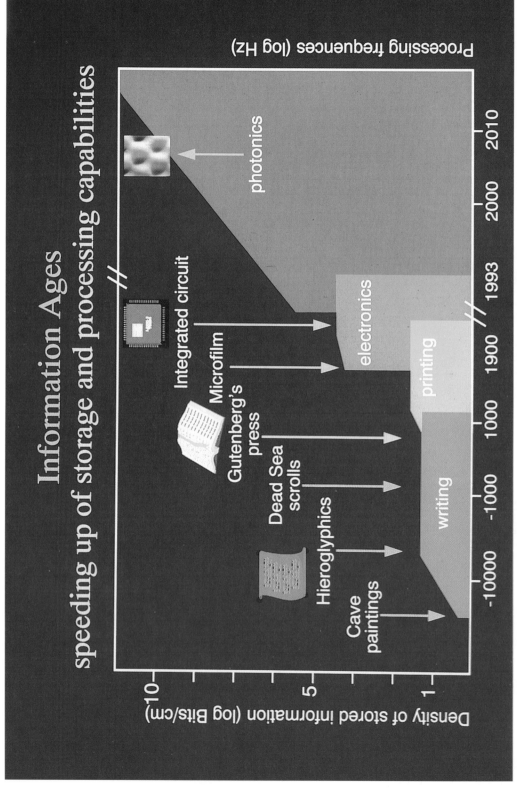

Information Ages
speeding up of storage and processing capabilities

36

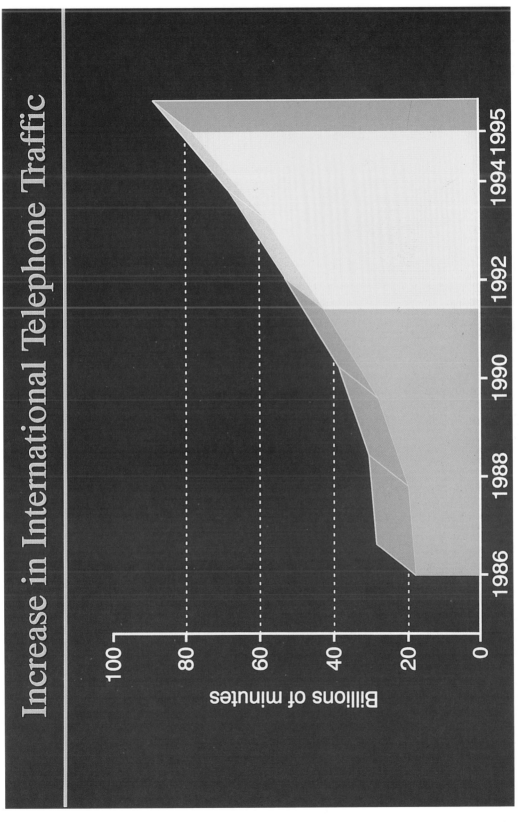

Increase in International Telephone Traffic

Billions of minutes

100 — 80 — 60 — 40 — 20 — 0

1986 1988 1990 1992 1994 1995

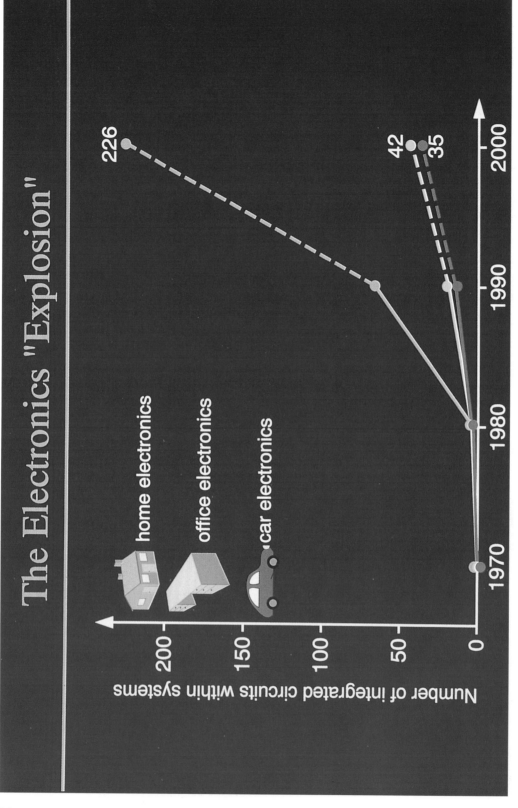

The Electronics "Explosion"

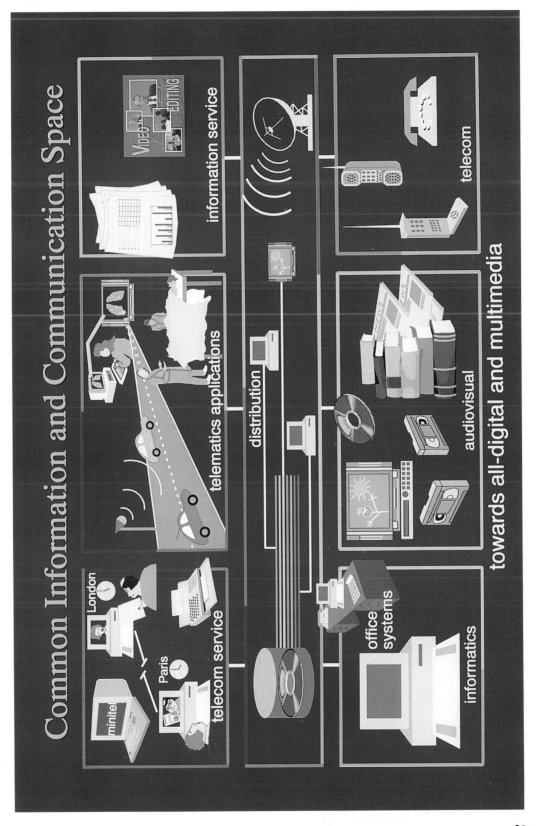

39

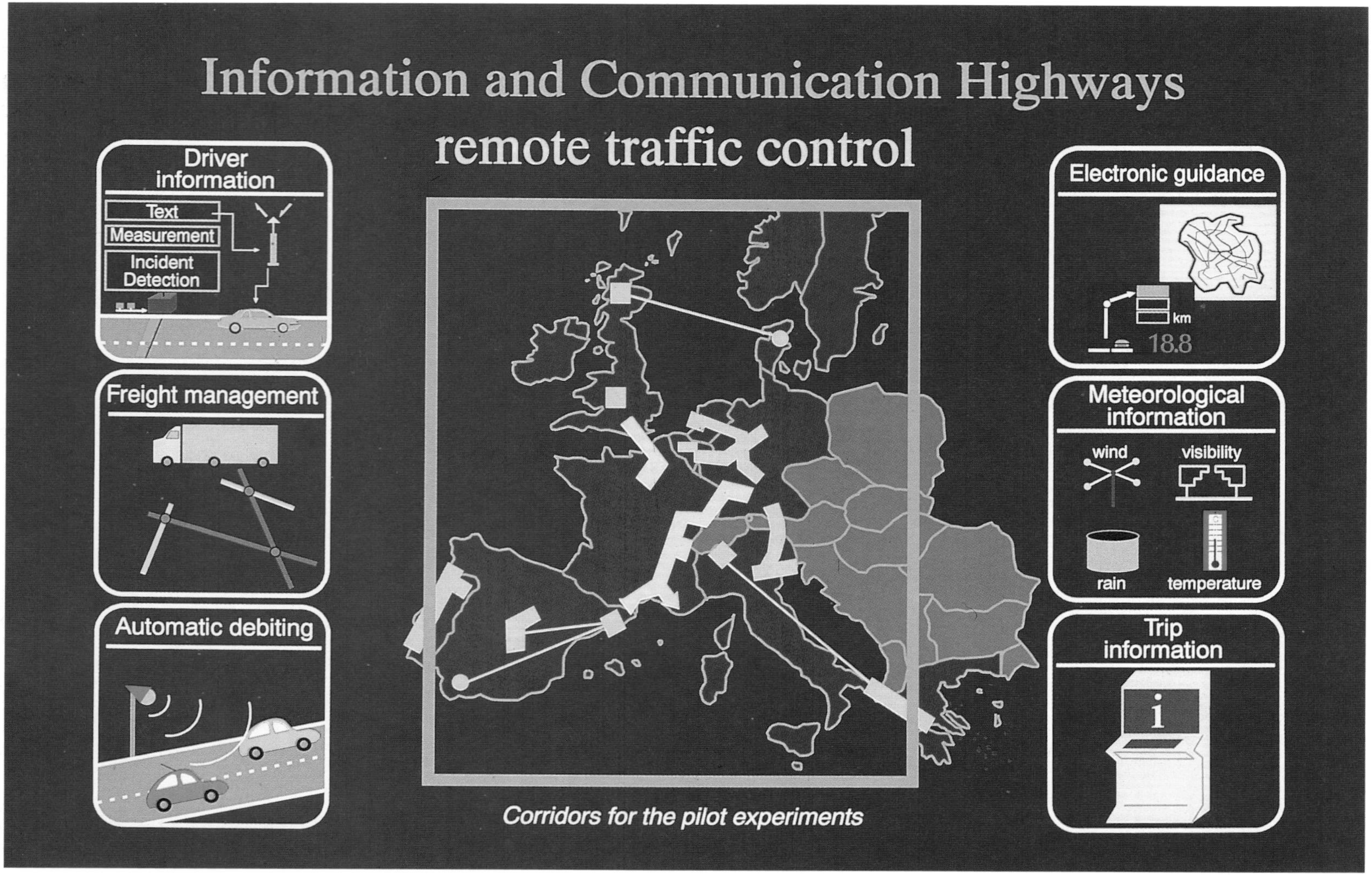

Information and Communication Highways

remote traffic control

Electronic guidance

188 km

Meteorological information

wind · visibility

rain · temperature

Trip information

Driver information

Text
Measurement
Incident Detection

Freight management

Automatic debiting

Corridors for the pilot experiments

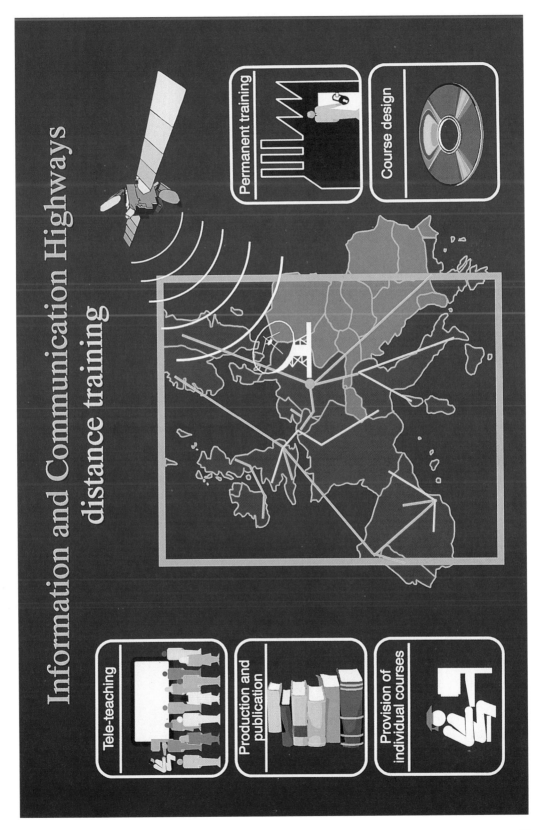

41

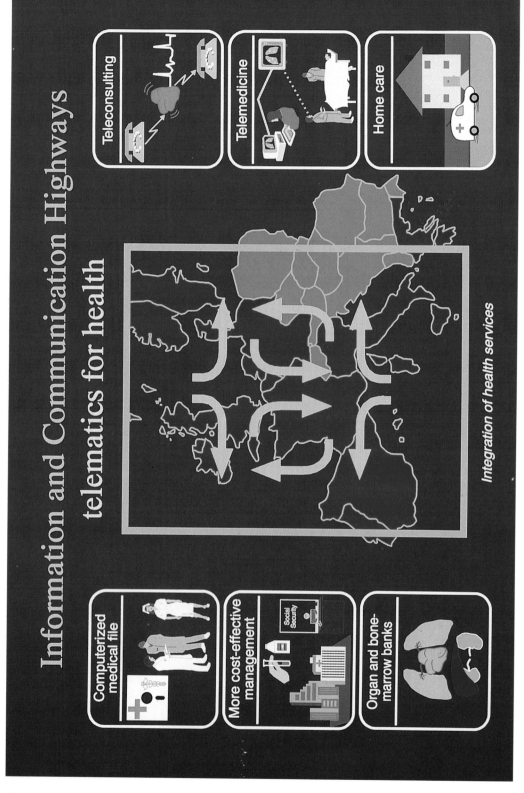

Information and Communication Highways

telematics for health

Teleconsulting

Telemedicine

Home care

Computerized medical file

More cost-effective management

Social Security

Organ and bone-marrow banks

Integration of health services

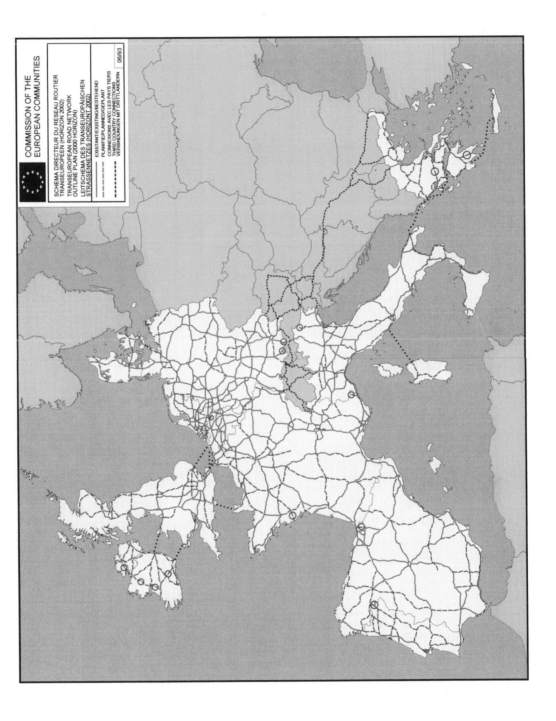

43

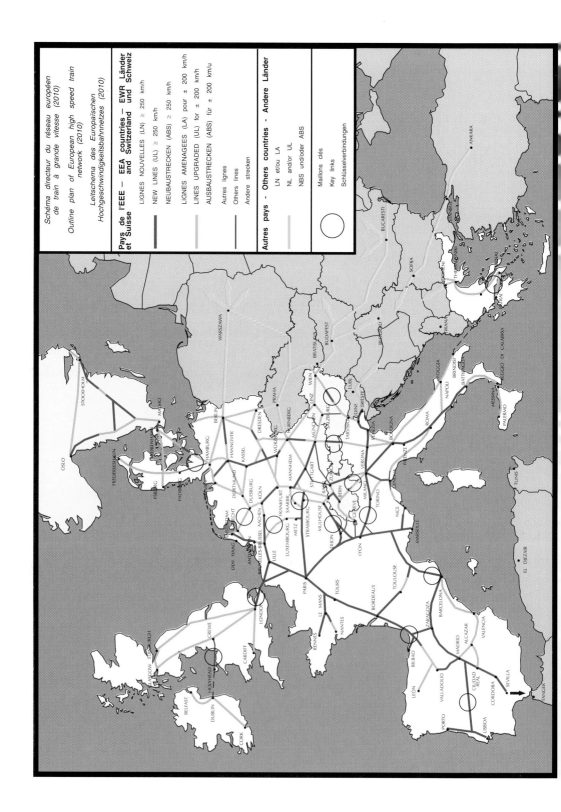

Schéma directeur du réseau européen de train à grande vitesse (2010)

Outline plan of European high speed train network (2010)

Leitschema des Europäischen Hochgeschwindigkeitsbahnnetzes (2010)

Pays de l'IEEE – EEA countries – EWR Länder et Suisse and Switzerland und Schweiz

LIGNES NOUVELLES (LN) ≥ 250 km/h

NEW LINES (UL) ≥ 250 km/h

NEUBAUSTRECKEN (ABS) ≥ 250 km/h

LIGNES AMENAGEES (LA) pour ± 200 km/h

LINES UPGRADED (UL) for ± 200 km/h

AUSBAUSTRECKEN (ABS) für ± 200 km/u

Autres lignes

Others lines

Andere strecken

Autres pays – Others countries – Andere Länder

LN et/ou LA

NL and/or UL

NBS und/oder ABS

Maillons clés

Key links

Schlüsselverbindungen

44

RESEAU EUROPEEN DE TRANSPORT COMBINE - EUROPEAN NETWORK OF COMBINED TRANSPORT - EUROPÄISCHES NETZ DES KOMBINIERTEN VERKEHRS

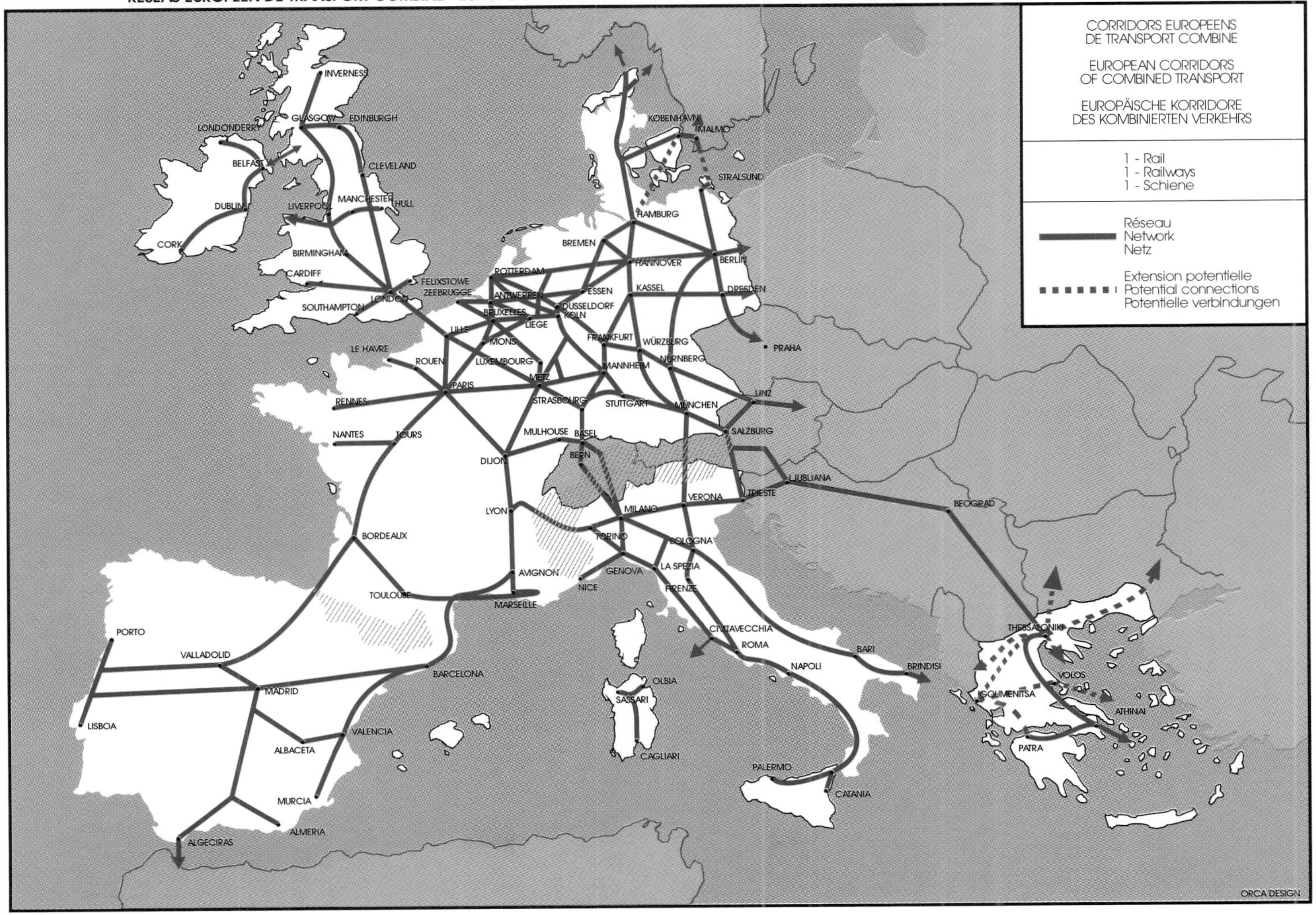

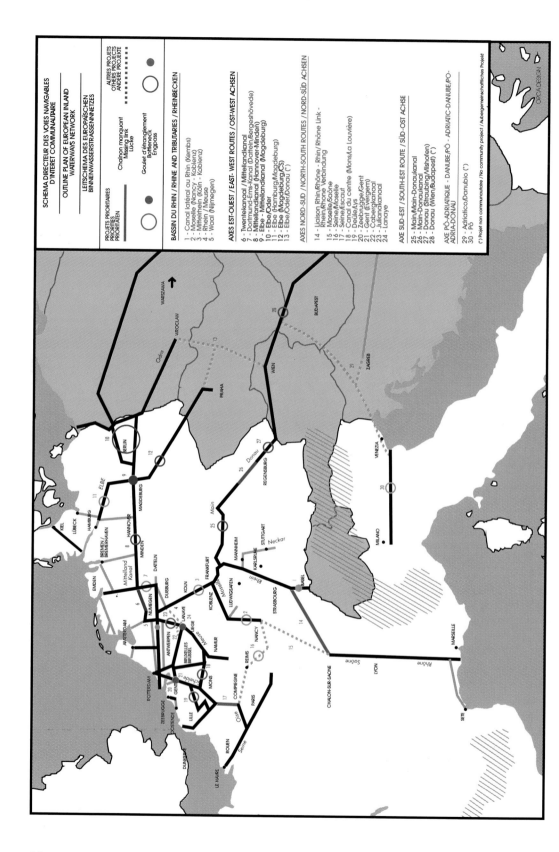

SCHEMA DIRECTEUR DES VOIES NAVIGABLES
D'INTERET COMMUNAUTAIRE

OUTLINE PLAN OF EUROPEAN INLAND
WATERWAYS NETWORK

LEITSCHEMA DES EUROPÄISCHEN
BINNENWASSERSTRASSENNETZES

PROJETS PRIORITAIRES
PRIORITY PROJECTS
PRIORITÄTEN

AUTRES PROJETS
OTHERS PROJECTS
ANDERE PROJEKTE

Chaînon manquant
Missing link
Lücke

Goulet d'étranglement
Bottleneck
Engpass

BASSIN DU RHIN / RHINE AND TRIBUTARIES / RHEINBECKEN

1 - Canal latéral au Rhin (Kembs)
2 - Moselle (Nancy - Koblenz)
3 - Mittelrhein (Köln - Koblenz)
4 - Rhein / Meuse
5 - Waal (Nijmegen)

AXES EST-OUEST / EAST-WEST ROUTES / OST-WEST ACHSEN

6 - Twentekanaal / Mittellandkanal
7 - Dortmund-Ems-Kanal (Datteln/Bergeshövede)
8 - Mittellandkanal (Hannover-Minden)
9 - Elbe - Mittellandkanal (Magdeburg)
10 - Elbe/Oder
11 - Elbe (Hamburg/Magdeburg)
12 - Elbe (Magdeburg/CS)
13 - Elbe/Oder/Donau (*)

AXES NORD-SUD / NORTH-SOUTH ROUTES / NORD-SÜD ACHSEN

14 - Liaison Rhin/Rhône - Rhin/ Rhône Link -
Rhein/Rhone Verbindung
15 - Moselle/Saône
16 - Seine/Moselle
17 - Seine/Escaut
18 - Canal du centre (Mons/La Louvière)
19 - Deûle/Lys
20 - Zeebrugge/Gent
21 - Gent (Evergem)
22 - Caberg/canal
23 - Juliana/kanaal
24 - Lanaye

AXE SUD-EST / SOUTH-EST ROUTE / SÜD-OST ACHSE

25 - Main-Main-Donaukanal
26 - Main-Donaukanal
27 - Donau (Straubing/Vilshofen)
28 - Donau (Wien/Budapest) (*)

AXE PO-ADRIATIQUE - DANUBE/PO - ADRIATIC-DANUBE/PO-
ADRIA-DONAU

29 - Adriatico/Danubio (*)
30 - Po

(*) Projet non communautaire / No community project / Außergemeinschaftliches Projekt

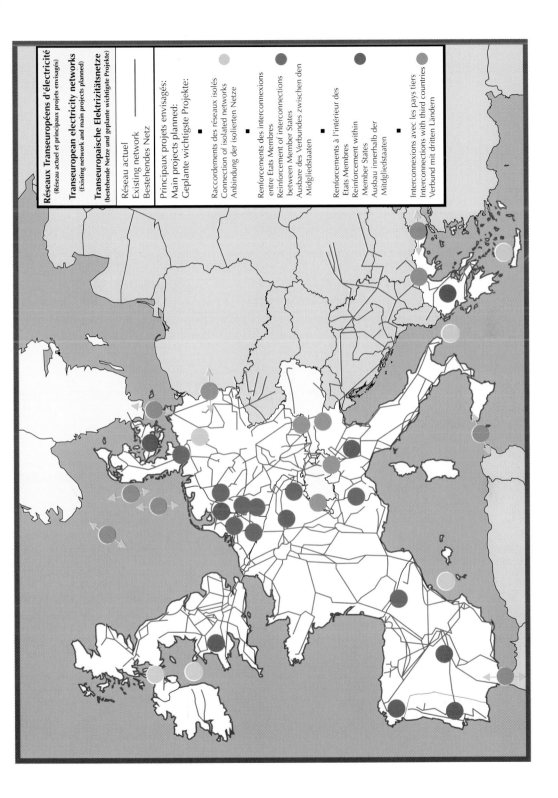

Réseaux Transeuropéens d'électricité
(Réseau actuel et principaux projets envisagés)

Transeuropean electricity networks
(Existing network and main projects planned)

Transeuropäische Elektrizitätsnetze
(bestehende Netze und geplante wichtigste Projekte)

Réseau actuel
Existing network
Bestehendes Netz

Principaux projets envisagés:
Main projects planned:
Geplante wichtigste Projekte:

Raccordements des réseaux isolés
Connection of isolated networks
Anbindung der isolierten Netze

Renforcements des interconnexions
entre Etats Membres
Reinforcement of interconnections
between Member States
Ausbare des Verbundes zwischen den
Midgliedstaaten

Renforcements à l'intérieur des
Etats Membres
Reinforcement within
Member States
Ausbau innerhalb der
Mitdgliedstaaten

Interconnexions avec les pays tiers
Interconnections with third countries
Verbund mit dritten Ländern

47

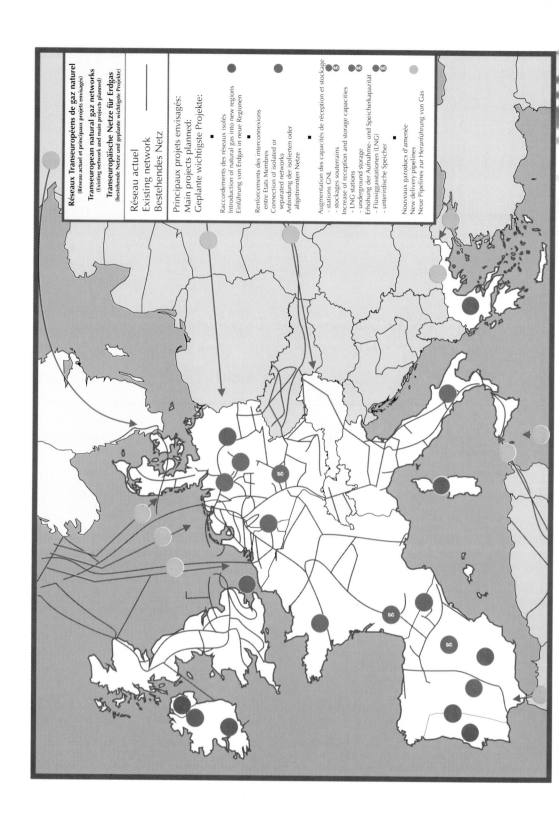

Réseaux Transeuropéens de gaz naturel
(Réseau actuel et principaux projets envisagés)

Transeuropean natural gaz networks
(Existing network and main projects planned)

Transeuropäische Netze für Erdgas
(bestehende Netze und geplante wichtigste Projekte)

Réseau actuel
Existing network
Bestehendes Netz

Principaux projets envisagés:
Main projects planned:
Geplante wichtigste Projekte:

Raccordements des réseaux isolés
Introduction of natural gas into new regions
Einführung von Erdgas in neue Regionen

Renforcements des interconnexions
entre Etats Membres
Connection of isolated or
separated networks
Anbindung der isolierten oder
abgetrennten Netze

Augmentation des capacités de réception et stockage
- stations GNL
- stockages souterrains
Increase of reception and storage capacities
- LNG stations
- underground storage
Erhöhung der Aufnahme- und Speicherkapazität
- Flüssiggasstationen (LNG)
- unterirdische Speicher

Nouveaux gazoducs d'amenée
New delivery pipelines
Neue Pipelines zur Heranführung von Gas

PART B

The conditions of growth, competitiveness and more jobs

(Preparatory work)

I — GROWTH

Chapter 1

The macroeconomic framework

Community unemployment has increased steadily since the beginning of the 1970s with the exception of the second half of the 1980s, when nine million jobs were created through a combination of appropriate national policies, a favourable external environment and the dynamism resulting from the prospect of the single market. Overall, however, since the early 1970s demographic factors have led to an increase in the number of people seeking jobs, while the number of jobs available stagnated or increased only modestly. Other developed economies have been patently more successful in responding to the challenge of increasing job creation.

The causes of the Community's poor relative performance in this area are numerous and deep-seated. The most important ones can be summed up under the headings of a suboptimal macroeconomic management of the economy and of an insufficient effort of adaptation to the changes which have taken place in the structure of the Community's economy and in its international environment. The 1980s saw a change of policy orientation. The emphasis shifted towards creating more stable macroeconomic conditions and towards easing the pain associated with structural change rather than slowing it down. This reorientation brought positive results in the second half of the decade, providing good growth but not enough new jobs. In 1992-93, however, there was a loss of confidence brought on in part by actions outside the economic sphere. This and other errors put the economy into its worst recession.

To the extent that the present problems are the result of inadequate policies in the more or less recent past, there is nothing inevitable in this state of affairs.

In addition, there is a number of factors which are favourable to a rapid return to sustained growth and which can and should be exploited. The Community's achievement in creating the world's biggest single market is a major asset on which it will be possible to build once the recovery sets in. The recession, painful as it is, has speeded up the process of adaptation of firms to the new environment.

The world economy has continued to grow over recent years and a number of developing countries have experienced very high rates of growth. The presence of new vibrant economies in Asia and, soon, in Eastern Europe constitutes a huge opportunity and not a threat to our standard of living. These countries will be buying on world markets as much as they will earn with their exports. The rest of the world is now experiencing again positive rates of growth of between 2 and 3% while world trade outside the Community is expanding by 5 to 6% in real terms. Finally, the price of oil is now back to the low levels recorded in the mid-1980s.

Over recent years, comprehensive analyses have been made. They show that there is no miracle remedy, but they point to the existence of a wide range of measures to help growth, competitiveness and employment. **The challenge is now to appreciate the order of magnitude of the likely effects of the various measures, to determine their appropriate mix and to implement the preferred strategy with determination. This will not be easy. The factors which have hindered in the past the implementation of the right policies are largely still present. Attacking the sources of the present unemployment problems requires, therefore, a clean break with the past.** This will only be possible if a large consensus on the necessary course of action to be followed can be developed: within each country, between management and the labour force in industry and among the members of the European Community.

This chapter outlines the macroeconomic framework which policies must create and within which the structural interventions outlined in the following chapters will be most successful.

1.1. Views of the Member States

In their contributions to the White Paper, the Member States broadly agree on the **assessment** made. They shall call for a clear analysis of the serious economic situation with a view to enlisting the help of all those involved in the economic process in finding remedies requiring sacrifices that have to be shared fairly.

The problems of employment and competitiveness — about which governments, the European Council, employers and trade unions have all expressed serious concern — are the result of developments which have been witnessed for a number of years but do not appear to have provoked an adequate political response. The pressures stemming from changes in the world economy are only aggravating the situation. At the same time, production processes and, consequently, the nature of employment have undergone radical change comparable, in certain respects, to the changes brought about by the industrial revolutions. The performance of economies depends on their capacity to adapt to these new circumstances, and it is precisely in this area that the Community is lagging behind.

The macroeconomic framework in the Community is being affected by certain **fundamental imbalances** which have caused a vicious circle to be created. The current levels of public expenditure, particularly in the social field, have become unsustainable and have used up resources which could have been channelled into productive investment. They have pushed up the taxation of labour and increased the cost of money. At the same time, the constant rise in the labour cost — affecting both its wage and non-wage components and caused, at least in part, by excessively rigid regulation — has hindered job creation. As a result, the level of long-term investment has fallen and the lack of confidence among those involved in the economic process has caused demand to contract.

The vital need to restore a **stable macroeconomic framework** as a basis for sustainable, job-creating growth is felt by all Member States. They all point to the link between the efforts to redress the economic situation and the process of economic convergence within the framework of economic and monetary union, which is generally viewed as the right instrument for addressing structural problems. A number of Member States advocate use of the economic policy guidelines provided for in the Treaty on European Union as a specific means of tackling these matters.

1.2. The problem

The level of unemployment in the Community has reached very serious proportions. After five years of steady decline, the jobless totals in the Community started to rise substantially again at the beginning of the 1990s. In addition, Community unemployment is characterized both by a high rate of long-term unemployment, which is nearing almost half of the unemployment total, and by its impact in particular among low-skilled people.

Particularly worrying is the substantial loss of ground in the recent past. There are, of course, identifiable economic reasons for this, in particular the effect of very high interest rates on investment, excessively high budget deficits in some Member States, unsustainable exchange rates and the problems of monetary instability. But the rapidity of the downturn indicates also the importance of the 'confidence factor', the decline in consumer and business confidence linked both to economic pressures and to the uncertainties arising from other causes, in particular the difficult ratification of the Maastricht Treaty. On present trends, a stabilization of the rate of unemployment cannot be expected before the end of 1994. By that date, more than 18 million citizens could be out of work: a figure equal to the total populations of Belgium, Denmark and Ireland.

The difference between the unemployment rates currently experienced in the major global economic areas — 10.5% of the civilian labour force in the Community against rates of about 7 and 2.5% in the USA and Japan respectively — has given rise to questions about the existence of a specific European unemployment problem. An examination of the Community's past performance and a comparison with the other major areas, however, suggests that no hasty negative conclusions ought to be drawn.

Before the first oil-price shock unemployment was low and the Community compared well with its principal competitors. The rate of unemployment in the Community was lower than that in the USA in each year of the period 1960-80. Even compared with Japan, which has successfully held down unemployment over a long period, the Community's performance only started to diverge radically in the period following the first oil-price shock.

To understand how the Community's unemployment performance deteriorated over time it is necessary to take a long-term perspective. To this end it is useful to distinguish between four main periods: (a) the period up until the first oil-price shock, (b) the period from the first oil-price shock to the mid-1980s, (c) the second half of the 1980s, and (d) the present period of slow growth or outright recession.

(a) The 1960-73 period was highlighted by very high rates of GDP growth (4.8% a year). While growth was high, the employment content of that growth was quite low. However, the low rate of job creation (0.3% a year) was not a problem over this period as the labour supply continued to grow at similarly modest rates (also 0.3% a year). As a result, unemployment in the Community remained relatively stable over this period and its average level was 2.6% (see Chart 1).

Chart 1
Unemployment in the Community
(percentage of the civilian labour force)

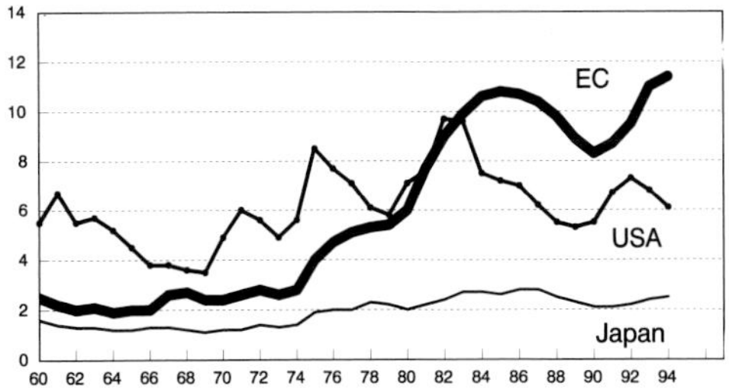

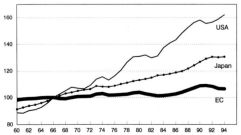

(b) During the subsequent period 1974-85, the rate of growth dropped substantially to a figure of 2.0% a year. The employment intensity increased, but not enough to maintain positive rates of increase in employment. As a result, employment creation stagnated (private-sector employment

actually declined, but this decline was offset by an increase in the public sector) just at the time when demographic factors led to sharp increases in the labour force (0.7% a year). This led inevitably to a continuous and sharp rise in the rate of unemployment from a rate of less than 3% in 1974 to a peak of 10.8% in 1985.

(c) During the years 1986-90, the fruits of the structural adjustment and policy reorientation which had taken place since the beginning of the 1980s were reaped and the Community experienced stronger rates of growth: 3.2% a year. Even if this average rate of growth was a far cry from that experienced during the 1960s, it was sufficient to generate a very strong increase in jobs since the employment intensity remained at the higher level reached during the previous period. Employment increased by 1.3% a year during this period, and unemployment was reduced from 10.8% in 1985 to 8.3% in 1990.

(d) Since 1991 the rate of increase of GDP slowed down substantially and in 1993 it became negative for the first time since 1975. Unemployment started its present worrying upward path which accelerated sharply when employment declined in 1992 and 1993.

This rapid overview of the Community's past employment performance shows clearly that the Community's economy, with the exception of the period 1986-90, has always been characterized by low employment creation (see Chart 2 and point (b) above) and that the origin of its unemployment problems go back to the

Chart 2
Job creation in the EC, USA and Japan
(index : 1960-73 = 100)

55

beginning of the 1970s, when it proved unable to increase its rate of job creation to match the increase in the number of people seeking employment.

By contrast, the USA has been able to respond to an even larger increase in the number of people looking for jobs with a strong increase in employment creation. Japan has also managed to increase its rate of job creation. The increase was less substantial than that recorded in the USA, but was more or less in line with the rate of increase in the country's active population. Where these two regions differ strongly, however, is in the way the increase in job creation was achieved. In the USA the job creation of the last 20 years resulted essentially from a modest rate of output growth and a very high employment content (low average productivity) of that growth. Japan, on the other hand, experienced an employment content of growth lower than that of the Community (a higher average productivity) but was able to couple that with a much stronger rate of output growth.

Chart 3

Active population in the EC, USA and Japan
(index : 1960-73 = 100)

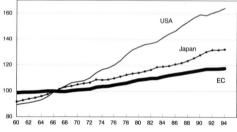

The macroeconomic causes of unemployment

As the contributions received from the Member States show, it is now largely acknowledged that the decline in the rate of job creation in the Community after the first oil-price shock is **to a very large extent the result of poor macroeconomic policies.** Structural and external factors also played a large role, in particular the inadequate adjustment of industrial structures towards new market opportunities both within the Community and elsewhere in the world, but the main explanation for the poor

unemployment performance of the Community over the past two decades is to be found in the constraints that unresolved distributional conflicts and insufficient structural adjustment placed on macroeconomic policies.

Low investment is one striking consequence. Lower rates of capital accumulation in turn took their toll on the competitiveness of the Community's economy and on its productive capacity which is now expanding much more slowly than in the past. The potential rate of growth, i.e. the rate of growth at which it can grow for many years without experiencing overheating problems, is now estimated to be much less than it used to be in the 1960s: just over 2% against more than 4.5% (see Chart 4).

Chart 4

Actual and potential rate of GDP growth in the Community

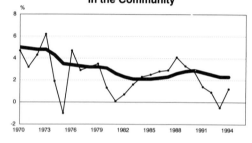

The present recession is, to a large extent, a consequence of the combination of a lower potential rate of growth and of policy errors which led to actual rates of growth in excess of the potential rate. At the end of 1987, the fear that the stock exchange crash might provoke a slump led to a worldwide substantial loosening of monetary policy. However, at that time the rate of growth of the Community's economy was already picking up although this was not yet fully reflected in the available statistics. The prospects opened by the single market project and the eventual feeding through of the positive effects of lower oil prices had just sparked off a period of strong investment expansion which was revealed by the statistics only in the spring of 1988.

The monetary stimulus, therefore, came on top of a positive underlying trend. Given

56

that no compensatory tightening of budgetary policy took place, the Community's economy experienced in 1988 a very strong rate of growth: 4.1% (against the 1.3% forecast by the Commission's services — and many other forecasters — in January 1988).

This rate of growth, although not very high in historical terms, was higher than the potential one. Given that the rate of growth remained above potential until 1990, tensions appeared. Inflation accelerated sharply in 1989 and wages followed in 1990. Since the authorities were committed to a stability course, monetary policy became more restrictive. This unbalanced policy mix had obvious negative consequences for investment and growth. The fiscal impulse resulting from German unification complicated things further. On the one hand, it sustained growth when world demand was faltering, but, on the other hand, it imposed an additional compensatory tightening of monetary policy and led to an even more distorted policy mix and a deeper recession.

The conflict between, on the one hand, budgetary and wage trends, which adapted very slowly, and, on the other hand, the continuing pressure exerted by monetary policy constitutes the single most important factor behind the present recession.

Employment intensity

The **employment intensity** is the relationship between the rate of growth of an economy and its rate of employment creation. Very often it is measured by the so-called *'employment threshold'*, which is a purely descriptive measure for the employment content of growth. This threshold is the percentage change above which the growth rate of GDP leads to increases in employment. Contrary to a widespread belief — the phrase 'growth without jobs' is often heard — the employment intensity of growth has not deteriorated over recent years. In fact it is now higher (the employment threshold is lower) than in the 1960s and it has hardly changed over the last 15 to 20 years (see Chart 5).

The employment intensity of growth is determined by numerous factors, such as the relative cost of labour (especially for unskilled work) and capital, working time including part-time work, the sectoral composition of employment, technological developments and a large number of microeconomic conditions. It is difficult to isolate the effects on employment of any of these factors so it is therefore easier to focus on the broad overall relationship between growth and employment, i.e. the **employment threshold.**

The employment threshold corresponds by definition to the trend of the apparent labour productivity of the economy as a whole. Thus, lowering the employment threshold means lowering the overall productivity of the economy. But there is no contradiction between calls for increased productivity growth in all sectors open to international competition and at the same time calling for measures which increase the weight of sectors where productivity increases are low. In fact, the process whereby the increased productivity emanating from the high-productivity sectors feeds through to all sectors of the economy is at the heart of any development model. Productivity must increase to guarantee the international competitiveness of a country and to increase the amount of material wealth distributable among the whole community. At the same time, as the wealth of a country increases, so can the relative importance of certain sectors, with usually a high labour content, which help distribute the wealth so created and at the same time improve the conditions for additional increases in this wealth.

1.3. Unemployment can be reduced

The Commission recommends that the Community sets itself the **objective of creating at least 15 million new jobs, thereby halving the present rate of unemployment by the year 2000.** This can only be a **target,** but it would be of great importance for our citizens, in particular for the young who see poor prospects of employment ahead of them. A target of this order of magnitude is the minimum required to make a significant dent in the human waste represented by unemployment.

The target, although ambitious, is not out of line with the past performance of the Community's economy or with what the performance of other economies would indicate to be possible. Over the next five to ten years, the Community labour supply will probably increase by about half a percentage point a year. Demographic trends will account for most of this increase. The population of working age is expected to increase by around 0.3% a year, a rate substantially lower than that of the last 20 years. In line with past trends, the rate of participation (0.7% a year) is also expected to increase once jobs again become available, thus providing the rest of the assumed increase in the labour supply. Half a percentage point a year is therefore the rate of increase in employment the Community needs just to keep unemployment stable. To the year 2000 this means creating almost five million jobs only to prevent unemployment from increasing. A reduction in unemployment to about half its present level (i.e. to 5 to 6% of the active population) by the year 2000 deadline requires the creation of an additional 10 million jobs.

If, as a result of structural changes, participation rates were to increase faster than what past experience suggests, then either the unemployment target would have to be revised downwards or the ambitions regarding employment creation would have to be scaled up.

Achieving the target of creating at least 15 million jobs by the year 2000 implies that from 1995 onwards, once the present recession is overcome, employment creation remains steadily a rate of increase of around 2% a year, certainly an impressive and ambitious target.

Between 1984 and 1990, a slightly shorter period of time than the one separating us from the year 2000, the Community economy was able to create more than nine million net new jobs. Between 1988 and 1990, the average annual rate of increase in employment was 1.6%. The proposed target requires a performance better than that of these years, but the difference is not so large as to suggest that it may be out of reach. Other economies have done even better. The USA, for instance, has recorded an annual average rate of increase in employment of 1.9% over the 17-year period 1974-90!

The immediate policy objective of the Community must be to overcome the recession and start creating jobs again. Section 1.6 deals with this objective. The choice of the policies which will have to be implemented to overcome the recession is conditional, to a certain extent, on the medium-term growth pattern which is considered most appropriate to bring about the required increase in employment. It is therefore useful to identify the medium-term growth pattern which is to be aimed at before discussing the policies needed to promote a recovery since the latter must be consistent with the former.

The present recession is resulting in a large net destruction of jobs (about four million jobs lost in 1992-93). But the Community's present unemployment problem has more deep-seated causes. The combination of the current potential rate of growth and of the employment intensity of that growth is not sufficient to generate the necessary increase in the number of jobs. If growth were to return only to a rate close to the current potential rate of growth (just over 2%), the present employment intensity of growth would not even allow increases in employment which kept pace with the increases in the labour supply and consequently unemployment would go on rising.

A higher rate of job creation can be achieved through various combinations of faster growth and higher employment intensity. The contributions received from the Member States and the EFTA countries contain a wide range of measures which help to reduce unemployment. Some measures aim essentially at increasing the rate of growth, others aim to increase its employment content while a few produce positive effects in both directions.

It is not necessary, nor would it be wise, to seek to lay down in advance what precise combination of growth and of greater

employment content of growth should be achieved. Efforts must be undertaken in both directions at the same time. Given the difficulties in making progress in these areas, which both lie outside the direct control of policy-makers, there is no risk of going too far in either direction.

However, there are significant differences in the scope for progress towards faster sustainable growth and in that towards a higher employment intensity. In addition, the social implications can be quite different and there are some important trade-offs. It is therefore right to examine the degree of realism and the implications of the main different alternatives: modest growth and very high employment intensity, and stronger growth and higher employment intensity.

(a) Modest growth and very high employment intensity

Pessimism over the chances of achieving stronger growth and worries over the environmental consequences of such stronger growth lead to predictions that the necessary rate of job creation would only be attained through a relatively modest rate of growth and a much higher employment content of this growth. Some people think it more desirable to aim, for instance, for a combination of a return to rates of growth close to the present potential rate of growth of the Community (just over 2% a year) and the achievement of an employment intensity much higher than the present one (a gap between output growth and employment growth of less than half a percentage point).

This proposition is usually inspired by the performance of the USA. Indeed, between 1973 and 1990 the USA experienced a rate of growth, 2.3% per year, but labour productivity grew by 0.4% per year, hence a growth in employment of 1.9% per year on average over the 17 years. This growth practically matched a growth in the labour supply which was much higher than in Europe and held down unemployment to cyclical fluctuations around a nearly constant average (5.6% in 1972, 5.5% in 1990). During the same period, however, real wages per head grew by 0.4% a year compared with 1.5% a year in the Community.

It is not clear, however, whether an increase in the employment intensity of the order of magnitude required to achieve this growth pattern is actually possible in the European economic and social context.

An increase in the employment intensity of Community growth to match the US performance would require the implementation, on a large scale, of measures increasing the willingness of employers to hire workers and in particular:

(i) a considerable downward widening of the scale of wage costs in order to reintegrate those market activities which at present are priced out of it;

(ii) a reduction in all other costs associated with taking on or maintaining labour, e.g. social security rules.

The experience of the last 15 to 20 years suggests that such an increase may be very difficult to achieve. During the 1980s, some progress has been made in reviewing the regulations that hinder job creation and substantial wage moderation has lowered the relative price of labour as a factor of production, but the employment intensity of growth in the Community has hardly changed (see Chart 5).

Chart 5

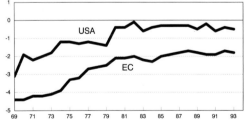

Employment intensity of growth

(Gap between employment and output growth)

Probably, the progress that has been made towards increasing it has only offset other factors working in the other direction such as productivity gains resulting from the introduction of more efficient production techniques and the rationalization made possible by the completion of the single market.

In addition, such a growth pattern would have important implications for wage trends. Since more employment would be created for a given rate of growth, the apparent productivity of labour (real GDP per person employed) would by definition be lower. As a consequence, the room for real wage increases would also be smaller. Given the need to improve investment profitability, at least to improve the present weak competitive position of the Community, gross real wages per head would have to remain practically stable. Furthermore, budgetary consolidation might lead to a decline of average net real wages.

Some other macroeconomic implications must also be stressed. This lower growth scenario would also be less positive for the rest of the world since it would mean slower increases in imports with detrimental effects on the developing countries and East European countries' exports and income developments. In addition, there may be some unwelcome social aspects of the specific measures leading to a more employment-creating growth. In particular, the downward widening in the wage distribution would result in a substantial real decrease in the lowest wages. This would not be possible without a lowering of unemployment compensations and social protection schemes. Combined with the expansion of part-time work, this would also, *ceteris paribus,* widen the existing income distribution towards larger inequality and, at the limit, could create 'working poor' unable to survive decently from their wages and thus lead to a form of exclusion just as damaging as unemployment. If the spirit of the European social model is to be kept, compensatory measures would have to be taken (e.g. negative income taxes for the lowest income groups) with significant budgetary costs.

(b) Stronger growth and more employment intensity

The difficulties and problems abovementioned suggest that the necessary pace of job creation is more likely to be achieved by a growth pattern combining a more modest increase in the employment intensity of growth with a stronger rate of growth. For instance, if from 1995 onwards the Community could achieve an **increase in the employment intensity of growth** of between half and one percentage point (i.e. a gap between output growth and employment growth of between 1 and 1½ percentage points against about 2 points at present) combined with a sustained rate of growth of at least 3% a year, then the unemployment target for the year 2000 would also be achieved. Roughly two thirds of the new jobs would come from stronger growth and about one third from the higher employment intensity of growth.

Real wages per head would be able to increase moderately, but given the resulting increase in employment (2%) the real value of total wages would increase by between 2 and 2½% in real terms. This would be curtailed somewhat by the effects of the necessary budgetary consolidation, but would still leave room for a more substantial real improvement in living standards and an adequate increase in private consumption.

Rates of growth of this order of magnitude are consistent with an environmentally sustainable growth pattern. Indeed, they will make it possible to create the resources to reduce present pollution levels. In addition, stronger investment will also have positive environmental effects since it will accelerate the introduction of new, less-polluting techniques.

An increase in the employment intensity of growth of the order of magnitude of the one envisaged in this second scenario, while not being easy to achieve, would not require the drastic measures needed to reach the performance of the USA. In addition it could be achieved with the consensus of most of those concerned thus improving the chances of implementing at the same time the macroeconomic policies required to achieve higher growth.

This question of how to increase the employment content of growth is dealt with more specifically in Chapter 8.

1.4. The road to higher employment creation

Increasing the rate of growth which the economy of the Community can sustain for many years and increasing the employment content of growth requires a strategy based on **three inseparable elements:**

(a) the creation and the maintenance of a **macroeconomic framework** which instead of constraining market forces, as has often happened in the recent past, supports them;

(b) determined actions in the structural area aimed at increasing the **competitiveness** of European industry and at removing the rigidities which are curbing its dynamism and preventing it from reaping the full benefits of the internal market; an adequate framework for the developing of new market opportunities should be set up;

(c) active policies and structural changes in the **labour market** and in the regulations limiting the expansion of certain sectors (notably the service sector) which will make it easier to employ people and which will therefore increase the employment content of growth.

The necessary actions in the structural area will be discussed in other chapters of the White Paper. This section draws the attention to the most important macroeconomic factors so as to underline a series of important implications and to help identify some useful intermediate policy targets. Its conclusions help to identify the framework which must be implemented to guarantee that actions in other areas translate in actual faster job creation.

Faster growth is a necessary component of any strategy aimed at reducing unemployment significantly. The achievement of this goal depends on a series of elements, some of which are outside the direct control of Community policy-makers. A healthy world economy and the maintenance of an open trading system are obvious examples. But to a very large, and actually increasing, extent the achievement of faster growth depends on implementing the right policies within the Community.

The real challenge facing policy-makers is not just to increase the rate of growth, already a daunting task, but to ensure that the higher rate of growth can be maintained over many years, i.e. to ensure that from

1995, growth remains at the required higher level up to and beyond the year 2000 and that the overheating which appeared in 1989/90 does not arise. This implies increasing the productive capacity of the Community's economy, in other words **increasing its potential rate of growth.**

Given that the capital/output ratio changes very slowly over time, a sustainable increase in production requires an **increase in the available stock of capital.** In turn, this presupposes an increase in investment leading, over time, to a much higher **share of investment** in GDP. This might have to **increase from the present 19% to somewhere in the 23-24% region** (see Chart 6). A shift of this magnitude can only be accomplished over many years.

Chart 6

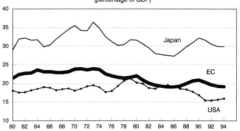

Investment shares : EC, USA and Japan
(percentage of GDP)

Fortunately, however, the actual rate of growth of the Community can reach the target value of at least 3% faster than the potential rate of growth since during the initial years it will be possible to exploit the spare capacity created by the present period of sub-potential growth.

Economic policy must therefore aim at fostering a higher rate of growth and, at the same time at encouraging investment so that it will grow faster than consumption. This relatively slower real expansion of consumption is the price that society must pay over the next few years to ensure a more equitable distribution of the access to gainful employment and to ensure its future overall prosperity.

Higher investment would produce positive results over and above the mechanical relationship between capital and output just mentioned. It would, for instance, accel-

61

erate the incorporation of new technologies into the production process thus leading to more efficient and more environmentally sustainable production. The competitiveness of the economy of the Community would be greatly enhanced.

Creating the conditions for investment-led growth, however, is another difficult task. A necessary, but not sufficient condition, is to make sure that investment profitability increases. But improving business confidence is the key element.

(i) **Increasing investment profitability** requires distributing productivity increases among capital and labour. During most of the 1980s, real wages increased in the Community on average by one percentage point less than productivity. This could constitute an acceptable rule of thumb to be followed to achieve the necessary improvement in profitability and competitiveness. Together with the expected growth in employment, such an increase would provide for a steady expansion of households' real disposable income and of private consumption.

(ii) **Improving business confidence** calls for a series of other actions which range from the maintenance of a stable macroeconomic environment and an adequate level of demand growth, to a determination to continue the process of structural adjustment and the launching of bold projects which demonstrate the will and ability of governments to promote growth (further trade liberalization in the GATT framework and the total opening-up of the single market, trans-European networks, far-sighted R&D efforts, other infrastructure projects, etc.).

An increase in investment, however achieved, has to be accompanied by a corresponding **increase in the rate of national saving** to prevent the appearance of inflationary pressures and balance of payments disequilibria. The Community's current account is presently recording a deficit while its position as an advanced industrialized group warrants a surplus so as to allow it to transfer real resources to the developing world. The necessary increase in the rate of national saving must come essentially from an increase in public saving (reduction of public deficits) since the savings behaviour of the private sector (households and enterprises) is very difficult to influence (see Chart 7 which shows how little it has changed over time). The deterioration in national saving which has taken place in the Community over the last 30 years is due almost entirely to the deterioration of the position of the public sector.

Chart 7

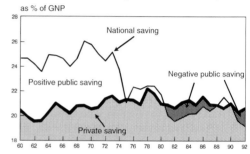

National Saving in the Community

1.5. The policies to reduce unemployment

The analyses conducted over many years have identified many policy actions which influence the rate of growth and the employment intensity of growth. Most of these actions have already been tried and have achieved some success. Their implementation is not painless as very often these actions imply a trade-off between sacrifices now and rewards at a later date. It is not surprising, therefore, that their implementation has almost always been discontinued or not pursued for a sufficiently long period of time.

Combination of macroeconomic and structural policies

The combination of the measures is also important. Very often an appropriate combination yields a result greater than the sum of the gains to be expected from each individual measure. In addition, **there are strong interactions between macroeconomic and structural policies.** Structural policies increase the effectiveness of macroeconomic policies through the removal of some of the constraints that limit their use; the positive effects of structural policies become apparent only in a sound macroeconomic context which allows stronger growth and, finally, implementation of structural policies becomes easier in a context of stronger growth.

The policies required to consolidate growth and to increase its employment content coincide to a large extent, with the policies which are needed to bring the Community's economy out of the recession. The seriousness of the present situation increases the likelihood that these policies will be implemented with sufficient determination. **But the most serious challenge facing policymakers will be to maintain the awareness of the need to implement appropriate macroeconomic and structural policies even when the recession is overcome.**

Once the best policy mix for the attainment of the medium-term goal of higher growth with a higher employment intensity is identified, it will be necessary to assess the extent to which it also contributes to achieving the immediate objective of overcoming the recession. Should it prove insufficient, it will be necessary to examine whether other policy actions of a shorter-term nature are possible without endangering the achievement of the more important medium-term goals. This assessment will be conducted in Section 1.6.

(a) Structural policies

The depth of the present crisis is largely due to insufficient progress in adapting the structures of the Community's economy to the changing technological, social and international environment. Although a consensus emerged during the 1980s on the need to accompany and accelerate structural change instead of trying to slow it down, the pace at which the European economy adjusted to change was only able to match, but not to surpass, that of its major competitors, with the result that vulnerability to cyclical downturns and external shocks remained high. Nevertheless, a mentality in favour of change and willingness to undertake a fundamental reassessment of corporate performance has grown up in Europe over the past decade. In order to achieve optimal results, however, this positive development must now be assisted and fostered by public authorities through the identification and removal of remaining barriers and obstacles to the successful implementation of strategies for change by firms. Only through the structural adaptation of industry can the twin requirements of higher productivity and more jobs be achieved.

Action in the structural area is essentially the responsibility of Member States. However, many of the policy areas that have a decisive impact on structural adjustment and competitiveness are either influenced by various Community policies or are primarily dealt with at the Community level. The Community can therefore play a very useful role in implementing appropriate actions in the fields where it has primary responsibility such as trade and competition policies.

A competitive environment is basic to an efficient allocation of resources and stimulates investment innovation and R&D. However in rapidly changing economic circumstances (globalization of markets, speed and cost of technological change) major restructuring and adaptation by firms is necessary. To meet this challenge they need to be able to restructure unilaterally or bilaterally in cooperation with other firms (mergers, strategic alliances, etc.). This restructuring can be facilitated and speeded up by the timely and judicious use of the available instruments such as State aids, cooperation between companies, etc. This proaction by firms and States needs to be distinguished from anti-competitive practices by firms or States that can slow the necessary structural adjustments.

Structural action can equally help to create the right business and consumer environment by making sure that the legal and regulatory infrastructure that has been created as the basis for the single market operates fairly and efficiently. In particular, the Community can **make sure that the regulatory environment in which business and consumers operate is stable and predictable, and places the minimum bureaucratic burden on economic operators,** particularly small and medium-sized businesses. Finally, the Community can support, encourage and coordinate efforts by Member States to accelerate the diffusion throughout the European economy of those technologies, like information technologies and biotechnologies, that will shape our society in the future and represent the key factor in shaping global competition in the decades to come. These policy issues will be further examined in the following chapters.

The Community needs an adequate framework for the developing of new market opportunities. In Europe some sectors are traditionally the exclusive preserve of non-market services or public utilities, in particular when it comes to the fulfilment of public needs. Reforms aiming at separating the different functions of public authorities with regard to the supply of such services, as producer, purchaser and regulator, in sectors such as health care, telecommunications, etc., should enable the needs of users to be better served at less cost for public finances and with market creation potential.

In recommending actions to be implemented in the Member States it is sometimes not very useful to make general statements since the individual situations are very different. Calls for a specific type of action to solve one particular problem in a country, where the problem is very serious, are resisted by individuals in other countries where the problem never arose or has already largely been solved. The following paragraphs attempt to identify areas for action common to the largest possible number of Member States. The recommendations must be seen as a framework within which Member States will have to identify their individual scope for action.

The necessary structural measures will be discussed in the other chapters of the White Paper. Here it will suffice to mention that action will have to be taken in **three main areas:**

(i) **Greater flexibility** should be introduced in the economy as a whole. In particular, the **regulatory framework** should become more enterprise-friendly.

(ii) Strategies should be developed to create an **efficient labour market** able to respond to new competitive situations.

(iii) The **international environment must be kept open** to allow the Community to participate fully in the development of those areas of the world where the biggest potential of unsatisfied demand presently exists and which are likely to experience the highest rates of growth over the next decade.

(b) Macroeconomic policies

The main task facing macroeconomic policy-makers is to eliminate the conflicts among policy objectives which have plagued the Community over the last 20 years and, more acutely, over recent years. Eliminating these conflicts will make growth, employment and real convergence compatible again with price stability and nominal convergence and will ensure that progress towards EMU will go hand in hand with stronger employment creation. In a stable and supportive macroeconomic framework market forces will be able to deploy themselves unhindered and the possibilities opened up by the internal market will be realized.

At the macroeconomic level, the first medium-term objective will be to maintain the **stability of monetary policy.** Monetary authorities have, over recent years, behaved in a way which is consistent with an inflation target of between 2 and 3%. It is necessary that budgetary policy and wage behaviour adapt to this objective as soon as possible and remain compatible with it. Interest rates will come down once inflationary expectations are stabilized and the perspective of lower budget deficits is established.

In addition it will be essential to make policy coordination more effective and to maintain exchange-rate stability and the EMU perspective. This will help to reinforce the stability of the macroeconomic framework, it will increase the credibility of policy-makers and will shorten the delay until it will be possible to reap the full benefits of monetary union. The implementation of a growth-oriented strategy, such as the one presented in this document will add credibility to the commitment to exchange-rate stability.

Budgetary policy will have to contribute to the medium-term goal of more growth and employment essentially in two ways: i) achieving debt sustainability and ii) contributing to the necessary increase in national saving. The first goal is necessary **to reduce the burden that unbalanced budgetary policies exert on monetary policies and on fiscal flexibility.** The Maastricht criterion for budget deficits (less than 3% of GDP) will constitute a useful reference point in the pursuit of this first goal. With a return to stronger growth the budget deficit criterion could be met by the Community as a whole by 1997. Individual countries may reach this target sooner or later than the Community average depending on their starting positions.

In a longer-term perspective, budgetary policy will have to contribute to increased national saving. This will require increasing substantially public saving and will imply budget deficits significantly below the 3% reference value indicated in the Maastricht Treaty (between zero and one percentage point).

An essential element of budgetary restraint policy will be the adoption of measures to improve the financial situation of the social security system.

Wages

There is a widespread consensus on the need for continued wage moderation and on the positive results it could produce. In their joint opinion of 3 July 1992, the social partners at the European level presented a consensus view for appropriate wage developments: 'The conduct of wage negotiations is under the responsibility of the social partners. The more credible and socially acceptable economic policies are, the easier the social partners can *anticipate low or decreasing inflation rates in the results of their wage negotiations.* This would reduce the strain on monetary policy and contribute to the reduction of short-term interest rates. Furthermore, wage developments have to take into account the requirements of the profitability of employment-creating investment, the competitiveness of enterprises on world markets and the implications of full economic and monetary union. The non-inflationary and sustainable growth process, thus generated, would

provide the appropriate scope for real wage increases which underlines the interrelation between the European integration process and rising living standards.' The difficulties arise when these general principles are translated into actual wage decisions.

There is evidence of **inconsistency between the stability objectives of the central banks and past and current wage behaviour** which bears part of the responsibility for the continuing high level of short-term interest rates. This can be shown by some simple calculations. Under normal conditions, nominal wages per head could increase by an amount equivalent to the inflation target of the monetary authorities (2 to 3%, as noted above) plus that part of the increase in productivity which can be distributed to labour. In the present situation, the increase in productivity results only from a shedding of labour in excess of the decline in production and does not correspond to any distributable creation of wealth. At present, therefore, nominal wages per head should not increase by more than 2 to 3% a year. However, notwithstanding a recent substantial decline, current trends in some Member States and in the Community as a whole are still higher than this figure thus giving cause for concern to monetary authorities.

The elimination of this conflict is a necessary condition for the return to growth in the present situation, but once the Community's economy is again on a sustained growth path, it will be important to ensure that wages continue to increase in line with the stability objective and the need to allow for an increase in investment profitability and competitiveness (the rule of thumb of *'productivity minus one percentage point'* identified in Section 1.4.). It must be underlined that these EC-wide prescriptions should give room for an appropriate differentiation according to Member countries, regions and vocational qualifications.

1.6. Overcoming the recession

The first requirement that the policies to be implemented must satisfy to overcome the recession is that of being consistent with the aim of the medium-term growth pattern. Within this framework, overcoming the recession calls above all for a **restoration of confidence.** Business leaders, the workforce and citizens in general must be convinced

65

that the authorities will be able to correct the present imbalances and maintain over many years a sound and stable macroeconomic environment.

This requires measures in both the macro-economic and structural areas. Macroeconomic policy actions can rapidly change the environment in which businesses operate, but structural actions are essential to the improvement in their confidence. The effects of structural policies will be felt essentially in the medium term, but determined actions are now vital in convincing economic agents that action is under way which will bring results later.

In addition it will be essential to give a new and visible impetus to the process of cooperation at the international level. Rapid implementation of the provisions of the Maastricht Treaty, conclusion of the Uruguay Round of trade negotiations, and bold new initiatives *vis-à-vis* the countries of Eastern Europe and of the Third World would be very important signals.

As soon as the recovery sets in, the economy will be able to reap fully the benefits of the structural adjustment which has taken place over the last decade and of the completion of the internal market. These structural measures bring substantial efficiency gains which during periods of slow growth remain unexploited.

Improving rapidly the quality of the policy mix

Lower interest rates constitute a powerful instrument to boost the Community's economy in the short term. Interest rates have already come down significantly over the last 12 months. However, given the depth of the present recession they still remain too high in many countries, especially at the short-term end. Under these circumstances, the first requirement is to create the conditions for further substantial reductions in short-term interest rates. This calls essentially for expected budgetary and wage developments to be kept in line with the monetary authorities' stability objectives. Any lowering of short-term rates not warranted by appropriate budgetary and wage behaviours would risk being offset by expectations of higher future infla-

tion and higher long-term rates. On the other hand, if credible plans for budgetary consolidation and agreements leading to more moderate wage increases were to materialize, expectations would be favourably influenced and central banks might be able to lower short-term interest rates in advance of actual developments.

A substantial lowering of short-term interest rates throughout the Community would reduce tensions within the ERM and would improve the financial position of firms and public budgets. The scope for reductions is large: interest rates could come down substantially in Germany if the appropriate policies are implemented while in other countries the reductions could be even larger to the extent that interest rate differentials can be reduced. A further significant reduction would signal to economic agents that the worst is over, that monetary policy had been loosened as much as it was possible and that nothing would be gained by further postponing any investment decision which may have been contingent on the availability of the best financing conditions.

A lowering of short-term rates in the Community would have a positive impact on the competitiveness of European enterprises. Together with the restoration of confidence, this would trigger an export/investment-led cyclical upswing in the Community.

Budgetary policy

Action in the budgetary area depends on an assessment of the likely impact on demand and on business and consumer confidence of changes in the present budgetary stance. In 1991 and 1992, Member States have allowed budget deficits to deteriorate since it was considered that this would lend a measure of support to domestic demand. At the beginning of 1993 additional efforts at the national level took place in the framework of the Edinburgh growth initiative. By mid-1993, however, Member States reached a consensus [1] that no room for manoeuvre in the short term was available: any additional deterioration in budget deficits was more likely to depress overall demand,

---

[1] EPC Opinion of 8 July 1993 and EcoFin Council conclusions of 12 July 1993.

through its negative effect on confidence, than to support it. On the contrary, they recognized the need for concrete, credible, medium-term consolidation programmes.

The immediate target of these programmes should be to prevent further deterioration in budgetary positions and to create the prospects of consolidation once the recovery sets in. The severity of the necessary adjustment will depend on the specific conditions of each Member State, but efforts in this direction are required in almost all countries. In addition, all governments should attempt to switch expenditure as far as is practicable, towards those items which most directly influence growth prospects: education, R&D, infrastructure investments, etc.

Wages

The previous section highlighted the existence of an inconsistency between the inflation target pursued by monetary authorities and actual wage behaviour in many countries. The sooner this inconsistency is eliminated, the sooner short-term interest rates can be reduced. In some cases, however, the gap is so large that progress will inevitably take some time. Tripartite agreements between the social partners and governments should be exploited where possible.

Developing a broad social consensus

The continuation of the EMU process is a key element to secure a stable macroeconomic framework enabling the achievement of higher, sustainable, growth. The Community has long acknowledged the negative influence exchange-rate instability has on business confidence and there is a powerful case for arguing that the full benefits of a single market can only be reaped in a monetary union. These considerations have been at the basis of the Treaty on European Union and maintain their validity today notwithstanding the ERM crisis of the last 12 months. A group of countries so closely knit by a web of trade and financial links as the European Community needs a stable monetary environment both internally and externally.

To restore the credibility of the EMU process Member States must retheir commitment to this goal and back up their words with actions. Economic policy coordination between the Member States must be made more effective. This calls essentially for the development of a consensus as broad as possible on the policy framework outlined in this document and apportioning in each Member State the efforts which will be required from all parties (using social dialogue procedures wherever possible). Those in employment must be convinced that the measures called for in this document will work and that the solidarity they will show in accepting some sacrifices will effectively result in those now deprived of gainful employment being given a real chance. Increased efforts to improve the situation of the public finances in order to meet the criteria set out in the Maastricht Treaty will require an update of the convergence programmes which remain useful instruments for the development of a debate leading to such a consensus. The guidelines for economic policy aimed at dealing with deficiencies identified in this paper should be agreed as a matter of urgency, if business confidence is to be restored.

A Community dimension

The success of such a policy course in restoring growth depends, however, on various factors which are to a greater or lesser extent outside the control of policy-makers; in particular business and consumer confidence and the performance of the Community's main trading partners. It is very likely that given the severity of the present situation and the size of the budgetary adjustment which will be inevitable in many countries, that the recovery will be modest and hesitant. This may call for an intensification of the Community initiatives agreed at the European Council meetings in Edinburgh and in Copenhagen. In a climate of growing business confidence, various Community projects, such as the trans-European networks, lend themselves to initiatives which can mobilize large financial resources, coming essentially from the private sector, to finance useful projects.

II — COMPETITIVENESS

Chapter 2

The conditions
for growth and greater
competitiveness

A — Towards global
competitiveness

For the level of employment in the Community to improve, firms must achieve global competitiveness on open and competitive markets, both inside and outside Europe. It is the responsibility of the national and Community authorities to provide industry with a favourable environment, to open up clear and reliable prospects for it and to promote its international competitiveness. This responsibility is now enshrined in the Treaty on European Union. Back in 1991 the Council of Ministers adopted guidelines for a Community industrial policy geared to such an objective.

The globalization of economies and markets, which involves the intensification of international competition through the emergence of a potentially unique worldwide market for an expanding range of goods, services and factors, brings out the full importance of that responsibility on the part of national and Community authorities as regards competitiveness. We must increasingly think in terms of competitive rather than comparative advantages. Comparative advantages traditionally relate to endowment in factors such as natural resources and are therefore fairly rigid. Competitive advantages are based on more qualititative factors and can thus be influenced, to a large degree, by corporate strategies and by public policies. In such a context, factor mobility and the capacity to combine factors effectively and to organize the social consensus on the share-out of value-added are becoming much more important than the initial factor endowment.

The Community will be able to improve its global competitiveness considerably provided it achieves a substantial recovery in its invest-ment ratio (see Chapter 1). **For this, it enjoys significant comparative advantages:** the potential of its labour force and the social consensus enabling that potential to be exploited, its valuable scientific and technical know-how, its integrated market, the density and quality of its infrastructures, the improved financial structures of its firms, and the diversity of its culture and regions. An economy based on the creation, dissemination and exploitation of knowledge will be one of the dominant features of the 21st century, and against such a background a number of these competitive factors will play a crucial role in generating a recovery in growth and an increase in employment.

The completion of the Europe-wide frontier-free market on 31 December 1992 and the improvements in its operation envisaged by the strategic programme will allow firms to benefit from economies of scale, reduce their administrative and financial costs, have easier and more competitive access to private-sector and public-sector procurement, and cooperate more efficiently with one another. This will give the Community a firm and well-organized base from which to tackle the new problems posed by international competitiveness.

However, the Community will also have to overcome the handicaps which have contributed to the erosion of its competitiveness within the Triad (Community, United States and Japan) in recent years: Apart from the macroeconomic policy imbalances that have contributed to the real appreciation of Community currencies, there is firstly, as emphasized by the Member States, the problem that their industries are not sufficiently well represented on expanding new markets, either in geographical terms or in terms of products, with its firms sometimes at a disadvantage in the face of the dominant positions held by certain international groups and the growth of strategic alliances. Secondly, the regulatory environment is still too rigid, and administrative and managerial traditions too centralized and compartmentalized. Lastly, government policies are often still too defensive and do not take sufficient account of the new constraints imposed by global competition.

Four overriding objectives must be pursued jointly by industry and the authorities if the Community's industrial competitiveness is to generate the highest possible level of employment:

- **Helping European firms to adapt to the new globalized and interdependent competitive situation.**

- **Exploiting the competitive advantages associated with the gradual shift to a knowledge-based economy.**

- **Promote a sustainable development of industry.**

- **Reducing the time-lag between the pace of change in supply and the corresponding adjustments in demand.**

This chapter analyses the Community's strengths and weaknesses when it comes to tackling these challenges and then goes on to identify the main components of a policy of global competitiveness.

2.1. Views of the Member States

Among the factors having a major impact on the competitiveness of the Community economy, Member States point particularly to the following: the negative effects of public deficits on investment; impaired functioning of the labour market leading — whether in terms of cost, skills or flexibility in the organization of work — to a mismatch between supply of and demand for labour; inadequate assimilation of new technologies combined with failure to exploit properly the results of research and technological development, leading to difficulties in concentrating the production of goods and services in leading-edge and high value-added industries.

A number of Member States report market rigidities or distortions in resource allocation caused by government intervention, either through excessive regulation or through various restrictions on competition. Some Member States point to the heavier burden which the ageing of the population is imposing on the economy, and one Member State establishes a link between competitiveness and the smaller number of hours worked on average in the Community compared with its main partners.

2.2. The Community's competitive position in a globalized economy: Strengths and weaknesses

Since 1989 the Community has experienced a gradual decline in the growth rate of the production of goods and services. [1] Although the trend in its industrial competitiveness is also worrying, it does have considerable strengths on which it can draw in order to redress the position and to manage its transition to the 21st century successfully.

Weaknesses

In the fierce competition prevailing on world markets, Community industry is handicapped by the deterioration in its commercial competitiveness, by its failure to establish itself sufficiently on expanding new markets, by an unduly low level of R&D investment and by productivity rates which still lag behind those of its major competitors. Most Member States agree with this assessment.

(a) The **trade performance** of Community industry has deteriorated since 1980, as the downward trend in the rate of cover of imports by exports shows (see Figure 1).

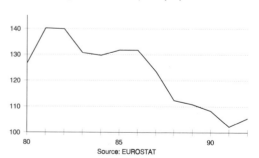

Figure 1: Cover of imports by exports

Source: EUROSTAT

---

[1] In the remainder of the text, the term 'industry' is used to cover the production of both goods and services.

In recent years, Community industry has not only lost market shares as a result of the growing power of the newly-industrialized countries, as was foreseeable, but has also had to give ground to the United States of America and Japan.

The situation has deteriorated *vis-à-vis* the USA because of the adverse trend of exchange rates. In the case of Japan, the reason is rather a failure to move into expanding new markets as quickly as Japanese industry. The erosion in the market shares of Community industry has been accentuated by the growing proportion of world trade accounted for by the newly-industrialized countries of South-East Asia.

Community industry's trade performance is fairly uneven. A large part of industry (two thirds in terms of activity) lost market shares between 1986 and 1991, either as a result of increased import penetration of the Community market or because of losses on the export front, or through a combination of the two.

(b) **Community industry improved its position on markets experiencing slow growth** (railway equipment, cotton, textile and sewing machinery, miscellaneous textiles, tanning and dressing, animal slaughter and meat preparation, grain processing and ethyl alcohol distillation), while **its performance deteriorated on markets with high value-added** such as office automation, information technology, electronics, and medical and surgical equipment. Its structure is therefore not yet geared to that of expanding new markets. This time-lag is all the more damaging in that these high-value-added markets are characterized by rapid growth in the apparent productivity of labour, high wages and salaries, and a diffusion of technological progress into other markets.

Apparent labour productivity in Community manufacturing still lags a good way behind that of US and Japanese industry. There is no sign of any narrowing of the gap (of more than 10%) with the USA and, despite the progress achieved, the gap between Europe and Japan is still around 40%. Closing this gap will necessitate in particular a significant recovery in the investment ratio. Productivity growth plays a key role in international competitiveness while, at the same time, making for an improvement in domestic living standards. Both the level and the growth rate of productivity must be taken into account. The factors influencing productivity growth are technological development, investment, the rate of capacity utilization, the size and skills of the labour force, management skills, the organization of production and the use of resources such as energy and raw materials.

(c) **Corporate investment in R&D** is one area in which the Community must make major efforts. In recent years, annual average growth in R&D expenditure has been highest in Japan (10%). Next comes the Community (8.1%), followed by the USA (7.9%). The 1992 break in the trend of corporate R&D expenditure in the Community (and in Japan) is very worrying in this respect (see Figure 2).

Figure 2: Growth of R&D expenditures

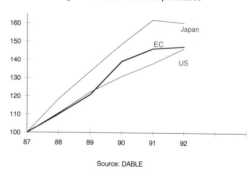

Source: DABLE

Strengths

However, Community industry can draw on major strengths to help it adapt to the new conditions of world competitiveness. It has a low level of indebtedness, and its profit margins are comparable to those of its competitors. It has been able to restructure itself in step with the moves to establish the single market. Its labour force is highly skilled. It has a high density of efficient infrastructures.

(a) **Community firms have kept control of their level of indebtedness** in recent years, albeit at the cost of some ageing of their capital stock. Their indebtedness is at present much lower than that of their competitors. Community firms are thus comparatively less vulnerable to any increases in interest rates, but they will also benefit comparatively less from further interest-rate reductions (see Figure 3).

Figure 3: Indebtedness of firms

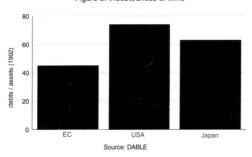

Source: DABLE

Japanese firms too face major problems in adapting to the decline in consumption and to the adverse effect of the strengthening yen on the volume of their exports.

(b) When the competitive environment became tougher at the end of the 1980s, Community and US firms **cut their profit margins significantly.** Japanese companies, which traditionally operate with smaller profit margins than their Community competitors, also saw their profit margins squeezed, albeit to a lesser extent. These developments have had the effect of narrowing the gaps between these three trading blocs (see Figure 4).

However, in both Europe and the United States, profit margins differ appreciably from one market to another, much more so in fact than in Japan. In Europe, industries facing relatively little international competition still achieve high profit margins, whereas in industries more exposed to international competition profit mar-

gins have shrunk to worrying levels and, in some cases, have actually disappeared.

Figure 4: Trend of profit margins

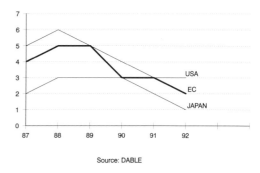

Source: DABLE

(c) Labour costs are an important element **underlying the competitiveness** of European industry, though by no means the only one. Unit labour costs depend on wage and non-wage costs compared with labour productivity. Thus high labour costs can be compensated for by high productivity to maintain competitive advantage. It is when costs are not aligned with productivity that problems for competitiveness arise. In relative terms, the large rises and falls in unit labour costs compared with those of the Union's leading competitors which have taken place since 1980 have been reflected by fluctuations in bilateral exchange rates between the ecu and the US dollar and yen.

Labour costs affect competitiveness differently with regard to other developed countries and to those in the process of industrialization. Non-cost items such as quality, delivery, design and customer focus can assist in maintaining competitiveness, but attention to relative costs, including labour costs, remains important. Compared with newly industrializing countries, particularly those just entering that path such as China, the **differential in labour cost is too great** for any significant employment gains to be made in Europe from wage reductions in manufacturing industry. Only high productivity and superior products will enable Europe to **maintain a competitive advantage.**

74

2.3. The main lines of a policy of global competitiveness

(a) Helping European firms to adapt to the new globalized and interdependent competitive situation

In the wake of the globalization of economies and markets, **it is no longer possible to divide industry and geographical areas into clearly identified and relatively independent segments.** European firms are engaged in production both within the Community and on third markets. Their competitors increasingly have subsidiaries in the Community. There is a multitude of international agreements between firms: more than 400 international strategic alliances have been entered into by large firms in each of the last five years.

European firms have to compete with international, polyvalent groups. The boundaries of traditional industrial sectors are becoming less and less sharply defined. This is particularly evident in the sphere of 'multimedia' activities. Firms engaged in telecommunications, information technology, consumer electronics, programming and network management combine and come together in extremely complex groups and alliances which will very largely determine the creation and distribution of assets, including cultural assets, over the next decade on expanding new markets of key importance for the future.

Industrial globalization means that **new balances must be sought between competition and cooperation. Four avenues** are particularly important in devising a policy of global industrial competitiveness:

(i) **Capitalizing on the Community's industrial strengths,** so as to safeguard productive and innovatory capacities as well as a diversified, job-creating industry that is spread throughout Europe, particularly on markets with a high-growth potential, such as health, the environment, biotechnologies, multimedia activities and culture. This aspect must take account of changes stemming from the globalization of markets, production and operators and from the industrial policies of the Community's main competitors.

(ii) **The development of an active policy of industrial cooperation,** notably with the transition economies of Eastern Europe and with the high-growth economies along the Pacific rim. As far as the **countries in Eastern Europe** are concerned, much closer industrial cooperation is necessary in order to ensure simultaneously a rapid modernization of their economies, a better division of labour within Europe and optimum exploitation of mutual interests. Cooperation must be based on closer links between public support and private initiatives and on speedier progress in establishing the legal framework, investment conditions and guarantee arrangements which our firms require. For the industries concerned, this could be accompanied by a transitional period to allow the necessary structural adjustments to be carried out under the best possible conditions. As far as the **Pacific area** is concerned, increased market penetration by European firms can be greatly facilitated by concerted efforts on the part of the public authorities to remove the regulatory, administrative and indeed cultural obstacles which have hitherto impeded or deterred such penetration.

(iii) **The establishment of a coherent and concerted approach to strategic alliances,** the uncontrolled development of which could result in the creation of oligopolistic situations prejudicial to competition at world level. The growing number of industrial and technological alliances will have an impact on all markets. These effects must consequently be assessed simultaneously and in a concerted manner by the competent authorities pending the introduction of appropriate international rules, particularly in the competition field, so that the Community is not placed at a disadvantage by the strict rules it imposes on itself in this connection. In addition, Community firms must be able to rely on **flexible instruments of cooperation,** in legal and tax matters as well as in others, to allow them to enter into the alliances that are necessary to counterbalance the weight of some of their US and Japanese competitors.

(iv) **The targeting of measures to remove obstacles to the smooth functioning of markets** in areas that severely penalize European firms' sales and growth potential. European firms' capacity for exporting to, and setting up in, other countries is sometimes far from being fully exploited because of the difficulties stemming from the structural impermeability of certain markets. **Pinpointing such barriers to growth and introducing specific measures** to remove them may help significantly to improve Community industry's opportunities for selling its products on the markets concerned. This could be modelled, for example, on the 'trade assessment mechanism' set up with Japan to identify the nature and causes of the Community's poor trade performance in Japan in those sectors in which Community industry is in a strong competitive position at international level.

(b) Exploiting the competitive advantages associated with the gradual shift to a knowledge-based economy

The wealth of nations is increasingly based on the creation and exploitation of knowledge. Optimum advantage must be taken of this new form of progress available to Community firms since it is an area in which the Community enjoys a substantial head start.

The shift towards a knowledge-based economy is reflected in particular in the externalization of certain activities by industrial firms and by the faster growth of services. It does not mean that manufacturing industry is declining in importance, since this sector is at the very heart of this development and continues to determine the overall competitiveness of the productive system.

The key elements in competitiveness that are now of greatest importance are no longer confined to the relative level of the direct costs of the various factors of production. They include in particular the quality of education and training, the efficiency of industrial organization, the capacity to make continuous improvements in production processes, the intensity of R&D and its industrial exploitation, the fluidity of the conditions under which markets operate, the availability of competitive service infrastructures, product quality and the way in which corporate strategies take account of the consequences of changes in society, such as improved environmental protection.

Even more crucial is the capacity to incorporate all of these elements into coherent strategies. Between 75% and 95% of firms' total wage and salary bill is now accounted for by functions linked to organization rather than to direct production, for example information technology, engineering, training, accounting, marketing and research. **Organizational capacity** is thus one of the key components of a firm's competitiveness.

A number of these factors, such as training, research and services, may be grouped together under the heading of **'non-physical' (i.e. knowledge-based) investment, to which government policies must in future accord at least the same priority as they do to physical investment.** This type of investment is becoming the key element in bringing about growth that is durable, creates skilled jobs and is economical in its use of resources.

This does not entail any increase in public deficits, but it does presuppose far-reaching reforms:

- **As regards taxes: The relative weight of taxation borne by the various factors of competitiveness should be adjusted** in such a way as to reduce those components of taxation which act as employment disincentives and to increase those conducive to more efficient and less polluting use of scarce resources.

- **As regards the criteria governing the use of national and Community financial instruments:** There should in particular be **a review of the criteria governing the admissibility of aid to industry,** which, under most existing schemes, encourages firms to increase the capital intensity of production and to boost their physical as opposed to their non-physical investment in order to improve productive efficiency. The aim should be to take fuller account of the creation of value-added and the non-physical content of growth.

- **As regards the priorities governing the use of public funds:** Investment in training, research, the promotion of innovation and, generally speaking, the non-physical components of value-added must be treated at least as favourably as traditional forms of investment. The aim should be twofold: **to promote the emergence of new generations of products** that make optimum use of all the technologies available on the world market, and to encourage the dynamic incorporation of innovation into processes, products and organization. An essential precondition is that there should be an **increase in research activities** by Community firms and greater selectivity in government assistance.

- **As regards the regulatory framework:** More must be done to ensure the efficient operation of the single market, notably by streamlining and **rationalizing rules and regulations** so as to make it easier to establish new forms of labour organization and to move away from 'Taylorism'. A **policy that focuses on quality** and is consistent with the Community's approach to standardization must be pursued in order to exploit the know-how of Community firms and avoid market fragmentation.

(c) Promote a sustainable development of industry

A policy of pollution prevention, in particular through a generalized development of clean products and processes, will not only prevent rapidly increasing clean-up costs but also stimulate a faster diffusion of R&D results. The first-mover advantage that will result will contribute to a strengthened overall competitiveness of European industry.

The significance of the so-called Eco-industry as a quickly expanding industrial market is now widely accepted and, according to OECD studies, will expand considerably this decade. It covers not only the supply of goods and services to firms for pollution control or abatement but also the expenditures made for the environment in the general context of improved production methods or products, as well as the markets for environmentally-sound products (green products).

In the present context of global competition, the technologies employed in, and the organizational requirements for, the successful introduction of clean technologies are often similiar to those associated with the new manufacturing paradigm. The concept of lean (e.g. less energy, fewer raw materials) constitutes a significant improvement regarding the environmental friendliness of production processes and fosters the competitiveness of the industries concerned.

Moving beyond production processes to product markets provides an additional dimension for industrial competitiveness. Markets for environmentally-sound products provide an incentive for firms since they represent in any case a source of potential profits. As stricter environmental requirements are imposed on export markets, the application of clean technologies becomes a condition of access to these markets.

To promote the sustainable development of European industry, the Community should:

(i) increase substantially and coordinate R&D efforts in the field of clean technology;

(ii) develop economic incentives to support the diffusion of R&D results into products and processes.

(d) Reducing the time-lag between the pace of change in supply and the corresponding adjustments in demand

As in the case of previous industrial revolutions, there is an appreciable time-lag between:

- changes in supply, where faster modernization is now under way through the use of increasingly efficient technologies, resulting in a rapid increase in labour productivity and thus releasing substantial human resources;

- changes in demand, which are lagging behind changes in supply because of cumbersome rigidities in income distribution, in modes of consumption, in the relatively low level of receptiveness to innovation within the Community, in the geographical structure of growth and in the unsatisfactory functioning of markets.

It is imperative that an attempt be made to reduce this time-lag so as **to make optimum use of the human resources released as a result of the increasing productivity of the productive system.** This can be done only by helping to broaden the sales opportunities for Community industry through policies geared simultaneously to demand, to supply and to improving the interaction between them.

On the demand side, this means:

- **Pursuing initiatives aimed at speeding up a concerted recovery in consumption at world level and helping to bring about a revival in demand for Community industry.** The asymmetries stemming from the continuing large differences in the degree of openness of markets as between the most open areas, foremost amongst which is the Community, and those which, for structural or political reasons, remain largely protected are reflected in a chronic growth deficit at world level. **Resolute support for initiatives to bring about a concerted recovery in demand and for the opening-up and industrial modernization of the protected countries** is essential in order to make up this 'shortfall' in growth.

- **Looking at the various measures liable to promote the emergence of new markets for goods and services.** This is a reference in particular to those markets geared to improvements in **environmental** protection (on which Community firms are particularly competitive), to the exploitation of biotechnologies and to the creation, management and dissemination of information. In this respect, the emergence of **'multimedia' activities** that exploit the scope afforded by the digitalization of information in all its forms (written word, image and sound) will engender major upheavals that will benefit those firms and economies capable

of establishing themselves on these new markets. [1]

On the supply side, we must:

- **Encourage continuing structural adjustment in Community industry.** This means facilitating privatization processes, which can, in large measure, help to speed up such adjustments.

Community industry has not sufficiently exploited all the opportunities afforded by the rapid growth of markets in Asia and Latin America.

- **Underpin the dynamism of SMEs.** It is clearly more difficult and relatively more costly for SMEs than for very large firms to find their proper place in the globalized economy, to have access to world technological capital and to avail themselves of the most sophisticated management techniques and business services. The policies in support of SMEs must, therefore, take account of these new constraints and be strengthened accordingly.

Lastly, better interaction between supply and demand must be strongly encouraged by:

- **facilitating partnerships between large firms and their subcontractors.** Effective cooperation between component assemblers and suppliers is one of the essential preconditions for reducing the total time involved in innovation, optimizing R&D expenditure, reducing overheads, ensuring the technical homogeneity of products and improving product quality. The steps already taken in this direction by industry are proving extremely positive and deserve increased support from the public authorities;

- **improving the interfaces between producers and users.** Although wide-ranging, this objective is of particular importance for **research** if more rapid and more sensitive account is to be taken of market requirements in RTD policies and if there is to be greater complementarity between Eureka and the Community research programmes. The research

---

[1] See the chapter on 'The information society'.

effort, which is insufficient overall, must be stepped up, become more focused and be more effectively exploited as regards its applications. Ensuring the broadest possible dissemination of information and facilitating contacts between all those involved through the establishment of multidisciplinary cooperation are both necessary in order to foster not only competition in the development of technologies but also effectiveness in exploiting them;

- **stimulating the development of 'clusters' of competitive activities that draw on the regional diversity of the Community.** The proliferation within the Community of 'clusters' that combine industrial, technological and geographical advantages may hold one of the keys to job creation. This requires the active involvement of all the actors concerned, something which can be greatly facilitated by **structural measures** taken at Community and national level. In this area, as in the preceding ones, **the main emphasis should be on a horizontal, transsectoral and multidisciplinary approach.**

These guidelines are summarized in the attached table.

Conclusion

So as to establish the bases for such a policy of global competitiveness and ensure that its positive effects on employment come through as rapidly as possible, the Commission proposes that the European Council adopt the following objectives and guidelines:

(i) **Government intervention in industry must be refocused on horizontal measures and on growth markets** where there is strong potential for European industry to develop, such as health, the environment, biotechnologies, multimedia activities and culture. This also means that precise and short-term deadlines should be set for restructuring activities whose development prospects are not satisfactory in terms of markets.

(ii) **The machinery and criteria for government intervention** that creates conflict between the promotion of industrial competitiveness and job creation **must be reviewed.** In so doing, the tax burden must be redistributed so as to lighten the burden on labour and increase the burden on the use of natural resources. The criteria for granting public assistance must be reviewed so as to take better account of value-added and so as not to encourage an unjustified increase in the capital intensity of production. The regulatory framework must be transparent, stable and predictable.

(iii) **The promotion of non-physical, knowledge-based investment** must be made the top priority of the general policy in support of investment. Training, research and know-how in general must be treated as proper targets of investment in their own right. The necessary consequences should be drawn notably as regards changes in tax and accounting rules.

(iv) **A dynamic policy of industrial cooperation** must be set in motion, starting with the countries of Eastern Europe and with the Pacific area. The details of such a policy must be established as a matter of urgency in collaboration with the private-sector and public-sector operators concerned, on the basis of clearly identified mutual and reciprocal interests.

(v) Measures must be taken shortly to **strengthen the competitive functioning of markets.** A European approach should be developed that takes account of the proliferation of strategic alliances, particularly in the field of competition, so as to prevent the development of dominant positions at world level. Machinery for pinpointing problems in the functioning of markets and for assessing their industrial implications must be set up so as to identify and tackle rapidly the obstacles facing European firms against the backdrop of global competition.

(vi) **The coordination of moves to facilitate a revival in consumption and reinforce the** interaction between changes in supply and demand at both international and Community level must be strengthened. Priority should be given to employing all the resources available, and in particular structural policies, in order to speed up the development of clusters of competitive activities that draw on the Community's regional advantages. The networks for collaboration between operators (SMEs and large firms, producers and users, public and private actors) must be improved along multidisciplinary and multisectoral lines. Lastly, there must be **a European policy on quality** that complements the policy on standardization and is geared to promoting activities with a high value-added.

Guidelines for a policy of global competitiveness

Objectives	Means
1. *Helping European firms to adapt to the new globalized and interdependent competitive situation*	• capitalizing on the Community's industrial strengths • developing an active policy of industrial cooperation • establishing a concerted approach to strategic alliances • targeting measures to ensure the competitive functioning of markets
2. *Exploiting the competitive advantages associated with the gradual shift to a knowledge-based economy*	• reforming tax policies so as not to create employment disincentives and to promote incentives for the efficient use of scarce resources • developing a policy to encourage 'non-physical' investment (training, research, technical assistance) • bolstering policies to streamline and rationalize rules and regulations • reviewing the criteria governing the use of public instruments in support of industry so as to enhance their impact on the growth of value-added and employment • launching a European policy aimed at quality
3. *Promote a sustainable development of industry*	• increase substantially and coordinate R&D efforts in the field of clean technology • develop economic incentives to support the diffusion of R&D results into products and processes.
4. *Reducing the time-lag between the pace of change in supply and the corresponding adjustments in demand*	*Demand-side measures:* • pursuing initiatives aimed at facilitating a concerted revival in consumption at world level • promoting the emergence of new markets *Supply-side measures:* • encouraging continuing structural adjustment by supporting privatizations • underpinning the dynamism of SMEs *Measures to improve the relationship between supply and demand:* • facilitating partnerships between large firms and their subcontractors • improving the interfaces between producers and users • establishing collaboration networks so as to develop clusters of competitive activities

B — Making the most of the internal market

The agreement under the Single European Act to establish an area without internal frontiers in which the free circulation of goods, services, capital and persons is ensured represents the single most important step that the Community has made towards a rational economy and greater prosperity. **Ensuring that this ambitious objective** is translated into practical reality is an essential condition for economic growth, competitiveness and employment in the Community.

The Community has met most of the original targets which it set itself for the establishment of a single market. The one outstanding failure to date is the maintenance of physical controls on the free movement of people, although the economic impact of this gap may be limited as the most economically-significant parts of Community legislation in this area, i.e. recognition of the right of establishment and of professional qualifications, are already in place.

The establishment of a genuine single market in the Community is not, however, a matter of once-and-for-all enacting Community legislation within a deadline. It is a continual process of ensuring that, as far as possible, a single legislative framework governing economic activity is enforced and, where necessary, developed in a coherent way within a continually changing environment. The decisions of individual enterprises and citizens are the hard core of a working single market. The challenge before the Community now is to make sure that they are not hindered from taking full advantage of it and to respond quickly to any signs if it is not working well.

Views of the Member States

Making the most of the opportunities offered by the single market is perceived in the Member States' contributions as one of the keys to making the European economy more competitive. Liberalizing sectors that have not yet been opened up to competition (energy and telecommunications in

particular), developing standardization in certain areas, monitoring the application of single market legislation more closely, removing tax barriers and harmonizing certain taxes are seen as priorities. Several Member States stress the need for the single market to create a propitious business environment; in this context, they suggest streamlining existing administrative rules and procedures, carrying out cost/benefit analyses before going ahead with new measures, and studying ways and means of reducing the cost of red tape for businesses.

2.4. The development of a strategic programme

The Commission has therefore decided to publish in parallel with this White Paper a strategic programme for the internal market which provides a comprehensive view of priorities for action in this area and which will serve as a 'road map' for the development of the single market.

The strategic programme contains **three parts:**

(a) Completing the legislative programme

The Commission will press for **early decisions** on the limited number of measures identified in the 1985 White Paper which have not yet been agreed, as well as on new proposals aiming at securing the free movement of people.

It has to be recognized that the internal market is not yet a reality in certain sectors where national legislation and the granting of exclusive rights deny access to the market and prevent competition in any form. For energy, telecommunications and postal services, for example, proposals have been made but these may have to be strengthened in order to achieve liberalization while ensuring that public policy objectives, such as 'universal service', are fully realized where appropriate. Further liberalization of the transport sectors is also needed, notwithstanding the considerable progress in recent years.

(b) Managing the Community area

This part of the programme is intended to ensure that the necessary arrangements are in place to permit adopted legislation to be applied effectively and efficiently, so that individuals and enterprises will be able to take full and fair advantage of the possibilities which the internal market offers them. This is not a bureaucratic exercise. It is a joint effort by the Community Member States and enterprises to avoid unnecessary costs, to ensure fair competition, to build up the confidence of both producers and consumers — a condition for economic recovery — and to guarantee that the single market is a practical reality.

The main priorities are **effective control of national transposition of Community law,** a reinforcement of administrative cooperation between Member States in the application and enforcement of Community law, notification procedures to prevent the emergence of new barriers to free movement, the auditing of national enforcement measures and measures to facilitate legal redress where Community law is infringed.

The need for **administrative cooperation** also requires the establishment of an efficient, reliable and user-friendly **system of communication and data exchange between administrations.** Until it is operational, unnecessary costs resulting from inefficient administration will be borne by the economy as a whole. What is called for is:

(i) an accelerated, progressive and wide-ranging introduction of an electronic mail network;

(ii) a high degree of coordination between the 13 administrations involved;

(iii) a series of flanking measures in order to facilitate the operational use and further development of the network.

It is proposed that this initiative to establish an effective communications network — **a new trans-European network for effective administration** — be taken by the Community public authorities quickly in order to facilitate the priority objective of the efficient management of the internal market,

while contributing directly to reduced costs for business and the citizen.

(c) Developing the single market

A dynamic view of the single market is necessary for the Community's achievement to be sustained and preserved. The third part of the strategic programme aims to ensure that the internal market can **develop to meet new needs** and to launch new initiatives to ensure that a continental-scale open market is fully realized. Not all such initiatives will be of a legislative nature; they also include close cooperation between the Commission and the Member States, and between public authorities and the private sector.

The following **objectives** are identified in the strategic programme as essential for this purpose:

(i) improving the evaluation of the effectiveness of Community rules including, when appropriate, the need to simplify them;

(ii) providing a more favourable environment for business. This is the central part of the programme, including initiatives to ensure greater competition, protection of intellectual property, cross-border payments and direct and indirect taxation, standardization and quality policy and a package of measures designed to assist small and medium-sized enterprises to operate more effectively. The resolute implementation of competition policy and control of State aids is one of the essential elements to ensure a greater flexibility of the system in order to increase competitiveness;

(iii) promoting the development of trans-European networks;

(iv) ensuring that the development of the internal market is sustainable. The commitment to 'sustainable and non-inflationary growth respecting the environment' in the Treaty on European Union must be reflected by action at Community level to ensure that measures taken to protect the environment are fully effective and compatible with a single market.

83

(v) ensuring a secure environment for the citizen, the employee and the consumer;

(vi) greater transparency in preparing any new Community legislation, if it were shown to be needed.

2.5. The impact of the internal market on growth, competitiveness and employment

It is impossible today to assess the full effect of all the measures designed to bring about a single market because they are not yet fully in force. Although the internal market has not reached its full potential, its credibility and irrevocability have exerted profound effects on business behaviour. On average, econometric calculations show that the contribution of integration to economic growth has accounted for around 0.4% per year in the period 1986 to 1992.

The following indications also suggest that **the internal market is acting as the catalyst for a shift in the competitive environment to** the benefit of the consumer and of greater prosperity in the years ahead:

(i) the removal of border formalities is facilitating cross-border trade, although internal market legislation to increase access to public procurement markets and to remove technical trade barriers have yet to make their impact widely felt;

(ii) the importance of intra-Community trade as a share of total trade has steadily increased (the share of imports rising from 53.4 to 59.3% of the total between 1985 and 1992, and exports from 54.9 to 61.3%);

(iii) the removal of controls on capital movements has allowed for a marked increase in the degree of integration of some Member States into international capital markets, which will facilitate cross-border investment and ease credit restrictions in some Member States which had contributed to higher costs of capital in those countries. Free capital movement also represents a precondition for effective liberalization of Community financial services markets. Direct investment through mergers and acquisitions in other Member States has increased sharply, the number of cases rising from 2 190 in 1987 to 4 553 in 1992;

(iv) the establishment of the internal market has been accompanied by a surge in intra-Community foreign direct investment, which has been heavily concentrated in those sectors most directly concerned by internal market liberalization;

(v) the internal market programme has also attracted considerable interest from overseas investors, particularly on the part of US, Japanese, and EFTA companies;

(vi) part of this investment has taken the form of a wave of cross-border mergers and acquisitions, which constitute a strong indication of companies' intentions to set up their presence on partner country markets;

(vii) in banking and insurance sectors, where obstacles to cross-border trade were particularly pronounced, there is evidence of a profound change in the nature of cross-border competition, reflected in a growing number of branches and outlets in other Community countries and in an increasing share of national insurance markets held by partner country producers;

(viii) portfolio investment in the Member States coming from other parts of the Community has increased significantly (between 1983 and 1990 it increased by five times in the UK, doubled in France and increased by one and a half times in Germany);

(ix) there are indications that the removal of non-tariff barriers is already facilitating intra-Community commerce and competition in the sectors most affected by the internal market programme (transport goods, electrical engineering, consumer electronics, office equipment, machine tools). Statistics which suggest that such an evolution is taking place are the increase in the proportion of a Member State's trade which is directed towards other Community countries, and the increasing share of national consumption which is met by intra-Community imports. This development implies increased presence on national markets and, by extension, greater competitive discipline on domestic enterprises.

In accordance with the Council resolution of 7 December 1992 on making the single market work, the Commission will be conducting a study from 1994 to 1996 on the impact of the single market, a period in which the relevant Community legislation will be more widely applied. This study will focus on individual sectors as well as on the possible macroeconomic effects.

2.6. Supporting the development of SMEs so as to make the internal market fully effective

For many SMEs, completion of the single market means a change in the environment in which they operate, although they do not always see any scope for actively exploiting the new opportunities available because of the lack of a European or international framework for their markets or production processes.

Unless the confidence of SMEs in the prospects opened up by the single market is restored, an important potential for growth will go unexploited. **The Community must therefore devise a back-up strategy designed to make it easier for businesses, particularly SMEs, to adapt to the new requirements of competitiveness** and thus ensure that economic operators are properly mobilized in support of growth, competitiveness and employment. SMEs play a crucial role in the link between growth and employment. On the usual definition of SMEs (fewer than 500 employees), they provide more than two thirds of Community employment (70.2%, of which 29% is accounted for by firms with fewer than 10 employees) and generate more than two thirds of Community turnover (70.3%) and between 65 and 85% of value-added in those countries for which data are available. They are considered to be the greatest potential job cre-

ators. In qualitative terms, SMEs play a major role in providing young people with their first jobs, thereby being instrumental in the training of the labour force, and they also help to provide productive employment for the less sought-after categories of individuals on the labour market since they recruit disproportionately large numbers of young people, women and unskilled workers and operate wage and productivity structures of their own.

However, the rate of SME failures, which, according to certain indicators, seems to be on the increase in most Member States, is a worrying factor as regards the maintenance and growth of total employment.

Analysis/assessment

However, SMEs are not short of strengths that can help them cope with the changes in the economic situation in the Community, notably the recession in the European economy and in the other developed countries.

The strengths of SMEs are, firstly, **their presence on expanding new markets** (activities less vulnerable to international competition, the service sector, market niches, the development of particularly innovatory technologies) and, secondly, **their internal organization** (flexibility due to the disproportionately high level of recruitment of certain labour-force categories, notably young people and women, and the greater willingness to adapt working conditions as and when necessary).

The weaknesses of SMEs will be determined by their structural capacity **to deal with the complexity of the administrative and legislative environment** (administrative and legislative requirements, including those performed on behalf of the authorities, such as VAT formalities and the deduction at source of employees' taxes and social security contributions; the introduction of new environmental or social security rules, and a new standardization/certification system as part of the arrangements for implementing the single market; barriers to the carrying-out of certain activities, notably in the service sector along the dividing line between market and non-market services); **to overcome financing difficulties** despite the increase in the number and diversity of the financial instruments available to firms; **to come to terms with the complexity of managing a firm and to develop strategic policies,** a problem which stems in particular from the fact that in small businesses most management functions are performed by the head of the business himself even though he does not always possess the necessary specialized skills and knowledge and that he has to switch between the production function and the management function.

2.7. Views of the Member States

In the contributions they sent to the Commission for the purpose of preparing the White Paper, most Member States highlighted the priority they give to measures to assist the activities and development of SMEs. Suggestions were made for improving access by SMEs to sources of financing, the results of research, and training. Other suggestions concerned support aimed at facilitating subcontracting and cooperation between SMEs and their participation in information, advisory and cooperation networks. Some Member States also emphasized the need for simpler administrative procedures and formalities, including those relating to social security, labour or tax rules, and for arrangements to promote job creation by SMEs. This shows that the Member States are aware of the need to step up their current efforts, which the Community could support through the action programme adopted on 14 June. However, to meet the expectations of Member States and firms, **a mass effect must be sought, in** partnership with the Member States, **so as to enhance the effectiveness, coherence and visibility of the measures in support of SMEs.** In this context, a number of specific measures can be launched by the Community under an **integrated programme.**

2.8. Proposals and remedies

In the light of the above assessment, it is essential to identify a series of back-up measures which the Community should launch with the broad aim of taking account of SME requirements within the single market, bearing in mind the need to increase competitiveness.

The general **objective** of such measures should be **to integrate SMEs more closely into the single market so as to underpin their competitiveness as** they take up the national, Community and international challenges facing them, with the accompanying dual aim of (i) helping to *preserve the number of jobs* in the Community by supporting existing SMEs and assisting with the renewal of the productive base, and (ii) *increasing the number of jobs* by supporting firms with a high-growth or employment potential.

To help enterprises face up to the dual challenge of growth and competitiveness, on the one hand, and employment, on the other, an enterprise pact for employment could be proposed.

As part of an integrated programme, such measures would be grouped together under **two headings:**

(a) *Making credible in the short term the potential available to SMEs in the single market*

Restoring the confidence of firms prior to encouraging them to increase their competitiveness and job-creating capacity requires **two types of action:**

(i) Identifying and alleviating the constraints of a tax, social security, administrative, financial or other nature that hamper the establishment or continued operation of SMEs

Concerted action with the Member States and the organizations representing SMEs could be proposed with a view to **examining existing legislation** that impedes the creation and development of businesses; action could be taken to **exchange information on best practices** for simplifying and harmonizing legislation and to **devise improvements** in priority areas (for example, payment terms, taxation and the transfer of businesses).

In view of the difficulties which social security and labour provisions pose for SMEs, particular attention should be focused on these aspects, both in terms of the rules applicable and in terms of simplifying their application, including the provision of information, so as to promote more flexible use of the workforce, particularly by very small businesses.

(ii) Improving the financing of firms

In this area, which is of crucial importance for SMEs, the first aim should be to give practical effect to the renewed calls by the Heads of State or Government for **an increase and improvement in the financial resources made available to SMEs** (Edinburgh and Copenhagen facilities, and Brussels decisions). Steps should also be taken to **improve relations between financial institutions and SMEs,** paving the way for more generous allocation of private finance to SMEs and **broader use of the most appropriate financial instruments.**

(b) Exploiting the dynamics of the single market in order to boost competitiveness in the medium term

(i) Supporting cooperation between firms

The Community could step up its efforts to foster cooperation between firms by providing **financing beyond the first stage of the search for partners.** It has already taken steps aimed mainly at encouraging the search for partners and initial contacts between entrepreneurs, but in many cases appropriate back-up (at national or regional level) for a given period would make it possible to follow up developments in a way that could increase the scope for cooperation between SMEs.

Another means of fostering cooperation would be to provide **support for participation by SMEs in enterprise networks** aimed at introducing flexible and specialized production systems. This concerns in particular the networking of subcontracting firms in the face of the threats posed by the major changes taking place in their relations with their main customers.

(ii) Improving the quality of management in SMEs

A key factor in safeguarding the competitiveness of SMEs and hence their long-term employment potential is an improvement in managerial skills in order to remedy the structural weaknesses of SMEs. The measures already taken in this field could be made much more effective if **coordinated action on the part of all intermediaries** placed emphasis on a number of key areas so that SME managers could become aware of the changes they need to make in their role.

There is a need to foster, in cooperation with the Member States and chambers of commerce and industry, **a demand for information, training and advice** in order to overcome the specific obstacles in business. Among these initiatives, appropriate advice could significantly increase the rate of survival among SMEs.

To achieve this, the potential existing among business intermediaries should be exploited to the full. In this connection, the Community could also look into the scope for **improving the supply of direct advice** to firms on the various aspects of their day-to-day management.

(iii) Supporting the development of firms with a high-growth potential

Among the smallest firms in the economy, the firms most likely to create a large number of permanent jobs are those with the determination and skills to expand their business either because their markets are not yet saturated or because they are in as yet uncharted markets. Such firms are to be found both in manufacturing and in the service sector; the problem, though, is to identify them.

Identification will be possible only if the firms themselves are encouraged voluntarily to gear up for growth. A number of measures that could be widely applied have been tried out in order to encourage SMEs to take the initiative, either by having recourse to a synergistic approach (membership of 'business clubs') or by way of an audit method (e.g. 'Euromanagement'). Coordination at Community level and quality control would make it possible to confer on firms taking part in technological audits recognition that they were capable of participating in national or Community RTD programmes.

(iv) Supporting employment growth in service SMEs

Recent work on the growth of service activities has highlighted the importance of improving productivity in this sector, a development which, far from creating a problem in terms of employment, would be a decisive factor in ensuring the growth of service firms and in the future competitiveness of the developed economies. We must thus turn our attention away from improving productivity in the classical sense to improving performance, that is to say a combination of quantitative development and better quality.

Improved performance depends first and foremost on conducting an awareness and mobilization campaign among service firms and their representative organizations. Through its role of anticipating and supporting changes, the Community can, in cooperation with the partners concerned, **assist in identifying and disseminating models** for service activities that could be developed in the future but have not yet been created for want of sufficient knowledge among individual creators of markets and their potential or of the technological changes likely to influence the provision of services and the market in services. It can also **support the development of professionalism in service activities,** this being essential if the growth and employment potential in these branches of activity is to be exploited, notably by identifying — pref-erably within the context of the social dialogue — professional profiles and by providing corresponding vocational training leading to the award of approved qualifications.

2.9. Guidelines for an integrated programme to assist SMEs

In order to strengthen, within the framework of broader partnerships, the effectiveness, consistency and visibility of the measures to assist SMEs, it is necessary to examine practical proposals for an integrated programme involving an initiative for SMEs.

As a matter of priority, the integrated programme should address three objectives from among all the measures set out above; these objectives correspond to measures which could not be implemented without appropriate financing or the scale of which would be restricted by the ability of the Member States or the intermediaries concerned to finance their general application in full:

(i) introduction of new financial facilities for SMEs;

(ii) support for cooperation between firms;

(iii) support for improvements in management quality.

Such a programme would have to assert the principle of **partnership between the Community and the Member States** in co-financing projects within the Community, would have to be **flexible** as regards **geographical priorities** and would have to ensure active cooperation on the part of SME intermediaries.

Chapter 3

Trans-European networks

3.1. The stakes

Traffic jams are not only exasperating, they also cost Europe dear in terms of productivity. Bottlenecks and missing links in the infrastructure fabric; lack of interoperability between modes and systems; non-communication between too many closed and scattered telecommunications circuits. Networks are the arteries of the single market. They are the lifeblood of competitiveness, and their malfunction is reflected in lost opportunities to create new markets and hence in a level of job creation that falls short of our potential.

The establishment of networks of the highest quality throughout the whole Union and beyond its frontiers is a priority task. It will require a joint, massive and sustained effort on the part of the authorities at all levels and of private operators. The potential to create jobs is substantial, both directly in the short term by initiating the large-scale projects proposed and through the beneficial effect in the long term on production conditions in Europe.

The Commission's analysis shows that the overall volume of direct investment to be mobilized by 1999 could amount to ECU 400 billion, of which ECU 220 billion would go to transport, ECU 150 billion to telecommunications and ECU 13 billion to energy transport. The sums involved are therefore fairly substantial. However, the possible gains in terms of employment creation, economic cohesion and as an aid to regional planning are no less considerable.

The message has not gone unheard. The new Title XII of the Treaty on European Union sets the framework. The objective of developing trans-European networks is to enable citizens, economic operators and regional and local communities to derive full benefit from the setting-up of an area without internal frontiers and to link the peripheral regions with the centre. The pol-itical impetus was subsequently given by the Copenhagen European Council: it called on the Commission and the Council to speed up the adoption of master plans in the field of transport, energy and telecommunications and the examination of the Commission's proposals on telematic networks; it also extended the duration and amount of the Edinburgh facility, so that in some cases Community financing might amount to 90%; furthermore, projects awarded a declaration of Community interest are to be given privileged access to Community financial instruments. The European Council, meeting in Brussels on 29 October, extended the scope of the Edinburgh lending facility to cover transport infrastructures.

Four master plans for transport and the plan relating to telematic systems are now in place. Discussions are already in progress in the Council on some of the plans, and the Commission intends to present the other draft plans shortly. Major obstacles persist, which are holding up implementation of the objectives of Article 129b of the Treaty within the stipulated framework of 'a system of open and competitive markets'.

It is necessary to step up the pace again. Networks can — and in the present economic context, must — provide fresh impetus. The Commission's analysis shows that the installation or completion of networks as a whole is progressing too slowly. There are many reasons for this, depending to a large extent on the specificities of each type of network concerned.

3.2. Opinion of Member States

Low-cost, efficient infrastructures are generally regarded by the Member States as being essential to promoting competitiveness; by creating trans-European networks, it should be possible to derive greater benefit from the internal market. Several Member States consider that the efficiency of infrastructures depends on their interoperability at Community level together with their deregulation, and on greater competition in the energy and telecommunications sectors in particular. In the transport sector, several Member States indicate that priority should be given to congested areas and transit, links to peripheral areas, traffic management systems, combined transport and high-speed rail links.

With regard to promoting networks, some Member States stress the need to apply market-oriented solutions and to encourage private-sector participation and financing. They are also keen to see rapid and optimum use of resources within the current budgetary constraints and with due regard to the subsidiarity principle.

Some Member States feel that account should be taken of links to the countries of Central and Eastern Europe in the planning of trans-European networks.

3.3. The four key elements of the initiative

On a general level, four factors of key importance to the proposals have emerged from the analysis:

(i) The state of the Community's and Member States' finances leaves virtually no margin to increase public financing beyond that already planned. The Commission's proposals take account of this fact and do not entail new public financing requirements.

(ii) The massive investment required in some sectors, particularly in transport infrastructures, necessitates new types of partnerships between private and public financing, backed by financial engineering encompassing all the different sources and types of financing.

(iii) The absence of open and competitive markets is hampering, to differing degrees, the optimum use of existing networks and their completion in the interests both of consumers and operators.

(iv) The inherent sluggishness of the preparation, planning, authorization and evaluation procedures creates major obstacles to the implementation of large projects.

The contributions from the governments of the Member States, as set out above, echo the substance of these points. All the contributions on the subject stress the importance of networks to the efficiency and proper functioning of the internal market, the linking up of peripheral areas with the centre and the impact on economic cohesion throughout the Community. The Member States broadly agree on the need for a greater role for private financing and better financial engineering. They also agree on the need to promote the most efficient use possible of networks by ensuring interconnection and interoperability. Some Member States stress the importance of creating or reinforcing market conditions, the need to respect the financial perspectives at Community level and the principle of subsidiarity.

Consequently, the objective of the Commission's proposals must be to **attract private investment in networks** by helping to create the conditions in which it will flourish, for example by removing the obstacles that persist, among others in the slowness of procedures at various levels, and by supplementing private investments with public funds where necessary. Stimulating the participation of private investors will have a direct effect on growth, competitiveness and employment in the Community, as it will advance projects which would otherwise not be implemented, however necessary and 'ripe' they may be, or which would suffer unreasonable delay. The Commission therefore proposes a pragmatic approach involving integrated projects.

The three types of networks involved each have different characteristics and suffer from different problems requiring a response tailored to their own particular operating conditions. These responses are examined further on. They have some points in common which make it possible to pursue a pragmatic joint approach. On the basis of a broad consensus between political and economic circles on the need to establish such networks, **a genuine partnership** should be sought **between all concerned**: the public authorities at all appropriate levels, in accordance with the subsidiarity principle, network operators, users, service providers, financiers, and industrialists. The large number of parties involved in itself represents a challenge since it is necessary for them to be able to combine their interests and resolve any possible differences of opinion.

For each type of network, the nature of the partnership may vary according to the problems to be resolved and the objectives to be achieved. For example, to resolve transport infrastructure financing problems, emphasis should be placed on the pivotal role of players capable of mobilizing private investment. On the other hand, in the case of telecommunications there is a need for a partnership with the network users in order to enable the market to be developed in response to their expectations. Where energy is concerned, the partnership should involve players capable of optimizing network efficiency without diminishing the requisite level of competition in this sector.

This partnership is simply a *modus operandi* to be applied discerningly on a Community scale, or on an even wider scale if the networks are extended. Arriving at a consensus on the solutions to be implemented is not the least of the difficulties. There needs to be a willingness to find joint solutions involving **measures at all decision-making levels:** Community, national, regional, public authorities, economic operators, etc. A strong political signal would enable this partnership to be implemented with a view to addressing the problems identified as pragmatically as possible.

Their respective roles are complementary and, as far as the public authorities are concerned, clearly defined in the various legislative and administrative instruments existing in the Member States. At Community level, the new Title XII of the Treaty defines responsibilities and their limits in the light of subsidiarity. Coordination among Member States is one of these responsibilities, and there are numerous and powerful elements and support instruments available at Community level for this purpose.

The initiative must be taken to unite all the levels of responsibility concerned and the necessary powers, and to write together the score for each of the projects selected. **The Commission proposes to act as a catalyst** in this respect.

It will be essential to play an active role at Community level to unlock private investment in the new open, competitive climate of the single market. Although the financing and implementation of the specific projects will have to be agreed on a case-by-case basis, it is equally important to **improve market conditions** in general by means of a framework favourable to the involvement of institutional and private investors. Various factors could influence the conditions on the financial markets, such as an innovative approach to guarantees and insurance in the framework of the European Investment Fund, interest-rate subsidies for Community loans or tax incentives to attract long-term capital. Direct financing would be another possibility. The Commission will present proposals on this matter.

Also at Community level, attention must be focused on **enhancing the role of the declaration of Community interest.** If this declaration is to have the desired profile and impact on the availability of private capital, projects to which it has been awarded should have easier access to Community financial instruments and benefit from a binding timetable for completion of the requisite administrative procedures.

3.4. Transport infrastructures: A financing problem

Financing problems are particularly apparent in relation to transport infrastructures, a sector with a major impact on employment in the construction industry.

By 1999, investment of ECU 220 billion will be necessary for trans-European transport networks alone, i.e. between ECU 30 and 35 billion per annum. The Community could mobilize ECU 90 billion of this, including the contributions from Member States. However, given the current state of Member States' finances, it is inconceivable that the remainder could be financed through the budget. Furthermore, the need for high-quality networks does not stop at the Community's external borders; it will be essential to extend the networks in particular within the boundaries of the

European Economic Area and to the East. The magnitude of the deficit is both substantial and worrying. Although the level of savings is still high, it has proved difficult to mobilize private-sector investments in this field. There are two reasons for this: firstly, and above all, any kind of risk inherent in a project dampens the enthusiasm of the private investor. This may concern feasibility, technical viability, authorizations, deadlines or competition from other modes. These elements need to be clarified, evaluated and conclusions drawn. The same response must be applied to the second disincentive, which is a natural follow-on from the first: uncertainty about the return on, and hence the profitability of, the investment.

The objective is therefore clear. In order to launch the process of reflection and preparation for the partnership immediately and effectively, **an initial list of projects** which are both of Community interest and have the potential to mobilize private economic operators **must quickly be drawn up.** To this end, the following selection criteria could be applied:

(i) **The Community interest** of projects, all of which must figure in the master plans for trans-European networks presented or due to be presented shortly, is obvious in the case of new transfrontier links of a strategic character (e.g. transalpine and Pyrenean links, sea crossings, links with the East); it is also clear in the case of projects which interconnect national networks and ensure their interoperability and access to networks, including transfer from one mode to another; and for projects which take account of the special needs of the countries on the periphery of the Community.

(ii) The **proposed financing** of these projects must allow for private investment, the magnitude of which will depend on an evaluation of the risks presented by each project or series of projects on a given network.

(iii) Priority will be given to projects capable of being implemented **at short notice,** i.e. which are sufficiently well prepared and feasible.

(iv) **Economic importance in terms of employment creation and industrial impact** is essential, over and above the economic viability of the project as such. The increase in the competitiveness of advanced technology products and services merits special attention in this context.

(v) Last but not least, only projects that have passed the **environmental** impact scrutiny will be eligible.

The Commission has drawn up an indicative list (see Annex) of 26 major projects, representing an overall investment of the order of ECU 80 billion, on the basis of which it will initiate discussions as soon as possible with the authorities concerned and the relevant economic circles.

Each project on the list will be evaluated jointly with all the actors concerned, in accordance with the partnership principle defined above. The evaluation will focus above all on the inherent risks of the project and the possibilities for covering them under acceptable conditions. It will also be necessary to identify the public financing sources that can be mobilized and the nature of the instruments that could be used to assess the expected revenue from the projected traffic and to consider the possible duration of the concession, the most appropriate legal formula for involving the interested parties, the management of the project, the administrative obstacles and the impact on the environment. The evaluation should lead to the presentation of an action plan for each project in the form which gives it the political profile necessary to speed it on its way and secure its financing.

3.5. Energy transport infrastructure: Towards better utilization of capacities

The reliability and efficiency of energy supplies are key factors in the competitiveness of industry and in terms of their effect on the consumer's pocket. There are various reasons for this, but among them, the **suboptimum use of existing networks and brakes**

on their desired expansion are a major problem in the central parts of the Community in particular, and one which is closely bound up with the situation on the market for electricity and gas.

Unlike transport proper, planning of trans-European energy transport networks is not in the first instance a financing problem. Investments in energy networks are generally more lucrative and do not require the same degree of financial support from the public sector. There are only some peripheral regions of the Community where public aid to certain projects is both necessary and useful. In such cases, the Community's Regional and Structural Funds and the EIB provide a suitable framework and market conditions do not, strictly speaking, pose problems.

What tends to be the problem is that **private sector investments are often hampered by administrative constraints.** These constraints are above all the consequence of **exclusive import and export rights, transport monopolies, limited possibilities to construct and operate gas pipelines and transmission lines.**

Removal of these constraints is essential to the relaunch of investment and network planning. Furthermore, the opening-up of markets and deregulation means greater competition and thus greater energy efficiency. The competitiveness of European industry would be generally strengthened as a result.

The development of energy networks also **helps to protect the environment,** by favouring the use of primary fuels with the least carbon dioxide emissions, and to intensify cooperation with non-Community countries in Europe and the Mediterranean region, the main suppliers in this area. Speeding up the development and more efficient use of networks is therefore vital. Gas consumption and imports are already increasing; in the case of electricity, interconnection and improvement of the management of electricity systems continent-wide falls short of what is considered essential to the proper functioning of the single market.

The slowness and complexity of administrative procedures are also an obstacle to energy networks. As with the other transport networks mentioned above, it would be worth examining giving more force to the declaration of Community interest.

In the light of estimates based on projects in progress, scheduled and planned by industry, the total amount of investment in trans-European electricity and natural gas networks could reach **ECU 13 billion by the end of the decade.**

Until now, Community action to promote energy transport networks has essentially focused on financing. The European Council has also called on the EIB to step up this type of aid. A first series of loans under the new facility has already been decided. The Commission intends to give specific financial support to feasibility studies, as an incentive to carrying out the technical, economic and environmental studies necessary to determine projects and mobilize the various funds and Community financial instruments and programmes, with a view to contributing to the financing of energy transport infrastructure projects whose implementation depends on such support.

However, on a more general level, the Community must **remove the obstacles to speedy establishment of these networks.** In view of the major obstacles already mentioned, the Commission is seeking the support of the European Council to ask the Council and European Parliament **to bring their work on completing the internal energy market to a rapid close.** The Commission, for its part, will re-examine the particularly controversial proposal regarding third-party access to the networks, as this entails a substantial limitation on the ownership rights of private companies and hence a barrier to investment, given the importance of the removal of national monopolies regarding imports and exports, line construction and sales.

3.6. Telecommunications networks: Creation of new markets

The establishment of trans-European telecommunications networks is a precondition for the creation of the 'common information area'. It is particularly important for the completion of the single market.

The social and economic stakes are high. Today, the telecommunications industries account for an annual market in terms of services of ECU 285 billion at world level and ECU 84 billion at Community level. The equipment market is worth ECU 82 billion at world level and ECU 26 billion at Community level. The expected annual growth rate until the year 2000 is 8% for services and 4% for the equipment market. It is estimated that this sector alone will account for 6% of GDP at the end of the century, not including the indirect effects on the economy as a whole of network installation and operation.

In the not too distant future, the telecommunications networks will be capable of instantly transporting and processing voice traffic, text and images between any locations, be they homes, offices or businesses, thanks to digitization techniques and electronic processing of information. These networks will therefore constitute the nervous system of the economy, and more generally of tomorrow's society.

With the aid of these new networks, it will be possible to transmit myriads of texts (commercial messages, newspapers, correspondence, training courses, catalogues, technical notices, etc.), images (films, medical images, graphics, etc.) and sound transmissions (voice traffic, music, etc.), stored and combined in databases, for use in the most diverse applications (leisure, education, medical care, tourism, manufacturing activity, etc.).

Although voice telephony networks and services are already international, the same is not true of other networks and services relating to information in text, data and image form. Such networks are currently developing at national level only.

If a common information area really is to be established, the **digital national networks** must, like the telephone network, be interconnected and managed in a coherent fashion in order to form trans-European networks which will provide access to a wide range of interactive services. Hence, the new telecommunications networks, themselves using different vectors (cables, terrestrial and satellite radio transmission, etc.) will have a beneficial effect on all economic activities and transform the way of life of Europe's citizens.

At present, this transition to interactive trans-European networks and services is being **held up by the fragmentation of markets, by insufficient interconnection and interoperability** and by the absence of mechanisms to ensure coherent management. Although these are obvious shortcomings, the problems concerning the telecommunications networks and services differ considerably from those of the other trans-European networks for the following reason: **supply of services is inadequate and, where it does exist, too costly, with the result that demand is also too low** as in this case it is supply which determines demand. As a result, demand is not manifesting itself, which in turn discourages the creation of a viable supply. This is a vicious circle. The general economic situation is aggravating this trend and the private sector will only invest in this area of services, which have been liberalized, if conditions are such as to limit the risks to an acceptable level.

To break this vicious circle and stimulate the creation of new markets, the Commission proposes to **identify strategic trans-European projects in collaboration with all the various parties concerned.** The aim will be to target our activities in order to identify potential new markets; to tackle obstacles to their development, be they of a financial, regulatory or standardization nature; and to define the specific details and functional characteristics of the services to be developed and the typology of potential suppliers. As in the case of transport networks, the national and Community authorities will restrict their financial involvement to a marginal, catalytic role.

This means that, taking account also of the conditions of competition on the world market, Community action will consist in **removing obstacles of a general nature** (problems of industrial property, security, training, protection of privacy, etc.), in providing R&D support to project implementation, in contributing to the performance of feasibility studies and in granting loan guarantees and interest-rate subsidies.

The strategic projects would be carried out at each of the **three** interdependent 'levels' that make up the telecommunications networks: the carrier networks for transmission of information, generic services and telematic applications.

With regard to the **networks that serve to carry the information** (voice, data, images), the objective would be to consolidate the integrated services' digital network and to install the high-speed communications network using advanced transmission and switching techniques (asynchronous transfer mode: ATM), which will help digitized multimedia services to make a breakthrough.

With regard to the generic (universal) services, which form the common basis for all telematic applications, three areas would be considered:

(i) access to information services, which should provide all users with user-friendly access to databases containing information of all types available in multimedia libraries, laboratories or administrations;

(ii) electronic mail, which will enable documents to be transmitted fast and cheaply. The market most concerned, apart from large undertakings and administrations, is that of SMEs;

(iii) interactive digitized video services covering the whole of the Community, the emergence of which it is vital to promote, as their general availability will revolutionize working practices, leisure and training. They offer new possibilities for customized services ('pay-as-you-view' and 'video on demand' services), creating new demand and hence jobs.

The general availability of such services in the Community will promote the development of **'teleworking'**, which will mean that the location of activities and access to available employment can be optimized.

Telematic applications are the third level, which concerns adapting the service to the specific needs of user groups. **Public administration in connection with the single market** is of particular interest here, as already discussed in Chapter 2.B. Exchanges of data and the coordinated, accelerated introduction of an electronic mail network between administrations involved in the management of the single market should also enable businesses and citizens to have easy access to the administrative information they require. This objective is being pursued in the framework of the Community TNA-IDA project.

Distance learning is another area of considerable public interest which will help to improve skill levels in an on-going fashion without the need for costly infrastructures. The same applies to telemedicine which is designed in particular to give practitioners remote access to specialist centres of excellence, to provide diagnostic aids and a basis for deciding on treatment, and to contribute to exchanges of research results in the fight against serious illnesses such as cancer and AIDS. Finally, the application of telematics to transport (road, maritime, air) is now becoming an important aspect in transport infrastructures.

It is estimated that the volume of financing to be mustered by public and private investors in the areas currently identified as being favourable to the creation of new markets in services, will amount to **ECU 150 billion from 1994 over a period of six to 10 years. The priority projects proposed until 1999 would amount to ECU 67 billion.**

Infrastructure for the trans-European transport network

Indicative list of projects

Project type	Member States involved	Indicative total cost (million ECU)	Maturity
1. Brenner axis; rail connection through the Alps	I/A/D	10 000	Studies in progress
2. Paris-Brussels-Cologne-Amsterdam-London (PBKAL); high-speed train: Belgium	B	2 500	Completion of feasibility studies
3. Paris-Brussels-Cologne-Amsterdam-London (PBKAL); high-speed train: Netherlands	NL	2 100	Completion of feasibility studies
4. Paris-Brussels-Cologne-Amsterdam-London (PBKAL); high-speed train: London-Tunnel access	UK	3 900	Completion of feasibility studies
5. Madrid-Barcelona-Perpignan; high-speed train	E/F	6 800	Studies in progress
6. Fehmarn belt crossing; fixed link between Denmark and Germany; estimated construction costs for the tunnel/bridge; new construction or upgrading of railway needs to be decided (preliminary cost estimates ECU 2 to 4 billion)	DK/D	4 500	Studies in progress
7. TGV Est; high-speed train Paris-Strasbourg	F	4 000	Studies under completion (F)
8. TGV Est; high-speed train Karlsruhe-Frankfurt-Berlin	D	8 500	Partially ready to go
9. Rotterdam-Betuwe line/(Cologne-Frankfurt-Karlsruhe-Switzerland-Italy); railway line (cost estimates for the corridor up to German/Swiss border ECU 9.6 billion)	NL (D/(CH)/I)	3 100	Studies under completion
10. Lyons-Turin; high-speed train/combined transport	F/I	6 200	Studies in progress
11. Urban by-passes for combined transport corridors and selected combined transport projects	D/F/I/E	2 300	Ready to go
12. Nuremberg-German/Czech border-Prague; motorway	D (Cz)	1 000	German part; ready to go; Czech part: studies finalized
13. Berlin-Warsaw-Polish/Belarussian border (Moscow); motorway (new construction)	D/(P)	3 200	Ongoing studies

Project type	Member States involved	Indicative total cost (million ECU)	Maturity
14. Patras-Athens-Thessaloniki-Greek/Bulgarian border; motorway	GR	1 500	Works in progress
15. Lisbon-Valladolid (Spanish/French border); motorway	P/E	2 000	Works in progress (P)
16. (Dublin)-Holyhead-Birmingham-Cambridge-Felixstowe/Harwich-(Benelux); road corridor (by sections)	UK (IRL)	1 000	Works partially in progress
17. Bari-Brindisi-Otranto; motorway	I	1 000	Studies in progress
18. Road traffic management system	EC	1 000	Technology available; programme to be designed; some centres already in place
19. New Athens airport (Spata)	GR	2 000	Studies in progress, construction consortium chosen; contract not signed
20. Air traffic management system for Europe (CNS/ATM); this includes also the satellite system Inmarsat-III (navigation payloads) and associated ground segment	EC	8 000	Definition of system completed; projects ready for implementation
21. Channel Rhine-Rhône	F	2 500	Studies in progress
22. Channel Seine north	F	1 500	Studies in progress
23. Connections between Elbe and Oder; inland waterways	D	600	Studies in progress
24. Danube upgrading: section between Straubing and Vilshofen; inland waterways	D	700	Studies in progress
25. Vessel traffic management system for Community waters	EC	1 000	Works in progress in E; demands from Cohesion Fund M.S
26. Multimodal positioning system by satellites system	D/F + European Space Agency	1 000	Studies in progress
Total		81 900	

Trans-European telecommunications networks:

Information highways	Target area for Strategic Projects	Investment required 1994-1999 *(billion ecus)*
Interconnected advanced networks	— establishment of high-speed communication network	20
	— consolidation of integrated services digital network	15
General electronic services	— electronic acces to information	1
	— electronic mail	1
	— electronic images: interactive video services	10
Telematic applications	— teleworking	3
	— links between administrations	7
	— teletraining	3
	— telemedicine	7
Total		67

ELECTRICITY NETWORKS

(a) Connection of isolated electricity networks

    a1: Northern Ireland — Scotland
    a2: Ireland   — United Kingdom
    a3: Germany   : Connection to the new *Länder*
    a4: Greece   — Italy
    a5: Greece   : Connection of Crete
    a6: Spain   : Connection of the Balears

(b) Improvement of interconnections between Member States

    b1: Germany   — Denmark
    b2: Germany   — Netherlands
    b3: Germany   — Belgium
    b4: France   — Belgium
    b5: France   — Germany
    b6: France   — Italy
    b7: France   — Spain
    b8: Belgium   — Netherlands
    b9: Belgium   — Luxembourg
    b10: Spain   — Portugal

(c) Improvement of electricity networks within Member States in conjunction with improved interconnections between Member States or with non-Community countries

    c1: United Kingdom : Wales
    c2: Denmark   : East-West link
    c3: Netherlands   : North-East area
    c4: France   : North-East area
    c5: Italy   : North-South and East-West links
    c6: Spain   : North-South link and lines along the coast of the Mediterranean and the Cantabrian Sea
    c7: Portugal   : Improvements regarding interconnection with Spain
    c8: Greece   : East-West link

(d) Creation or improvement of electricity interconnections with non-Community countries

    d1: Germany   — Sweden
    d2: Germany   — Poland
    d3: Germany   — Norway
    d4: Germany   — Austria
    d5: Italy   — Switzerland
    d6: Italy   — Austria
    d7: Italy   — Tunisia
    d8: Greece   — Balkan countries
    d9: Greece   — Turkey
    d10: United Kingdom — Norway
    d11: Netherlands   — Norway
    d12: France   — Switzerland
    d13: Spain   — Morocco

GAS NETWORKS

(e) Introduction of natural gas in new regions

  e1: Northern Ireland
  e2: Germany : New *Länder*
  e3: Corsica and Sardinia
  e4: Spain : New regions
  e5: Portugal : Whole country
  e6: Greece : Whole country, including Crete

(f) Connection of isolated or separated gas networks

  f1: Ireland — Northern Ireland
  f2: Great Britain — Continent
  f3: Germany : Connection of German network to gas
      Belgium : Pipelines coming from Zeebrugge
  f4: Germany : Connections to the new *Länder*
  f5: Spain — France
  f6: Portugal — Spain

(g) Improvement of reception capacities/LNG storage and underground storage

  g1: Ireland : Construction of an LNG station
  g2: Germany : Construction of an LNG station
  g3: France : Extension of LNG stations
  g4: Italy : Extension/construction of LNG stations
  g5: Spain : Extension of LNG stations
  g6: Germany : Creation of underground storage facilities
  g7: France : Creation of underground storage facilities
  g8: Spain : Creation of underground storage facilities

(h) New gas supply pipelines

  h1: Norway — Belgium or Netherlands: new project planned
  h2: Norway — Germany (Emden): Europipe project
  h3: Norway — Denmark-Sweden: Scanpipe project
  h4: Algeria — Morocco-Spain-France (Toulouse/Fos)
  h5: Algeria — Tunisia-Italy: capacity increase
  h6: Russia — Ukraine-EC: upgrading of existing gas pipeline system
  h7: Russia — Belarus-Poland-EC
  h8: Russia — Scandinavian countries-EC
  h9: Bulgaria — Greece

NB: LNG could be an interesting alternative to some gas supply pipeline projects that have not yet been finalized.

Chapter 4

Research and technological development

Research and technological development (RTD) can contribute to renewing growth, strengthening competitiveness and boosting employment in the Community. However, in order to achieve this a series of conditions must be satisfied: an adequate level of funding; an appropriate range of research activities; and effective mechanisms for transferring the results.

4.1. Opinion of the Member States

As it is difficult to increase public spending, the Member States agree on the need to promote investment in RTD **in the private sector** especially and to increase the effectiveness of their RTD through cooperation between companies and with universities and research centres.

Where **Community RTD** is concerned, emphasis is placed on **coordination** of RTD conducted by the Community and the Member States, focusing on key areas, simplifying procedures, in particular to facilitate the access of SMEs to RTD, and especially improving the **dissemination and application** of RTD results, notably by promoting standardization.

Among the practical measures proposed, mention is made of tax incentives for RTD investments, the promotion of companies specializing in new technologies, and the launching of major RTD projects.

4.2. Assessment of research in the Community

In the Commission's opinion, Europe's research and industrial base suffers from a series of weaknesses.

(a) Level of resources

The first of these weaknesses is financial. **The Community invests proportionately less than its competitors in research and technological development.** In 1991, for example, its total public, private, civil and military spending on RTD stood at some ECU 104 billion, compared with ECU 124 billion for the USA and ECU 77 billion for Japan. This was equivalent to an average of **2% of GDP in the Community, 2.8% in the USA and 3% in Japan** or, in relation to population, ECU 302 per inhabitant in the Community, compared with ECU 493 in the USA and ECU 627 in Japan. However, there are big differences between the Member States with research spending accounting for 2.6% of GDP in Germany, for example, but only 0.7% in Greece and Portugal. Investment by businesses is particularly weak, as they fund only 52% of all research in Europe compared with 78% in Japan, for example.

The Community also has **proportionately fewer researchers and engineers**: 630 000 (4 out of every 1 000 of the working population) compared with 950 000 (8 per 1 000) in the USA and 450 000 (9 per 1 000) in Japan.

Figures like these are meaningless in absolute terms and must be treated with caution. The use made of the funds is more important than the amount spent. And more important than the absolute number of researchers are their qualifications, their ability to meet the needs of developing industries and the extent to which the capital they represent is utilized. Nevertheless, on the whole this lower investment in both financial and human terms gives cause for concern.

(b) Coordination of research

A second weakness is the **lack of coordination at various levels** of the **research and technological development activities, programmes and strategies** in Europe. First, there is the lack of coordination between the national research policies. The Community's research budget accounts for only 4% of research spending by the 12 Member States. Even adding the resources allocated to joint European RTD activities in other frameworks (e.g. under Eureka, ESA, CERN, EMBL, etc.), the budget amounts to only 10% or so of the total. Despite the coordination called for by the existence of these activities and the need for the Member States to take them into account when defining their own policies, the national policies are still developed largely without reference to one another.

This lack of coordination is particularly marked between military and civil research activities in each Member State which are conducted within relatively self-contained institutional frameworks, between which bridges are only just beginning to be built. In some Member States military activities account for a large proportion of all research (44% in the United Kingdom, 37% in France and 17% in Spain).

One immediate consequence, which can vary in intensity from one sector to another but is generally relatively important, is the lack of coordination of **business strategies** too, not only with public research policies and with the activities of universities and public research centres in each Member State but also with the strategies of other European businesses.

(c) Application of research results

The greatest weakness of Europe's research base, however, is its **comparatively limited capacity to convert scientific breakthroughs and technological achievements into industrial and commercial successes**. In most major fields and disciplines, Europe is up to the highest standards in the world in terms, for example, of the number of publications by researchers and of references thereto. In certain fields heavily dependent on action by the public sector, such as telecommunications, transport or the aerospace industry, European firms can also point to indisputable technological successes. The European chemical and pharmaceutical industries are in the forefront on world markets. However, in all other fields of advanced technology, with a few exceptions, European firms have failed to convert their scientific and technological achievements into products and competitiveness.

This weakness stems from a **combination of factors**: the still inadequate links between universities and businesses, despite the pro-

gress made on this point in most Member States; the lack of risk capital to help firms through the development phase and the reluctance of private-sector financiers to invest in activities if they consider the risks too great or the return too uncertain; insufficient account of RTD in business strategies and the lack of coordinated strategies between businesses, universities and the public authorities (compared with Japan, for example); the lack of facilities or the regulatory obstacles to business start-ups by researchers and the lack of mechanisms for harnessing the knowledge and technologies generated by defence research; the targeting on markets which are too small and the weak capacity to foresee future needs and demand on the market, etc.

4.3. The solutions

(a) New directions for research

To restore the dynamic combination of technology, growth and employment, the Community and the Member States must take measures on several levels. These can be divided into two main groups. The first comprises measures aiming essentially at **restoring** the **competitiveness** of European businesses and **renewing growth**. One aspect will be to correct the traditional weaknesses of Europe's research and industrial base and to restore Community firms to the forefront of the world economy. The other will be to **extend the geographical coverage** and to **take account of the new needs of society** in the Community and throughout the world.

The effect of these measures to restore competitiveness on industrial activity in the Community will have a positive indirect impact on employment. Coordinated measures to take account of the new needs of society should in turn create a number of jobs. Alongside these measures, however, a second category of action should also be taken, targeted more specifically on improving the employment situation.

(i) Restoring competitiveness and renewing growth

To make European companies more competitive, action is needed on the three traditional weaknesses of Europe's scientific and industrial base. First, steps must be taken to allow **better application of the results of the research** carried out in the Community, i.e. the establishment of **operational mechanisms** at national and European level **for the transfer of technologies from university laboratories to companies, from one company to another and from the military to civil research sectors**. One key aspect must be substantially to step up the measures to improve the business environment, in the form of scientific and technical information, financial services, aid to protect innovations, training in new technologies, etc.

In this context, sufficient importance should be attached to small businesses. **Small businesses working in high-technology sectors**, producing capital goods and advanced consumer goods **or applying advanced technologies** in manufacturing industry, represent a significant potential source of growth. In the USA, a very large proportion of emerging technologies was first developed by small firms which are better equipped to anticipate the needs of the market and to react rapidly.

Beyond the coordination already existing in practice today, measures should also be taken to further effective coordination of research activities, strategies and programmes in Europe. **The first thing must be coordination between the national public research bodies**: the coordination structures now being set up between most of the major national bodies should be strengthened and institutionalized. **A forum for concertation and exchanges between the various European research bodies and centres** could also be set up. To encourage the development of concerted strategies linked to the Community's activities, a **science and technology assembly** could also be established, based on the Commission's existing consultative committees.

Companies, particularly firms conducting large amounts of research, should also coordinate their strategies more closely in the framework of Community projects. Based on or alongside existing consortia, **frameworks for intercompany cooperation** should be established at Community level. These frameworks for close cooperation

between potential users and makers of new products, component suppliers and manufacturers of the end-products would provide a means of deriving maximum benefit from the work carried out by companies' research departments and establishing consistent strategies, guided by earlier anticipation of the needs of the market. They could be planned in conjunction with the definition and implementation of major projects bringing together rival European companies for work on carefully targeted technological objectives.

With regard to overall research funding, the **objective of a gradual increase to 3% of GDP** should be borne in mind. It is not a question of 'more of the same research'. In view of the current budgetary constraints in all European countries, companies should bear a larger share of the spending. Their objective should be to achieve investment levels comparable to those of their rivals by providing greater funding for in-house research and work in universities. Appropriate regulatory and tax measures should be taken to make it easier for the private sector to bear such a higher share of research spending.

(ii) New geographical markets and new needs of society

In addition to competition and market forces, considerable potential for growth lies in **catering for a wider geographical area** than the Triad alone (European Community, USA and Japan) **and for the emerging needs of society**. The newly industrialized countries in the Pacific region compete with the Community in basic and intermediate technologies and will soon be able to develop more sophisticated technologies themselves. For several years they will offer a window of opportunity for companies in the Community. Countries such as these which are keen to acquire advanced production technologies but also, by virtue of their explosive development, face serious environmental problems, offer large potential markets.

Both as a source of high-level scientific and technical know-how and as a market for specific technologies and advanced production processes, **the countries of Central and Eastern Europe**, which are not only geographically but also historically close to the Community, provide further rich potential for innovations which Eastern and Western Europeans should harness together, by pooling their complementary skills.

Accompanied by measures to create viable demand in the countries concerned, the establishment of **truly effective mechanisms for transferring technologies to developing countries** would also provide Europe with substantial potential markets for specific products and requirements.

One key aspect of this broadening of the horizons of the Community's research should be **closer cooperation to implement very big programmes reflecting the biggest worldwide needs for the next century**: energy, global change and food.

New needs which could make a significant contribution to restoring growth are apparent in **three areas: the environment, health and the media**.

The market in environmental products and services, for example, covers pollution detection and monitoring technologies, environmental improvement technologies, clean technologies (i.e. improvements to conventional technologies to take greater account of environmental requirements) and ecotechnologies (entirely new technologies based on novel raw materials and energy sources). Added to this market in goods, there is also the market in services such as water treatment, waste processing, etc. On the basis of the latest estimates, this world market in environmental products and services is worth some ECU 190 billion per year now and could reach ECU 270 billion by the year 2000.

The second area is **health**. Alongside new molecules to treat diseases of the nervous system and degenerative and viral illnesses not yet properly controlled, the principal market concerned is in advanced preventive technologies and methods allowing treatment in the home by the patients themselves or by non-specialist staff, automatic monitoring and diagnosis systems, remote monitoring, etc.

In the field of the **media**, one category heading for vigorous expansion is the range of **multimedia products** (CD-ROM, CD-I, CD-TV, etc.) and the corresponding hardware. With their impressive capacity to store enormous quantities of text, sound and moving and fixed images on the same medium, combined with the possibility of multiplying the effects by linking up with telecommunications systems, these products will revolutionize the media industries. This market is worth an estimated ECU 1 000 billion per year today and is expected to grow by 16% a year over the next five or six years.

At the crossroads between satisfying the worldwide needs in the fields of energy, health and the environment and the requirements for competitiveness, biotechnology is one of the fields offering the greatest potential for innovation and a particularly rich source of growth. What is more, a significant proportion of the research and development work in this field is carried out by small and medium-sized businesses. However, in order to ensure development of activities in this field commensurate with actual and potential needs, steps must be taken to establish an appropriate regulatory framework, to harmonize the measures taken in the various countries and to define a global strategy bringing together the public authorities, research bodies, businesses and the various sectors of society concerned.

Impact on employment

The measures described above to restore competitiveness and take account of the new needs of society should have a **moderate, but indisputably positive indirect impact on employment**. The rise of the environmental industries could possibly have a great impact on competitiveness and should have at least the same effect in terms of safeguarding existing jobs as the concept of quality did a few years ago. By contrast, **there is undoubtedly potential to create jobs in the health and media sectors**. The development of new formulas for care in the home based on decentralized assistance and health-care technologies will create a need for health-care, assistance and training staff. The **new market in media products** in addition to, rather than in place of, existing printed and audiovisual media should also generate a whole cascade of new jobs.

Of course, the measures to encourage business start-ups in high-technology sectors should in turn have a positive impact on employment. In the USA, firms of this type are often started up by researchers leaving universities or big businesses. The increase in the number of firms of this type should create a certain number of jobs for development engineers, administrative staff, etc. The same applies to the measures to increase the total number of researchers and engineers in the Community. Of course, the primary objective should be **optimization of the available resources by adapting** the skills of the existing scientific and technical staff **to the new needs**. However, the creation of new jobs for researchers and engineers as fast as Europe's scientific and industrial base can absorb them would be the most effective means of ensuring a net increase in the resources allocated to research activities.

The policies and programmes conducted by the Member States and the Community should also aim at **promoting technologies which will save the maximum number of jobs or require or encourage the creation of new jobs** as long as they have an equal effect on competitiveness and growth and an equal capacity to satisfy the current and foreseeable needs of society. Tools and methods must be devised to determine the net impact of a wide range of technologies on employment.

(b) Specific means

(i) Measures by the Member States

Since most of the spending on research and development in the Community is under the control of the Member States, most of the measures mentioned must be taken at national level. **The provisions outlined should be put into practice in the national policies and programmes**. In view of the current constraints on research budgets and to ensure the most effective action possible in cost/benefit terms, **priority must be given to the indirect regulatory instruments** under the control of the Member States.

In the context of transferring a higher proportion of research spending to the private sector and of shifting government intervention from direct support to indirect instruments, **tax credit schemes for research** could be developed to encourage companies to invest more in science, even in the long term. Special formulas could be devised to **encourage companies to fund research by universities**.

The Member States could also study and **introduce schemes to lighten the social security contribution burden on firms and research bodies creating new jobs for researchers and engineers** together with financial or career **incentives for further on-the-job training for the scientific and technical staff in service**. In addition to its impact on employment, action in this field could also promote the dissemination of knowledge and of new technologies. Within the existing schemes to help business start-ups, formulas could also be defined for helping researchers to start up businesses. Financial instruments under the direct or indirect control of the national authorities could be adjusted to provide companies, particularly small businesses, with the risk capital to develop the innovations which they have prepared.

(ii) Community measures and concerted action

The Community itself should also take measures to back up these activities. The broad lines of the **fourth (1994-98) framework programme** currently being discussed already clearly point towards the establishment of mechanisms to coordinate the national efforts (research consortia) and industrial research policies (particularly in the form of support for Eureka projects), concentration on a limited number of key technologies with a major impact on many branches of industry, greater support for the dissemination of the results of the research carried out in the Community, establishment of a system of access to and participation in the programmes specifically for small and medium-sized businesses, etc.

In conjunction with the fourth framework programme and the preparations about to be started for the next programme, **new large-scale research projects should be defined in conjunction with the national research bodies and companies in fields with** a direct bearing on renewed growth and on areas generating jobs directly or indirectly. These initiatives, at the interface between different categories of need, could take the form of large integrated projects covering specific regions such as the Mediterranean, Baltic and eastern frontiers of the Community, which face a combination of demographic, environmental and industrial development problems, transfrontier regions, etc.

Implementation of the guidelines proposed will also call for **changes in the rules and instruments for Community research**. In practice, there are clearly limits to the single formula of 50% funding of the costs of pre-competitive research projects. Formulas creating a more flexible link between project-funding and the obligation to produce results, tailoring the level of public support to the economic and social importance of the results, will have to be explored. More practical formulas in terms of costs and benefits, such as low-interest loans repayable over very long periods, will have to be developed.

To facilitate the adoption of converging, proactive measures in the Member States, the possibility of **agreeing guidelines at Community level** on business start-ups, funding of the application of research results or changes in the conditions of employment for scientific staff will have to be studied. Steps will also have to be taken to ensure that the measures implemented are compatible with competition policy, notably on agreements and State aid. Finally, to maximize the impact of the measures taken at Community level and by the Member States, significant efforts will be required to **make the Community's research, external relations and commercial policies more compatible.**

Chapter 5

The changing society, the new technologies

Introduction

Information and communication technologies (ICTs) are transforming dramatically many aspects of economic and social life, such as working methods and relations, the organization of companies, the focus of training and education, and the way people communicate with each other. They are resulting in major gains in productivity in industry, and in the quality and performance of services. A new 'information society' is emerging, in which management, quality and speed of information are key factors for competitiveness: as an input to the industries as a whole and as a service provided to ultimate consumers, information and communication technologies influence the economy at all stages.

Comparable changes in productivity will be achieved by further progress in life sciences — biotechnology — through the creation of innovation in highly competitive areas of industry and agriculture.

The competitiveness of the European economy will to a great extent depend both on the conditions of utilization and on the development and application of these technologies. Since they are amongst the highest growth activities in industrialized countries, and they are also highly skilled labour activities, their potential for employment creation is considerable, in particular for the creation of new services. At the same time, potential drawbacks of widespread use of these new technologies, such as the risk of non-skilled people being left behind by progress in information technologies, should be combated through positive policies.

Various obstacles to an optimum exploitation of these technologies have been encountered in Europe, and they should be removed. The diffusion of best practice aimed at business should be promoted and the development of Community-wide applications favoured. To this end, an appropriate regulatory and political environment should be created and the implementation of trans-European telecommunication services stimulated. Training systems should foster the application of these technologies. Europe should implement the conditions that will allow it to maintain a sufficient level of mastery over technology and benefit from an innovative and competitive ICT industry, within an open and competitive environment.

Member States' views

The Member States' contributions on this subject place the emphasis on cooperation between the Community and the Member States to promote economies of scale; the Community could focus its efforts on facilitating the development of market forces, while ensuring free competition and promoting systems compatibility.

A — The information society

5.1. Introduction

This decade is witnessing the forging of a link of unprecedented magnitude and significance between the technological innovation process and economic and social organization. Countless innovations are combining to bring about a major upheaval in the organization of activities and relationships within society. A new 'information society' is emerging in which the services provided by information and communications technologies (ICTs) underpin human activities. It constitutes an upheaval but can also offer new job prospects.

With easier access to information, it is becoming increasingly easy to identify, evaluate and compete with economic activities in all sectors. The pressure of the market-place is spreading and growing, obliging businesses to exploit every opportunity available to increase productivity and efficiency. Structural adaptability is becoming a major prerequisite for economic success. The growing interconnection of the economy is leading to major productivity improvements in the production of goods but also in relation to services, and the borderline between goods and services is becoming increasingly blurred. Throughout the world there is a trend towards specialization and professionalization in economic activities which is gradually extending to subcontractors and service providers. To be able to compete worldwide, European industry must exploit all possible ways of improving its competitiveness by making growing and effective use of ICTs. It must favour innovative and attacking strategies aimed at acquiring market shares rather than simply adjusting by reducing its production costs.

Businesses are very much aware of the importance of applying ICTs in order to stay competitive. **The job situation has generally remained more favourable in companies which have introduced microelectronics than in those companies that have not used this technology.** The main effects have been job substitutions on the basis of different qualifications. The spread of ICTs within the Community has generated increases in productivity and in GDP, and a lower rate of inflation. The overall impact on employment depends to a large extent on how competitive the European ICT industry is: the better it performs, the greater the benefit in terms of the impact on employment. However, the current worrying employment situation within the Community cannot be blamed on the penetration of the ICTs into the industrial and social fabric.

The economic impact of technological progress on growth and employment depends on the innovation process, which has become interactive. The linear model of innovation, with the innovative act being isolated, has in today's world been replaced by complex mechanisms: innovation requires constant and organized interdependence between the upstream phases linked to technology, and the downstream phases linked to the market.

The means available to create, process, access and transfer information are remodelling relationships in our societies. One of the most important aspects of current developments is the breathtaking expansion in the means available to us to communicate and process information (sound, text, images) in digital form.

Companies' operations have become unthinkable without the use of ICTs. These technologies are enabling them to seek total integration of their own functions in space and time and in terms of their environment. The introduction of ICTs, globalization and international competition are forcing companies to rethink the way in which they organize their production. Where the general public is concerned, the penetration of ICT-dependent products and services into everyday activities is also striking. This generates new forms of economic and social organization, the structure of which is no longer subject to geographical constraints but depends on telecommunications networks or teleports: teleworking is emerging as a major social phenomenon. Authorities concerned with the management of public funds and wishing to provide their constituents with better quality services also call upon ICTs. Relationships between the general public and the authorities are changing, and more fundamentally the present boundaries between the role of the State and the market are altering.

Despite the undeniable progress that has been made, the penetration of ICTs is not an unmitigated success story. **The changeover towards an information society has placed severe demands on the adaptability of those concerned.** The risk of exclusion, for example, as a result of inadequate skills or qualifications and, more generally, the emergence of a two-tier society should not be underestimated. Europe must prepare itself for this changeover in order to capitalize upon the economic and social advantages while analysing and mitigating any adverse consequences: an increase in the isolation of individuals, intrusions into private life, and moral and ethical problems. It is important to **identify to a greater extent the employment possibilities** for those who encounter difficulties in integrating into a working world which is becoming increasingly complex and demanding. Social responsibility is a matter for employers, employees and the State. The information society is producing a significant acceleration of economic and social changes, and new and more flexible forms of employment are emerging which often require new forms of social protection.

5.2. A common information area

The move towards an 'information society' is irreversible, and affects all aspects of society and interrelations between economic partners. Creation of a common information area within the Community will enable the Community fully to seize these opportunities.

(a) What is a common information area?

The common information area consists of a number of indivisible levels:

(i) the **information** itself, converted and collated in electronic, i.e. digital, form (databases, document bases, image bases, CDI, etc.);

(ii) the **hardware, components and software** available to the user to process this information;

(iii) the **physical infrastructure** (terrestrial cable infrastructure, radio communications networks and satellites);

(iv) the **basic telecommunications services,** particularly electronic mail, file transfer, interactive access to databases and interactive digital image transmission;

(v) the **applications,** for which the above-mentioned levels perform the storage, processing and transmission functions, providing users with the specific services they need. Generally, users 'see' only the application to which they are connected; the transport side needs to be 'transparent' for them. Consequently, applications are the area where the greatest efforts must be made to improve the structuring of the information and user-friendliness. With the aid of the applications, their performance and the conditions in which they can be used, the common-information area will have an economic and social impact and can help to improve the employment situation;

(vi) **users,** who are not only trained in operation of the applications, but are also aware of the potential of ICTs and of the conditions required for optimum use thereof.

(b) What opportunities?

The common information area is a factor for economic and social improvement. In the current competitive context, access to and mobilization of information are becoming the central aspects of productivity and competitiveness, especially for SMEs. The capital and non-capital investment required to set up information technology infrastructures **directly supports growth** and contributes to structural improvements in the conditions of supply. The common information area is also a **factor for economic and social cohesion:** it will allow reconsideration of siting and make it possible to promote new decentralized methods of organizing work, for example, teleworking. It contributes to the performance of other major infrastructures, in particular transport infrastructures, and constitutes an aid for the protection of the environment and risk management. Last but not least, infrastructures are a powerful **lever for the development** of new services, and in this way can make a significant contribution to improving the job situation. In particular, certain services for which the State has been responsible hitherto, and which are subject to increasingly tight budget restrictions, could be transferred permanently to the market. There are many examples of such new services related to communication and social relations: education and training, culture, security, etc. They cannot be developed free of charge and be funded implicitly by the taxpayer. They call for the introduction of new methods of payment, such as the pay-per-use system.

Modern technologies are fundamentally changing the relationship between the State and the general public. The ordinary citizen can have access to 'public services' on an individual basis, and these will be invoiced on the basis of the use made of them. Transferring such services to the marketplace will lead to new private-sector offers of services and numerous job-creation opportunities. However, this will have to be accompanied by a reduction in user costs;

otherwise, no-one will be willing to make use of such opportunities. It will also be essential to ensure that this transfer does not entail social disadvantages.

(c) The policies pursued with the Triad (European Community, United States and Japan)

The move towards an information society, and the opportunities which it provides, will in the long run be as important as the first industrial revolution. It is difficult to predict the pace at which this change will take place. The economies which are the first to succeed in completing this change satisfactorily will have major competitive advantages. The USA and Japan are therefore attempting to speed up the process.

In the **USA,** the public authorities have a strong desire to maintain US technological pre-eminence, in particular on national economic security grounds, and are making technology the driving force behind a revival in US economic growth and competitiveness. The policy to establish information technology infrastructure spanning the entire USA is considered vital for the country's growth. The project to speed up the introduction of new high-speed networks, computer systems and communication technologies is not limited to investment in physical infrastructures. It also includes the development and installation of new technologies and applications.

In **Japan,** political awareness of the strategic importance of ICTs for Japan's economic development dates back to the 1960s, and a social consensus on the priorities and the means and programmes required was already achieved at that time. The recognized importance of 'information infrastructures' to maintain Japan's development has given rise to a programme under the new Japanese economic recovery plan.

The **Community** and the **Member States** have taken numerous steps to create information infrastructures: revision of the regulatory framework for telecommunications,

and in particular the liberalization of value-added services and a programme designed to culminate in 1998 in the liberalization of voice telephony, RTD support programme, stimulation of the development of data-communication systems of general interest, establishment of a standardization policy, and a policy of innovation and support for regional policy.

*

The development of an 'information society' will be a global phenomenon, led first of all by the Triad, but gradually extended to cover the entire planet. In pursuing its strategy, Europe should aim at achieving **three objectives:**

(i) from the outset, **placing its approach in a world perspective,** and therefore encouraging the international alliance strategies of its companies and operators; promoting where possible the development of open systems and international standards; working resolutely towards the opening-up of third country markets, in order to seek genuine reciprocity, and opposing any form of discrimination;

(ii) ensuring, at the same time, that the systems developed take due account of **European characteristics:** multilingualism, cultural diversity, economic divergence, and more generally the preservation of its social model;

(iii) creating the conditions whereby, in an open and competitive international system, Europe still has an adequate take-up of **basic technologies** and an efficient and competitive industry.

Fuller use of the potential offered by information and communication technologies can:

create new service markets;

facilitate provision of services by the private rather than the public sector, including a new partnership between the private and public sector, for example for training;

speed up administrative decision-making procedures.

5.3. The objective: To create new service markets

Europe has the know-how and experience to establish a common information area. However, to harness them, there needs to be a collective effort and a political framework so that the measures to be taken can be implemented as quickly as possible. This process will primarily be led by the private sector and underpinned by the emergence of new needs and new markets. It is therefore necessary to define the role of the public authorities unambiguously.

In the first instance, it will be their responsibility to address the 'societal' implications as a whole, avoiding exclusion phenomena, **maximizing the impact on employment,** adapting education and training systems, and taking due account of the cultural and ethical implications for the general public, including aspects relating to the protection of privacy.

The second task of the public authorities will be to **remove the remaining regulatory obstacles to the development of new markets.** However, investors' 'wait-and-see' attitude can also be explained by the fact that, for want of a communication infrastructure, demand cannot be expressed sufficiently clearly. To resolve this dilemma there is a need for the public authorities to provide encouragement, guidance and opportunities for concertation.

The third task of the public authorities is to **create the conditions whereby European companies develop their strategies in an open internal and international competitive environment,** and can continue to ensure that crucial technologies are mastered and developed in Europe.

The changeover towards an information society is a very complex process requiring new forms of partnership and cooperation between the public and private sectors. In the measures proposed below, the principle of subsidiarity must be applied fully between the private sector and the public authorities and also between the Community authorities and the national administrations.

A strategy for establishing a common information area must satisfy four specific requirements:

(i) diffusion of best practice and development of European ICT applications, which is the fundamental objective in view of the contribution which it can make to restoring growth and strengthening competitiveness;

(ii) liberalization of the telecommunications sector, which alone can release the market forces of the information society; users must be offered a broad range of options at attractive tariffs;

(iii) faster standardization, which alone can create a European information area from the fragmented communications areas;

(iv) trans-European telecommunications infrastructure, which is essential as the basic foundation of the information society.

The policy for creating a common information area should set the following priorities:

(a) Diffusion of best practice and development of European ICT applications. This is the fundamental objective in view of the contribution which it can make to restoring growth, strengthening competitiveness and improving the employment situation.

(b) Creation and enforcement of a legal, regulatory and political environment encouraging private initiative by opening up the market to competition, taking due account of the interests of the Community (the existence of universal services and the emergence of European operators) and of individual citizens (protection of data and privacy, security, etc.).

(c) Development of basic trans-European telecommunications services, which are a *sine qua non* for the free movement of information.

(d) Provision of specific training targeted on extensive use of information and on the needs of the ICT industries for qualified human resources.

(e) Technology take-up and improvement of the performance of the European ICT industries, a precon-

111

dition for adapting the applications to the specific situation in Europe, for making full use of technological progress and for maximizing the impact of the measures proposed on employment.

These five complementary priorities form an indivisible whole. The first sets the objective and the others are the means to attain that end. In the current climate of rapid technological and industrial change, action must be started as soon as possible to establish a European information infrastructure and give a positive lead to the strategic intentions and choices made by businesses. The instruments or bodies necessary to ensure the compatibility and interoperability of products and services must also be set up without delay.

(a) Diffusion of best practice and development of European ICT applications

Strict implementation conditions are needed to exploit all the potential offered by ICTs. In particular, the introduction of computer systems must go hand-in-hand with the identification of companies' strategic objectives, the functions and support to be provided by the system, and appropriate work organization. This is an area where the awareness of the user companies must be raised.

It is recommended that the following **action** be taken:

(i) **Diffusion of best practice** in the use of ICTs. Attention should be focused on the conditions under which ICTs are used: a programme for the diffusion of best ICT practice aimed at businesses, in particular SMEs, would significantly improve the impact of ICTs on their competitiveness and ability to create jobs.

(ii) **Launch of European applications projects.** The crux of the matter is not technology, but organization. In order to avoid a proliferation of uncoordinated and incompatible applications in Europe, several major applications projects should be launched to catalyse the market and promote greater

homogeneity in terms of standards in particular. Clear priorities must be defined. They offer the prospect of creating a market large enough to make investment in telecommunications infrastructure profitable and guarantee satisfactory amortization. They could concern:

Administrations, through an extended version of the IDA programme.

Major public services. On the basis of work already carried out, efforts should be concentrated on effective implementation of a limited number of major projects leading to a political commitment: an integrated air-traffic control system, a European road-traffic management network, a European medical information system, a network of research centres, a European distance-learning service, a 'computers in schools' programme or a European civil protection system.

Teleworking and telepartnerships. Teleworking and telepartnerships have an important part to play in the relocation of work and of businesses to the disadvantaged areas of Europe (rural areas, peripheral areas or old industrial areas, etc.). A European project could be launched to promote the development of teleworking and telepartnerships.

Greater involvement of ICT users in the creation and implementation of Community programmes.

Strengthening the coordination of programmes

(b) Creation of a regulatory and political environment

Creation of a common information area will depend primarily on private sector investment. It is therefore essential to create a legal environment which will stimulate the development of such investments and guarantee that they are used in the public interest. Several types of action can be taken to achieve these objectives, most of which have already been initiated, and should be intensified where appropriate.

(i) **Opening up to competition,** to provide the broadest possible range of services at the best price to suit the market.

(ii) **Universal service:** since the traditional operators are becoming increasingly independent of the State and are exposed to growing competition, it is necessary to define precisely the universal service obligations, their price and how they should be financed.

(iii) **Standardization:** given the standardization policy conducted hitherto at Community level, enhancing the efficiency of the present system means speeding up standardization processes, ensuring transparency in standardization (declaration *ab initio* of patents by standards proposers) and guaranteeing all companies equitable rights to exploit the patents underlying the standards.

(iv) **Protection of data and privacy,** in particular ensuring complete reliability of data transfer systems.

(v) **Security of information and communication systems:** both industry and Member States are calling for coordinated action to solve the problems of security of information and communication systems.

(c) Providing the Community with basic trans-European telecommunications services

European telecommunications face considerable difficulties, notably the incompatibility and non-interoperability of the national telecommunications services' networks. The principal problem is not technological, it is the result of the structure and organization of the market: the absence of telecommunications operators of a European stature and the non-existence of basic services at European level (electronic mail and file transfer, remote access to databases and interactive image transmission services). [1]

---

[1] It should be noted that standardization could lead to the introduction of European telephone paycards or a European 'Minitel' without the need for specific technological development.

The following **action** can be recommended:

(i) **development of support networks:** Euro-ISDN and integrated broadband communication (IBC) system. Mobile radio communications (GSM, PCN) are another area in which efforts should be made to speed up development;

(ii) **acceleration of the standardization process** and integration of standards into services, in particular those which are vital to service interoperability;

(iii) **strengthening of coordination,** in particular between telecommunications policy and the Structural Funds.

(d) Providing the right training

The competitive pressures on European industry require from all staff an increasingly high level of skills and an ability to use new technologies effectively. Managers need specific training to make them aware of the potential of ICTs and their organizational and socio-professional implications. Technicians and other workers need to have specific ICT-related aspects better integrated into the training for their basic trade. Schoolchildren and students should learn to use ICTs, in particular in order to resolve general education and training problems. Educating potential ICT users to enable them to make effective use of ICTs entails training as many people as possible in the basic skills and providing specialist training for some of them.

Europe has made a big effort to develop basic training in computer science, but **it does not have sufficient qualified staff, and insufficient attention has been paid so far to the application of new technologies in training and education systems.** In particular, the possibilities opened up by distance-training should be better exploited.

The following **recommendations** are put forward:

(i) There needs to be an in-depth analysis of the importance of the greatest possible number of people being given the basic knowledge for making the best possible use of **data-processing systems, and the conditions and resources necessary to achieve this;**

(ii) on user-oriented training: **generalize the use of new technologies in teaching and training, notably by developing appropriate software and training teachers and instructors;**

(iii) on producer-oriented training: it is essential to **train the engineers and researchers** which the European ICT industry needs and to coordinate the ICT-related training provided under the various specific Community RTD programmes.

(e) Harnessing technologies and improving the performance of Europe's ICT industry

Unlike its competitors, Europe's ICT industry does not have a firm hold on its home market. Europe must be given the applications necessary to meet its needs and the ability to devise the requisite applications software. A solid software industry base is inconceivable without close cooperation with equipment suppliers and early knowledge of how their equipment performs. Because of the speed of new developments, it is essential to know the specifications of equipment and components before they are available on the market, otherwise it is possible only to follow developments, which leaves very little scope for initiative. Having a strong European ICT industry would also help considerably in maintaining a scientific and technological community in Europe, and particularly in harnessing generic manufacturing technology.

It is recommended that action be taken in the following areas:

(i) **Promotion of 'strategy watch' at European level.** There should be action to raise awareness on strategy watch, to reinforce the measures already taken and to coordinate and rationalize existing resources in order to remedy the lack of strategy watch structures and organizations in Europe.

(ii) **Support for the R&D effort.** The rapidity of technological progress requires that the R&D effort be maintained and even reinforced. In the priorities of the fourth framework pro-

gramme concerning the generic technologies necessary for the emergence of an information and communication infrastructure special emphasis will be placed on taking into account users' and market needs and the general aim of making the economy as a whole more competitive. The impact of the programmes will be strengthened by involving users, and through training, coordination with national initiatives and Eureka and international cooperation. Careful consideration needs to be given to taking better account of the importance of incremental research, industrial realities and the interactive nature of the innovation process.

(iii) **Exploitation of RTD projects through industrial policy.** Specific action could be launched consisting in developing pilot demonstrations in those areas where market forces are slow to commercialize the results of RTD (multimedia, in particular).

(iv) **Adapting industrial and commercial policies to the new international situation.** Globalization of the economy and the existence of unfair competitive practices in the various markets of the Triad create competitive advantages which could seriously handicap European companies. In accordance with the Council resolution of November 1991,[1] higher priority should be given to specific measures aimed at levelling competitive practices and launching international cooperation programmes.

5.4. Conclusions: Combining our efforts

A Community policy aimed at establishing a common information area will help to increase competition and improve European competitiveness. It will help to create jobs. It should be backed up by specific measures aimed at facilitating economic

---

[1] Council resolution of 18 November 1991 concerning electronics, information and communication technologies (SN 211/91).

and social changes, and ensuring that all workers have jobs which reflect their qualifications. To this end, **steps should be taken to promote the creation of new jobs,** for example, in new social services.

Devising a policy to promote a common information area requires in particular the setting-up of an **efficient system for cooperation** between the parties concerned. Because of the Community's political structure, this is much more difficult than in the USA or Japan.

Establishing an information infrastructure will require urgent and structured measures. If these measures are to be credible and successful, it is important to define them clearly, to specify a timetable and to put in place resources or structures which will ensure that this timetable is respected. We must therefore combine our efforts in Europe and make greater use of synergy in order to achieve as soon as possible objectives aimed at building an efficient European information infrastructure and taking the necessary measures for creating new services.

It is proposed that a task force on European information infrastructures be established with a direct mandate from the European Council. This very high-level task force would follow guidelines set by the European Council and would have the task of establishing priorities, deciding on procedures and setting schedules. It would be required to report to the European Council within three months after first consulting all the parties concerned.

It would consist of one member of the Commission, several members of the governments of the Member States, representatives of the European Parliament and high-level representatives of industry, operators, users and financial institutions.

The task force should be set up before the end of 1993.

At the same time, the European Council should instruct the Council to speed up the work already being done aimed at setting up information infrastructures.

B — Biotechnology and its diffusion

5.5. As a result of intensive scientific research and major discoveries over the past four decades in molecular biology, biotechnology has emerged as one of the most promising and crucial technologies for sustainable development in the next century. Modern biotechnology constitutes a growing range of techniques, procedures and processes, such as cell fusion, r-DNA technology, biocatalysis, that can substitute and complement classical biotechnologies of selective breeding and fermentation. This confluence of classical and modern technologies **enables the creation of new products and highly competitive processes in a large number of industrial and agricultural activities** as well as in the health sector. This would provide the impulse to radically transform the competitiveness and growth potential for a number of activities and open up new possibilities in other sectors such as diagnostics, bioremediation and production of process equipment (biohardware). In terms of the quality of life, we should not underrate the important **potential of biotechnology for improving the environment** by correcting pollution and for improving health by preventing or remedying illness or other physical problems.

The Community has taken a number of initiatives, on the one hand, to promote the competitiveness of bio-industries and, on the other hand, to ensure the safe application of biotechnology. It implies mainly funding of research and development and the putting into place of a regulatory framework.

5.6. Potential of biotechnology and similarities with information technologies

Reinforcing the potential of biotechnology are a number of features which biotechnology shares with electronics and information technologies: it is science-based, the scientific input being the most crucial element of the technology trajectory; the gap between developments in basic science and their research and development applications and even further downstream is small and diminishing; a very major and growing stimulus can be expected for process equipment, instrument and engineering sectors; and finally **the impacts of the processes, techniques and hardware represented by biotechnology are across a number of sectors.**

The Community is highly competitive in these sectors which cover chemicals, pharmaceuticals, health care, agriculture and agricultural processing, bulk and specialized plant protection products as well as decontamination, waste treatment and disposal. These sectors where biotechnology has a direct impact currently account for 9% of the Community's gross value-added (approximately ECU 450 billion) and 8% of its employment (approximately 9 million). Beyond this, perhaps only modern biotechnology has the potential to provide significant and viable thrusts, compatible with CAP reform and not dependent on operating subsidies, to new energy/fuel and industrial outlets for agricultural raw materials. The important role of biotechnology in these sectors is likely to be to maintain employment by stimulating its productivity as well as to create highly skilled labour demand.

The following are two valid indicators of the potential of biotechnology: the pace of international innovative activity and the evidence of growth in output and value-added in products derived through biotechnology. Measuring innovative activity by patents filed for relevant products in the USA, the Community and Japan show that patents filed have increased from 1 100 per annum in the early 1980s to 3 350 per annum in 1990. In 1980 the Community was in a leading position, by 1990 the USA was filing 50% more patents than the Community. European Patent Office (EPO) statistics reveal a similar evolution: between 1980 and 1991 biotechnology patents filed with the EPO increased by a factor of 10, the most being filed by US-based companies.

Current global indicators of the growth prospects of the biotechnology industry are the following: in the USA the industry based on modern biotechnology had a turnover of over USD 8 billion in 1992, a growth rate of 28% with employment growing at 13%. It is estimated on the basis of the observed rates of diffusion of bio-

technology that the US biotechnology industry's revenues will grow at an average rate of 40% to reach USD 52 billion by the year 2000. The current industry size in Japan is officially put at USD 3.8 billion and is estimated by the Ministry of International Trade and Industry to reach USD 35 billion by the end of the century. In the Community, despite the emergence of a significant number of firms and a substantial growth in markets, primarily of bio-pharmaceuticals, to over USD 3 billion, at the current rate of growth, the value of output and employment is about the same as that in Japan. It is therefore clear that by the year 2000 with an estimated world market of ECU 100 billion for the biotechnology industry, the Community growth rate will have to be substantially higher than at present to ensure that the Community will become a major producer of such products, thereby reaping the output and employment advantages while at the same time remaining a key player in the related research area.

5.7. Factors favouring growth, competitiveness and employment in the Community

The sectors with the greatest potential for the applications of biotechnology are amongst the most vigorous and competitive sectors in the Community with a long record of sustained growth, productivity increase, and highly competitive trade performance.

The Community firms in these sectors (chemicals, pharmaceuticals, agricultural processing) are leading firms at a global level with important capabilities in the domain of innovation.

Among other factors favouring investment in biotechnology in the Community are the strong science base and infrastructure, the availability of skilled labour, and the high quality of process engineering and production facilities.

5.8. Unfavourable factors

The key factors that may jeopardize a significant expansion of biotechnological applications in the Community are the following:

(i) In a domain where the technology trajectory is crucially dependent on basic science, the **public research and development expenditure in the Community lags behind.** For the 1993 financial year publicly financed US biotechnology research and development expenditures are set to exceed USD 4 billion; in Japan in 1991 they exceeded USD 900 million whereas the Community's and Member States' expenditures totalled around USD 600 million. The fourth research and development framework programme's proposes ECU 650 million in biotechnology over five years. Member States have also programmes devoted to R&D in biotechnology.

(ii) **Privately financed research and development on biotechnology in the Community has not compensated for the shortfall in public funding;** on the contrary, available indicators identify a delocalization — an investment outflow, largely net, from Community companies mainly towards the USA and Japan of USD 2.2 billion since 1984. In the most vigorous sector of biotechnology, biopharmaceuticals, in 1990 67% of patents were held by US-based companies and only 15% by Community-based companies. There exists the risk that the Community will be a leading future market for biopharmaceuticals but not a leading future producer. There is an evident feedback between technology diffusion and private investment.

(iii) Regulation concerning the safety of applications of the new biotechnology is necessary to ensure harmonization, safety, and public acceptance. However, the current horizontal approach is unfavourably perceived by scientists and industry as introducing constraints on basic and applied research and its diffusion and hence having unfavourable effects on EC competitiveness.

(iv) Technology hostility and social inertia in respect of biotechnology have been more pronounced in the Community in general than in the USA or Japan. It has become clear that these issues should be examined in greater detail in order to properly address these concerns. Supporting actions such as those under the Biotech programme and the creation of a group of advisers to look at ethical issues have been undertaken.

5.9. Conclusions and recommendations

The potential of biotechnology to dramatically impact on competitiveness is greatest in certain sectors of the Community chemicals, pharmaceuticals, process equipments and appliances, agriculture and agricultural processing. These sectors contribute importantly to value-added and employment. The observed international growth in output of between 30 and 40% in the most vigorous of the biotechnology dependent sectors and the associated labour-intensive service activities (e.g. research, health care) has the capacity to provide a valuable stimulus to employment growth.

The means to achieve a fuller realization of the Community's inherent strength in biotechnology are to be found in overcoming existing constraints by creating appropriate channels for biotechnology policy development and coordination and by acting on the following **recommendations.**

(a) Given the importance of regulations for a stable and predictable environment for industry and given that they influence localization factors such as field trials and scientific experimentation, the Community should be open to **review its regulatory framework** with a view to ensuring that advances in scientific knowledge are constantly taken into account and that regulatory oversight is based on potential risks. A greater recourse, where appropriate, to mutual recognition, is warranted to stimulate research activities across Member States. Furthermore, if the Community is to avoid becoming simply a market rather than a producer of biotechnology-derived products then it is vital that Community regulations are harmonized with international practice. The development of standards will supplement regulatory efforts.

(b) The Commission intends to make full use of the possibilities which exist in the present regulatory framework on flexibility and **simplification of procedures** as well as for technical adaptation. To sustain a high level of environmental protection and to underpin public acceptance, it is important to **reinforce and pool the scientific support for regulations.** An advisory scientific body at Community level for biotechnology diffusion drawing on the scientific expertise within and at the disposal of the existing committees at national and Community level. An advisory body at Community level — scientific committee for biotechnology diffusion — could play a crucial role in intensifying scientific collaboration and in providing the needed support for a harmonized approach of the development of risk assessments underlying product approval. This body could also advise on the development of a further Community strategy for biotechnology.

(c) Since the Community is not matching efforts elsewhere in research and development expenditure, it needs to compensate for this through **focusing on the most vigorous biotechnology research and development domains and increased coordination** between the Community and Member States in order to avoid duplication, encourage collaborative research and improve efficiency of expenditure on research and development.

(d) The small and medium-sized research-oriented firms play an important role in biotechnology diffusion and the growth of this sector would substantially benefit from the creation of a **network of existing and new biotechnology science parks** in the Community linking together academic institutions, research laboratories and SMEs. This would create the possibilities for, on the one hand, greater educational investment in molecular biology and biohardware, and, on the other hand, the involvement of venture capital and other financial institutions. The Structural Funds could also play an important role.

(e) Member States should provide additional incentives to **improve further the investment climate for biotechnology** and to facilitate the transfer of applied research and development to the market place. These might include fiscal incentives respecting the existing Community guidelines that have a bearing on biotechnology innovation and investment.

(f) The commercialization of biotechnology will in certain areas require specific actions aimed at **further enhancing public understanding of the technology.** Member States should encourage interest groups to make objective information available and to encourage dia logue.

(g) It is necessary **to clarify further value laden issues in relation to some applications of biotechnology.** In view of this, the Commission will reinforce the role of the Group of Advisers on Ethical Implications of Biotechnology and other groups which examine in particular ethical questions related to biomedical research.

C — The audiovisual sector

5.10. Introduction

The audiovisual sector which covers programme production and distribution ('software'), to which equipment manufacturing ('hardware') can be added, has an economic importance that is often underestimated as compared to its unquestionable cultural significance.

The sector has an estimated current global market value, considering both its components, of ECU 257 billion. [1] The software sector represents 54% of the overall market value. [2] One of the main characteristics of the sector is that it is undergoing both a technological and regulatory transformation that will considerably affect its future growth and development.

---

[1] *Source:* OMSYC 1993 report.
[2] *Source:* OMSYC 1993 report.

5.11. Europe — Growth forecasts and employment

The European market has been among the fastest growing in the world with a current market growth rate of 6% a year in real terms, that is being sustained even in today's recessionary climate. The USA has benefited most from growth in Europe increasing its sales of programming in Europe from USD 330 million in 1984 to USD 3.6 billion in 1992. In 1991, 77% of American exports of audiovisual programmes went to Europe, of which nearly 60% to the Community, this being the second largest US industrial sector in export terms, while the European Union's annual deficit with the USA in audiovisual trade amounts to about USD 3.5 billion.

Some impressive growth figures that flow from recent studies clearly show that by the end of this century the demand for audiovisual products will double in Europe, expenditure on both audiovisual hardware and software growing from ECU 23 to ECU 45 billion.

Such growth will accelerate under the impact of new transmission technologies which will multiply and diversify the vectors for distribution (satellite TV, pay-per-view, video on demand, interactive TV, etc.). The number of TV channels is expected to increase from the present 117 to 500 by the year 2000 with an increase of TV broadcast hours from 650 000 to 3 250 000 over the same period. Moreover, encrypted programming hours are predicted to increase by a factor of 30, which implies fundamentally different (and greater) revenue flows.

The audiovisual sector has a highly labour-intensive structure. Staff costs make up 47% of typical film budget and on average 15% of TV channels' **operating** costs (i.e. not counting the personnel involved in **producing** the programmes which may be bought in or made in-house). The sector intrinsically provides many high-level 'grey-matter' jobs, like technicians, performers, script-writers, directors, and so on. It is thus potentially less vulnerable to competition from low labour cost markets.

Though there is a lack of reliable statistics on employment within the sector, it has been estimated that at least 1.8 million people are earning their living in the EC audiovisual services (i.e. in the software sector). [1] It is clear from the vigorous demand-side growth trend, accentuated by technological developments, in the audiovisual software sector in Europe, and from the nature and structure of the employment that it can provide, that there is remarkable potential for job creation in this sector. Recent estimates point to the doubling in the medium term of the share of household expenditure given over to audiovisual software products. In line with the increased growth predicted for the sector, on the condition that the growth is translated into jobs in Europe and not into financial transfers from Europe to other parts of the world, job creation could be of the order of two million by the year 2000, if current conditions prevail. Furthermore, bearing in mind that, if proper resources are deployed, there is a clear potential for an increase in our share of the market, it is not unrealistic to estimate that the audiovisual services sector could provide jobs, directly or indirectly, to four million people.

5.12. Conclusions

It is vital that the predicted growth in the European audiovisual market be translated into jobs in Europe? Given the intrinsic nature of audiovisual products (i.e. that they need to be amortized on large domestic markets) concerted national policies and policies at Community level are needed to achieve this objective. The aim must be to establish a growth-employment relationship that is positive within the European audiovisual sector and to prevent increasing resources from being diverted to job creation in other parts of the world, with Europe becoming a passive consumer of other countries' audiovisual products and with both its economy and culture depending on others. This thinking is behind the Community's firm stance in the

---

[1] *Source:* Eurostat.

GATT negotiations and behind the policy instruments that have been developed since the Rhodes European Council in 1988. Moreover, a Green Paper on audiovisual policy will be presented by the Commission during the first semester of 1994 setting out suggestions on how existing policy instruments in this field may be developed and refined in order to maximize their impact and contribute to guaranteeing not only the survival but also the growth of a viable audiovisual software industry in Europe into the year 2000. The stakes are high. The audiovisual sector is no longer a marginal one in economic or employment terms. On the contrary, it will be one of the major service sectors in the 21st century and should be given corresponding attention.

Chapter 6

The Community, an open and reliable partner

Summary

World economic relations are no longer limited to international trade in goods and services. In the world economy, the Community and all major partners are interdependent: Community policies must reflect and build on this reality.

The Community must keep up its efforts to bring the Uruguay Round to a swift conclusion covering all the problems now outstanding and paving the way for the transition to a world trade organization.

In the context of the liberalization of global trade and economic relations, the integration of Central and Eastern Europe and the former Soviet Union into the world economy will contribute to the strengthening of growth in these countries and the world in general. Similarly, the Community should for the same reasons support the smooth and gradual integration of the developing countries in the world economy.

The perspective of accession for the associated countries confirmed by the Copenhagen Summit lays the foundation for the development of a Europe-wide zone of open markets and economic cooperation which will stimulate growth in the associates and give a strong stimulus to Community exports and therefore growth. This process of integration will contribute to rendering European enterprises in West and East more competitive on world markets.

6.1. Diagnosis

The Community economy is a global economy. The Community accounts for one fifth of total world trade in goods; 12 million jobs in Europe depend directly on export of goods. Tradable services account for one quarter of overall goods and services exports. Nor are trade figures alone a good reflection of Community economic links worldwide. Direct investment by Europe in other countries accounts for over one third of foreign direct investment worldwide. The Community has strong links to preferential partners, but these do not dominate trade: Community exports to EFTA, Eastern Europe, the Mediterranean basin and ACP countries together account for only just over 40% of total exports.

Underlying this static picture, **the structure of the world economy is undergoing rapid change.** The post-war picture of inter-country trade, increasingly accompanied by international investment and with very large companies the privileged players, is less and less reliable. Trade in goods increasingly means interfirm trade in semi-manufactures. The development of informatics networks makes it possible for companies to cooperate more flexibly than by joint venture or franchise alone.

This means that **the key factors shaping business behaviour will be different.** Already, import duties are generally less important for exporters than domestic regulations (tax, safety, consumer protection). There is less and less scope for a nation State or an economic community to improve life for its businessmen by acting alone. Nor, even internationally, can trade policy action be taken without looking at possible policy linkages (trade/exchange rates, trade/environment, trade/security, trade/human rights) which were hardly addressed 10 years ago.

Integration in the global economy none the less depends on a **solid set of trade relations.** The analysis of competitiveness has already demonstrated that extra-Community exports of traded goods are too frequently concentrated in sectors where long-term prospects are for low demand. Nor are Community exporters sufficiently focused on the Asia-Pacific region, which has the highest medium-term growth potential. Community exports to some Asian markets have increased dramatically, underlining the mutual advantages of free trade. But we need to be more broadly present and to pursue further market-opening worldwide.

Nominal exchange-rate fluctuations may increase business uncertainty on third country markets and are a proper subject for Community activity (see recommendation (h) below) but do not seem to drive the underlying trend in Community competitiveness.

Perceptions of unfair trade abound. Some relate to traditional problems (dumping, subsidy, unilateralism), and some to the problem of free-riding in new areas of international policy coordination (social or environmental dumping, international impact of anti-competitive practices). There remains, too, a sense that market-opening is lagging behind economic growth and export performance in many, newly industrialized countries.

6.2. Member States' views

Several Member States' contributions underscore the benefits of an open market economy and free competition as advocated in the Union Treaty. This would enable the Community to turn its competitive advantages to good account in the framework of the international division of labour. Maintaining an open economy facilitates the allocation of resources to the places where they are most productive and, consequently, specialization in products and services with a high added-value and greater competitiveness. In the view of some Member States these arguments also hold good for products originating in countries with low wage costs as their development, coupled with an opening-up of their markets, offers new opportunities for European industry.

All Member States consider the conclusion of the Uruguay Round in the very near future to be necessary for the world economy. Several point to the need in future negotiations to take account of certain factors which have a bearing on trade, such as the environment, competition conditions and monetary aspects. There is no unanimity, however, on the inclusion in trade negotiations of social aspects or on the use and shape of trade policy instruments.

Most of the contributions highlight the benefits to be derived from the European

Economic Area and the progressive integration of the economies of Central and Eastern European.

Some Member States call for **international economic cooperation** to be stepped up significantly, notably in the G7 framework.

6.3. Europe in the world economy

Open markets with free competition is one of the objectives of the Treaty on European Union. It has a profound interest in promoting open markets, both inside and outside the Community. Open markets are a key element for international competitiveness. Within the Community they facilitate the international division of labour and the assignment of resources where they are most efficient. They also enable Community industry to purchase goods and services (for intermediate or final consumption) or raise capital in the best available conditions worldwide.

In the changing world economy, Europe itself is changing rapidly, presenting dangers but also great opportunities for the European Community.

The successful conclusion of accession negotiations with four of the EFTA countries will lead to the creation of an even more powerful industrial and trading Community.

Recent changes in Eastern Europe and the former Soviet Union have major implications for the Community, creating **new opportunities to expand the overall volume of trade** in the region and challenging the Community, and Community business, to play an active role in supporting these countries in their progress towards full market economies so that they achieve their full potential. The European Council meeting in Copenhagen laid down the parameters for developing future relations.

The integration of the associated countries of Central and Eastern Europe with the Community resulting from the decisions of the Copenhagen Summit will further reinforce the Continent's trading capacity and its competitiveness on world markets.

In the longer term, similar benefits and challenges for the Community can be expected from contributing actively to a smooth and gradual integration of the developing countries into the world economy.

6.4. Strategy

An open and comprehensive framework for trade and economic relations under internationally agreed rules, enforced multi-laterally, with strong coordination of policy-making in all areas beyond those rules, is the only recipe for maximizing growth in an **interdependent world.** But that recipe will only work if the Community economy regains a long-term competitive position on world markets.

The push for competitiveness and the search for a strong position in the global market depends on a long-term vision: 20 years, not two.

The open 'trade' system must be improved and extended to meet the challenge of global economic interdependence. In order to regain public confidence, it must be seen to respond to current concerns.

The Community must be seen to take full advantage of that system. Community institutions must respond more quickly to threats and opportunities. Community business must work harder at developing strong links to foreign firms and consumers.

We must avoid setting up international trade as either a panacea or a scapegoat for current ills. Strong export growth can ease necessary internal restructuring, but no action on the external front alone, however drastic, could resolve the current unemployment problem.

Community priorities must reflect structural change in world markets, both the long-term prospects of fast-growing regions such as Asia and the immense opportunities created by adjustment in Central and Eastern Europe and the Commonwealth of Independent States (CIS).

These latter opportunities must be seized as they represent not only large future markets but also will present opportunities to Community companies to improve their competitiveness on world markets. It will be necessary to push forward with the liberaliza-

tion of market access, and to develop the economic relationship in areas such as industrial cooperation, in order to maximize the benefits accruing to the Community and the associates from progressive economic integration.

However, the creation of new market opportunities in highly indebted countries will depend on the effective alleviation of the debt burden which strongly constrains these countries' capacity to import. The Community will work jointly with other partners in order to find a lasting and satisfactory solution to the debt problem.

6.5. Recommendations

(a) Reform the open market rules of the world economy

The Uruguay Round is an overdue first push towards the objective of strengthening GATT rules and extending them to reflect today's wider and more complex set of international economic relationships. We must reach a successful conclusion to the Round this year. Prospects for a favourable deal will not improve with time. Without a Uruguay Round agreement, the open trade system will come under sharp protectionist pressures: current Community trade flows as well as prospects for further growth will suffer.

In the remainder of this year and beyond, the Community's priorities are clear:

(i) Market-opening in both goods and services

The latest negotiations have produced progress in sectors where the Community is competitive, at least among major developed countries, and have laid the basis for further progress among all GATT participants.

Negotiations for accession to GATT by countries such as China and Russia will provide opportunities to secure clear commitments to continued market-opening.

The Community must make a positive contribution in order to unlock all these benefits.

123

Even if the Uruguay Round is concluded successfully, it is still based on a one-track approach to trade liberalization, dealing only with governmental obstacles to trade. It is important that multilateral rules are developed for the elimination of private conduct and structures which constitute obstacles to trade. Such obstacles are adequately dealt with in the Community through an active competition policy. However, the competition policies of its major trading partners are not geared similarly to the trade impeding effects of such private obstacles. Multilateral rules in this area should therefore re-establish a level playing field for Community companies and provide them with important additional trade opportunities.

(ii) Rules for a global economy

In a global economy, the range of policy areas where foreign decisions will affect Community companies is widening rapidly, while the scope for unilateral Community action to secure competitiveness gains at the expense of other economies is weakening. The strategy for all policy areas should be to seek common action with partners to meet Community objectives. This will require early action in a series of fields: some, such as intellectual property rules and investment, are covered in the Round, and others, such as environment and multilateral rules, which establish a level playing field.

(iii) A robust framework

This is essential to guarantee prompt action on outstanding issues. GATT is too loose a body to respond with the speed now essential in the face of new challenges, to integrate the range of policies that now interact, or to secure full compliance with increasingly complex multilateral rules. The trade impact of environment protection is one such issue which will have to be tackled immediately after the Round: the European Community wants to see a permanent environment committee in the new multilateral trade organization. A strengthened organization to manage the multilateral system is the essential guarantee that a Uruguay Round result will be of lasting value.

(iv) More harmonious rules

Special sectoral deals create intersectoral distortions which hamper economic growth in Europe. The Community is fighting in the Uruguay Round for an overall agreement that enables rules for textiles and clothing, agriculture and other sectors subject to GATT — recognized or covert trade restrictions, to be returned progressively to normal disciplines. The process can only be gradual, must bind all participants and must be set in the context of an overall strengthening of GATT rules as well as of the recognition of Community policies in the spheres affected. On this basis, it will be beneficial to Community producers as well as to the economy as a whole.

(v) Stronger rules

This is a necessary corollary to other action referred to above. Dumping and export subsidy remain threats to fair competition. GATT rules for preventing unfair competition must be strengthened. Safeguard action must also be made more effective and transparent, so that the Community can, as GATT foresees, take temporary action to allow industrial restructuring. Wherever possible, this action should be based on cooperative understanding with all involved rather than unilateral action.

(b) Streamline Community decision-making

Trade policy should be shifted towards the citizen (transparency, assessment of consumer interest) and towards greater Commission autonomy (subject to CFI control by the European Court). This will increase the confidence of Community producers that necessary decisions can be taken rapidly. But this will require not only legal powers but greatly increased Commission resources, and better cooperation from national administrations (e.g. statistical offices and customs). Key areas for resource increases include anti-dumping/anti-subsidy/safeguard action, the new policy instrument, the international dimension of competition policy, and action to prevent circumvention or fraudulent use of quotas under the Multifibre Agreement.

(c) Promote Community business strategies for the post-Round world

Uruguay Round market-opening measures will be implemented progressively. But it is not too early to focus debate on optimal strategies to generate Community gains (profit, market-share, new investments and business relationships) from the post-Round world market. This should look beyond the likely impact effect on world business confidence and anticipate the adjustment necessary to take account of new competitive situations in Community markets as well as overseas.

There is no need for Community duplication of Member State export promotion efforts. But at Community level, more effort is needed to produce Community-wide business organizations, and to develop Community organizations expert in regional rather than simply national export markets. Asia is a high priority for action in this regard. Positive developments in Latin America (the setting-up of NAFTA, Mercosur, etc.) open up increasing possibilities for action in this region as well.

The framework exists in embryo in the current web of bilateral agreements, and will be reinforced as those countries align themselves ever more closely on multilateral open market principles. The Community is both leading the cooperative effort of the G24 and developing, through TACIS and PHARE, its own instruments.

Broader business investment in these markets, whether bilaterally or in joint efforts with Asian or US business, is the element that must now be encouraged. Closer economic integration of this sort would accelerate the pace of reform to the East and reduce the examples of friction that inevitably result in sectors suffering structural overcapacity.

We should improve **coordination between export promotion and other policies** in order to increase export opportunities, particularly at the cutting edge of technological development. As policy cooperation becomes more extensive (for example on environment or biotechnology under the Community/Japan Declaration, or other-wise), the officials involved should be conscious of the scope for creating new forms of industrial cooperation or new markets for Community products.

The globalization of the economy raises the question of the adequacy of the current instruments of commercial policy. We should now be developing more positive tools of business and intergovernmental cooperation.

(d) Develop the relationship with Eastern Europe and the former Soviet Union

The Europe Agreements concluded with Poland, Hungary, the Czech and Slovak Republics, Bulgaria and Romania commit the parties to the creation of broadly based political and economic cooperation on the basis of a free trade area. In Copenhagen the European Council decided to accelerate the timetable for removing barriers to trade on the Community side, recognizing that greater market access was an essential support for the process of economic reform in these countries.

In addition to the framework for future trading relations, which has been established, it is necessary **to develop a broad and dynamic economic relationship,** by encouraging business and economic cooperation between Western and Eastern Europe and by providing a framework for cooperation, including the application of common competition rules in the wider European area. One of the benefits of closer economic cooperation should be to reduce trade frictions by easing adjustment and minimizing recourse to trade defence instruments.

The Community is currently negotiating partnership and cooperation agreements with Russia and a number of other newly independent States, and defining the rules which will govern the future trading relationship and which will form a key element of these agreements. The Community has indicated its willingness to envisage establishing a free trade area with Russia in the future.

Finally, the Community must pursue the process of multilateral opening and integration among TACIS and PHARE participants and support appropriate regional cooperation so that the old model of hub-and-spoke preferences can be avoided.

In order for the former centrally planned economies of Europe to be able to implement market-oriented reforms successfully, the Community will need to adopt an innovative approach that, besides market-opening and financial support, includes the necessary transfer of skills. **Cooperation between Community enterprises and newly privatized firms** can play a key role in this regard.

(e) Anchor the southern Mediterranean region into the European economy

The Mediterranean neighbours, from Morocco to Turkey, represent the southern part of the European Union's future economic and social environment. With a rapidly growing population of some 200 million people at present, these countries represent as important an export market potential as Eastern Europe.

It is of vital political and economic importance for the European Union to develop this relationship into a closer economic symbiosis.

The first steps towards a possible Euro-Mediterranean free trade area have already been made: free trade agreement with Israel (1989), customs union to be completed with Turkey by 1995 and Cyprus, association agreement to be negotiated with Morocco in 1994, later with Tunisia and possibly with other countries of the region.

It is also expected that the successful outcome of the peace negotiations in the Middle East and the process of economic liberalization which is under way will boost the intraregional trade.

All these developments should, during the coming decade, lead to a substantial increase in entrepreneurial activity in the Mediterranean countries, marked by more direct investment, more joint ventures, more agreements of production sharing, and, in general, a much higher level of industrial and trading interaction.

These geo-strategic developments on Europe's southern flank are bound to have a positive impact on the European employment situation, thanks to the economic dynamics that will be generated in the Mediterranean basin.

For this potential to become a reality the Community must contribute actively to the process of economic and social transformation which has already started in these countries, towards more open, regionally integrated and efficient economies.

(f) Improve competitiveness

Trade and economic policies cannot substitute for the development by business both of saleable products and of the means to deliver them to world markets on time and at the cost and quality needed. As to social costs, the fear of so-called social dumping would be misplaced if it related to a belief that in certain countries the level of social protection is kept artificially low in order to gain a competitive advantage elsewhere. We should not accept too simple a picture of high-wage industrial countries and low-wage developing countries. Differences in worker wages alone can be misleading. It is true that modern technology spreads much faster and more easily than in the past to different areas of the world. But poorer education, lower skill levels, lower levels of capital investment overall and inadequate infrastructure can all offset the possible advantage to be derived from low wages.

This is not to say that the Community has no difficulty in competing with labour-abundant countries. But **European competitiveness is falling not principally because of the impact of international social cost differentials in some sectors, but because we ourselves suffer structural distortions in Europe.** In developing countries, more elaborate social protection becomes a generally held political objective as national income rises to a level where those objectives are attainable. In the long run, a major part of the solution will consist in helping these countries to set up the conditions necessary for the development of domestic demand and rise in the standard of living.

126

The search for greater competitiveness both by trade and other policies does not imply that social protection should be undermined in Europe or ignored abroad. We are rightly proud of our record in this respect, which compares with the best in the world, and we are right to remain committed to establishing European-wide standards for social protection wherever appropriate.

The Community and its Member States can take every opportunity to raise with the countries concerned the need to bring forward their own legal changes. We can encourage this by positive measures, for instance by providing legal advice or technical cooperation where required. These are legitimate objectives of development aid and economic cooperation. But trade policy is not an instrument for the achievement of those objectives.

We rightly object to unilateral action by others to impose on Europe their view of how the world should be run. The international organizations responsible for multilateral rules must themselves judge Community compliance with these rules. The same principle must apply to judging others' compliance.

There are **three fronts** on which to act:

(i) Inform better the current Community debates on social dumping, explaining why the Community wants multilateral rule-making and should not allow individual countries to set up as the unilateral judge of others' domestic laws or of others' compliance with international agreements;

(ii) Develop a positive Community economic cooperation policy to increase social standards worldwide but without introducing unilateral trade discrimination as a lever;

(iii) Prepare for the discussions that will be necessary, in the International Labour Organization and elsewhere, after the Uruguay Round, of how best to strengthen compliance with current and future agreements in the field of social policy.

(g) Pursue a balanced policy on preferential agreements

As worldwide levels of protection fall, the importance of trade preferences diminishes, except in the case of newcomers to the world market-economy open trading system.

Preferences remain an important signal of the Community's political commitment to one or other of its neighbours or partners, but should **be made compatible with the health and stability of the multilateral system.** Nor should special bilateral economic relationships be limited to trade preferences: economic integration cannot be achieved only through reduction of tariffs and non-tariff barriers, however. It also requires the elimination of distortions of competition resulting from anti-competitive behaviour or State aid.

(h) Delocalization

Increased direct investment is good for jobs, for reducing trade imbalances and trade frictions, for developing Europe's cultural understanding of other countries, and for the projection of Europe's identity among its trading partners. It is most useful as a stimulus to the world economy where trade barriers are low, so that increased international investment should go hand in hand with efforts towards further market-opening, in particular in the newly industrialized countries.

There are no Community restrictions on foreign investment, although some Member States continue to vet investment in certain sectors. We encourage investment, but also encourage inward investors to integrate fully in the European economy. We do not want so-called 'screwdriver' operations, nor are they likely to be an attractive formula in the long term for European-based operations, since we have high labour costs and a screwdriver operation depends on low labour costs. For us, the future lies in inward investment which is fully integrated in the local economy, with research, development, marketing and management functions located in Europe alongside manufacturing, sales and service. This indeed is the trend, not least because there has been a sharp rise in mergers and acquisitions as a proportion of overall foreign investment in Europe.

Little by little, foreign investment in Europe has come to be accepted by European citizens as the first step in closer cooperation between sectors in Europe and their counterparts in key markets overseas. The same is not yet true of European outward investment which has been criticized for over 30 years as a means of 'exporting jobs'. The argument maintains that outward investment simply deprives Europe of value-added activities, increases our imports and decreases our exports. This is not a correct analysis. **Over 80% of Community overseas investment goes to other members of the OECD. Less than 10% goes to the newly industrialized Asian countries and Latin America.** In some parts of the Community, the level of investment in low-salary countries is even lower: 4% of overseas French investment, for example, a figure that has changed very little over time. Industrialists who invest outside Europe tend to do so to supply markets other than their own, reimporting barely 10% of their total intracompany purchases from the low-salary countries where they have invested.

(i) Work multilaterally to minimize exchange-rate fluctuations

Coupled to macroeconomic imbalances and the resulting current account problems of major trading countries, exchange-rate fluctuations increase prevailing levels of uncertainty and increase trade friction, thus reducing business confidence and delaying recovery.

This is a problem which cannot be tackled by the Community in isolation but requires a multilateral solution in which there is **better coordination between the macroeconomic and structural policies** of major international economies and not only exchange-rate targeting. The Community can encourage this by building on its own internal policy coordination of economic policy through regular surveillance.

Recent developments within Europe have not made action on this front any less urgent. Community interests will only be given proper weight in world discussion of exchange-rate issues when we are seen by the rest of the world to be back on the course towards EMU.

(j) The international dimension of competition policy

Competition policy in most countries has traditionally been seen as a purely national prerogative. The Community was the first to practise a policy which tried to deal with the impact that distortions of competition had on trade. Originally only applied within the Community, this approach has been gradually extended to trade with the Community's main trading partners in Europe as well. Thus, competition policy has played a major role in furthering international trade and, in particular, the possibilities of our companies to export to other markets, hitherto closed by anti-competitive practices, State aids or public monopolies.

Not all the Community's main trading partners have followed a similar approach of applying their competition policies to open their markets to imports, however. Such policies are lacking in particular in a number of countries in East and South-East Asia, whose markets are closed not so much by tariffs and non-tariff barriers, but mainly by anti-competitive practices. The 'Keiretsu' in Japan and the closed distribution systems in several countries are but two important examples of this phenomenon.

It should be a Community priority to seek to establish rules governing these competition problems. Ideally such rules should be multilaterally agreed, in order to give them the broadest coverage possible. As indicatedabove, the present GATT Round does not deal with the issue, even though certain codes (in particular the TRIPS and Services Codes) include provisions on restrictive business practices. The Multilateral Trade Organization, created as part of the Round's package, should cover competition policy issues as part of its immediate agenda, focusing especially on restrictive business practices and cartels. The aim should certainly be to agree on minimum substantive rules, but more importantly to lay down procedures to ensure enforcement of these rules by each of the contracting parties. For it is only through their enforcement in individual cases that the positive market opening effects can be achieved.

The right of recourse to GATT panels should be strengthened, as should the effectiveness of their adjudications. Achieving effective rules of this kind will be difficult and time consuming but it is high time that the process began.

In the short term, therefore, the first step is to seek agreement on a system of mutual consultation and cooperation with competitive authorities elsewhere in order to forestall potential conflict. The Commission has concluded an administrative agreement with the antitrust authorities of the United States of America in order to limit such conflicts through a process of consultation, cooperation and coordination.

If the agreement, which is presently being reviewed by the Court of Justice, is upheld, it can form a model for other negotiations. Discussions to this end were already held with the Canadian authorities and other candidates could follow. As one of their main objectives is to limit conflicts in cases of enforcement, such agreements can only be concluded with authorities which actively enforce their competition rules.

III — EMPLOYMENT

Chapter 7

Adaptation of education and vocational training systems

7.1. Training — the catalyst of a changing society

There can be no doubt that education and training, in addition to their fundamental task of promoting the development of the individual and the values of citizenship, have a key role to play in stimulating growth and restoring competitiveness and a socially acceptable level of employment in the Community. However, it is essential to grasp the nature, extent and limits of this role. Given the economic and social problems they are facing today, which are cyclical in certain cases and essentially and more profoundly structural in others, **our societies are making many pressing and sometimes contradictory demands on education and training systems.** Education and training are expected to solve the problems of the competitiveness of businesses, the employment crisis and the tragedy of social exclusion and marginality —in a word, they are expected to help society to overcome its present difficulties and to control the profound changes which it is currently undergoing.

Certain of these demands and expectations are fully justified. Moreover, all other things being equal, it is the countries with the highest levels of general education and training (for example, Germany or Japan) which are the least affected by the problems of competitiveness and employment. However, education and training should not be seen as the sole solution to the most urgent questions. **It is** only within certain limits, and **in combination with measures in other areas** (industrial and trade policies, research policy etc.) **that they can help to solve immediate problems.** There is no doubt that they could play a significant part in the emergence of a new development model in the Community in the coming years. However, European systems of education and training will be able to do this only if they are suited to the task. Indeed, it is the place of education and training in the fabric of society and their links with all economic and social activity which must be re-examined. **In a society based far more on the production, transfer and sharing of knowledge than on trade in goods, access to theoretical and practical knowledge must necessarily play a major role.**

These adaptation measures will inevitably have to be implemented progressively, and their effects will be felt only with the passing of time. Nevertheless, by the extension of a certain number of steps taken by the Member States and the Community in recent years, well-planned education and training measures should still produce positive results in **three** areas: **combating unemployment by training young people and retraining staff made unemployed by rises in productivity as a result of technological progress; boosting growth by strengthening the competitiveness of businesses; developing a form of growth which produces more employment** by improved matching of general and specific skills to changes on the markets and to social needs. In order to determine with accuracy the shape and content of the measures needed, it is essential to diagnose the current state of education and training in the Community.

7.2. Opinion of the Member States

The contributions of the Member States highlight the dual role played by the system of vocational training:

(i) training is an **instrument of active labour market policy;** it adapts vocational skills to market needs and is therefore a key element in making the labour market more flexible; the training system plays a major role in combating unemployment, making it easier for young people to enter the labour market and promote the re-employment of the long-term unemployed;

(ii) investment in human resources is necessary in order to increase **competitiveness,** and especially in order to make it easier to assimilate and spread new technologies.

133

As far as labour market policies are concerned, the contributions of the Member States all point to the need to promote **continuing** training in various forms (sandwich and supplementary training, systems of rotation and training leave); several Member States believe that priority should be given to **preventive measures** for low-skilled people whose jobs are more likely to be under threat and to measures for integrating the unemployed and young people into the labour market.

The Member States agree on the need for **greater involvement of the private sector** in education and/or vocational training systems and in drawing up education and training policies in order to take account of market needs and local conditions. This could be done, for example, by encouraging businesses to become involved in education and training systems and to integrate continuing training into their strategic plans.

The following suggestions have been made for specific improvements to training systems:

(i) the transition from the education system to the world of work should be eased by **increasingly practical orientation of training** and by ensuring that students have achieved a higher minimum level before they leave the education system;

(ii) education could be rationalized by providing a shorter period of general education which is better tailored to market needs and by promoting vocational training as an alternative to university;

(iii) there is a need to **improve coordination** of the measures implemented by the various authorities and bodies with responsibilities in the areas of training and the labour market.

Under the Treaty on European Union, the Community is to concentrate on promoting cooperation between Member States and on supporting national strategies for improving the results and quality of training, establishing an open education area in the Community by greater recognition of qualifications, and developing Community programmes for giving a European dimension to training.

7.3. The diagnosis

The most important thing to remember is that the situation differs greatly from one Member State to another. In some of them, the standard of basic education is satisfactory while the quality of vocational training is inadequate; in others, it is the continuing training element which is weak and the basic training which is strong; then again, continuing training may be well-organized but initial training deficient.

A diagnosis of the current situation in the Community in this area provides a mixed picture of weaknesses and a certain number of strengths.

(a) Weaknesses

The major weaknesses of the education and training systems can be found in the most frequently voiced criticisms by industry, parents, social analysts etc. The first is the **relatively low level of training in the Community, and especially the fact that too many young people leave school without essential basic training.** In the Community, the proportion of people of normal school-leaving age who leave the education system with a secondary qualification is 42%, against 75% in the United States of America and 90% in Japan. The proportion of young people in any age bracket who are in higher education in the Community is, on average, 30%, as compared to 70% in the USA and 50% in Japan.

There is a direct connection between this problem and the problem of **the failure of education, which is a particularly important and increasingly widespread factor of marginalization and economic and social exclusion.** In the Community, 25 to 30% of young people, who are the victims of failure, leave the education system without the preparation they need to become properly integrated into working life. Many of them join the ranks of the young long-term unemployed.

As shown by the initially surprising combination of a high rate of unemployment and a lack of skills in various areas, the second area of weakness is the **persistently inade-**

quate development of systems and types of continuing training, the inequality of access to this kind of training, the limited possibilities in this area for people employed in SMEs etc. These weaknesses have produced the second substantial group of unemployed people against a background of ever increasing strides in knowledge and an ever shorter life for technologies and types of work organization.

While the problem of the suitability of skills concerns primarily low- and intermediate-level **skills, there is also a real lack of skills in a number of areas related to the applications of science and technology and the interaction between them and society:** information technologies; applications of bio-technologies; applications of regulations on the environment; combinations of technical and management skills, etc.

With a university system faced — as it has been since the beginning of the 1970s — with the challenge of absorbing a growing number of students while maintaining the quality of its teaching, and the marginalization of — and increasing disaffection with — vocational education, the most developed systems of education and training in the Member States of the Community are, to put it another way, becoming subject to ever increasing constraints. They are weighed down by a combination of new expectations (improving the level of initial training and the ability of individuals to adapt to occupational and social changes throughout their lives) and old tasks (socializing people and imparting to them the basic values of citizenship).

In addition to these features, which are present in varying but significant degrees in all Member States of the Community, there are a number of **weaknesses at the specifically European level: the lack of a genuine European market in skills and occupations; the lack of mutual transparency and the limited recognition of qualifications and skills at Community level; the lack of a genuine European area for open and distance learning.**

(b) Positive aspects

Nevertheless, there are also positive points and encouraging developments.

Accordingly, in recent years there have been a number of **important qualitative and quantitative steps forward** in most Member States: a general improvement in the population's level of training; an increase in the level of school enrolment; the recovery or development of investment in education; an increase in the number of teaching staff etc. **Reforms of university systems and education policies and structures — some of them major** — have been devised and implemented, the effects of which should be felt throughout the 1990s: growing involvement of the private sector; decentralization of the management of education systems; an increase in local and regional initiatives.

These measures have been accompanied by changes in attitudes which have led to a *rapprochement* (not always without its risks) **between education systems and industry,** with the representatives of education systems showing increasing awareness of the need to provide training which prepares students for the world of work, and the representatives of industry realizing the importance of general education, in addition to purely vocational knowledge, given the development of new forms of work organization and the decentralization of responsibilities.

The Member States and the Community should now adapt the European system of education and training by building on the measures referred to above and continuing and bolstering the efforts already made.

7.4. Elements of a reform of education and vocational training systems

(a) General objectives and broad lines

The main principle of the various types of measures to be taken should be to develop human resources throughout people's working lives, starting with basic education and working through initial training to continuing training. By giving general currency to best practice in the various Member States at these different stages, we will succeed in developing an education and training system of the quality we are seeking.

In order to combat unemployment among young people with no skills, the objective should be to develop systems and formulas which **provide sound adequate basic training and establish the link between school education and working life.** The basic skills which are essential for integration into society and working life include a mastery of basic knowledge (linguistic, scientific and other knowledge) and skills of a technological and social nature, that is to say the ability to develop and act in a complex and highly technological environment, characterized, in particular, by the importance of information technologies; the ability to communicate, make contacts and organize etc. These skills include, in particular, the fundamental ability to acquire new knowledge and new skills — **'to learn how to learn' throughout one's life.** People's careers will develop on the basis of the progressive extension of skills.

In order to ensure a smoother and more effective transition from education to working life, **formulas of apprenticeship and in-service training in businesses** which allow people to gain skills in the world of work **should be developed and systematized.** Alongside the normal apprenticeship schemes, considerable effort should be devoted to developing **initial vocational training** in special training centres as a possible alternative to university. **Shorter and more practically oriented forms of training** should be encouraged, but students should still be provided with enough general knowledge to ensure a sufficient degree of adaptability and to avoid excessive specialization.

In their efforts to devise and implement education and training measures which are able to stimulate growth and employment, the Community and the Member States must also take account of the fact that 80% of the European labour force of the year 2000 is already on the labour market. All measures must therefore necessarily be based on the **concept of developing, generalizing and systematizing lifelong learning and continuing training.** This means that education and training systems must be reworked in order to take account of the need — which is already growing and is set to grow even more in the future — for the **permanent recomposition and redevelopment of knowledge and know-how.** The establishment

of more flexible and more open systems of training and the development of individuals' ability to adapt will become increasingly important, both for businesses, so that they can make better use of the technological innovations they develop or acquire, and for individuals, a considerable proportion of whom may well have to change their line of work four or five times during their lives.

Education and training systems will have an important role to play in this process of adaptation. There is an evident shortage in the Community of certain highly-skilled technical personnel, such as people who are capable of maintaining flexible manufacturing systems or handling systems for monitoring emissions of pollutants in firms. In many high-tech disciplines, Europe cannot yet call on the requisite manpower to do top-level research. This problem can be overcome by a joint effort on the part of specialized training and higher education establishments. **Cooperation between universities and the business world** is another basic way of transmitting knowledge, a vector for innovation and a way of increasing productivity in developing and potentially job-creating sectors.

Universities must also be given the resources they need to play their particular role in developing lifelong learning and continuing training. In association with public and private partners at national and regional level, they can **promote lifelong education,** for example by measures for training instructors, retraining primary and secondary school teachers, retraining middle and senior management, etc.

In order for these measures to be as effective as possible, it is necessary to **anticipate skill needs correctly and in good time** by identifying the developing areas and the new economic and social functions to be fulfilled, as well as the skills required for them. Even if real-time adjustment is not possible (since a certain period of adaptation is inevitable), the organization of as much research as is necessary in this area and the introduction of observation instruments and of mechanisms for transferring the information collected to the education system should make it possible to minimize the gap between required and available skills.

In order to ensure the success of this process of adapting the system of education and training and to implement the measures set out above, **it will not just be a question of increasing the level of public funding assigned to this area nor will the same increase be appropriate in all cases. The task is rather to reorganize educational resources** in association with the employment services.

Generally speaking, **the private sector, and businesses in particular, should become more involved in the work of vocational training systems.** In order to facilitate this process, **appropriate incentives (of a fiscal and legal nature)** should be developed. **The training dimension should be integrated into the strategic plans of businesses.** Provision should also be made for a significant proportion of the funding allocated for the compensation for the unemployed to be reallocated for training measures. In order to ensure optimum overall use of funding, **it is essential to improve the coordination between public and private training opportunities.**

The public authorities, apart from their role of providing incentives and setting the general framework for the measures, **would be responsible for setting guidelines and giving clear instructions on the objectives to be achieved at the various levels.**

Moreover, the systems of education and, above all, vocational training, have developed over the past two decades against the background of life dominated by work. Given the steady rises in productivity and the concern to distribute work more equitably — but at a rate and in a manner which are not yet known — there will probably be a further reduction of working time and a readjustment of the balance between working time and training time. New possibilities are emerging for **linking new patterns of working time with the development of training;** these possibilities should be explored and exploited. Experiments in this area, based notably on agreements between the various parties in businesses, should be multiplied, assessed and, where appropriate, generalized.

(b) The specific means

(i) Action at Member-State level or concerted action

By concerted action at European level, possibly even in a Community framework and with the aid of Community instruments, Member States should use the instruments which they control in an effort to achieve the goals set out above. A key aspect should be the **development of genuine 'training policies' with the involvement of the public authorities, businesses and the social partners.** In order to ensure sufficient transparency at European level and to make it possible for Member States to draw on the experience gained in other Member States and to adapt their measures to those conducted elsewhere, the policies and strategies implemented should lead to **the regular publication** and large-scale distribution of **documents setting out objectives and providing descriptions and assessments.**

Particular attention should be paid to the continuing training of staff in SMEs, which account for a significant proportion of businesses in the Community and represent a potential for innovation which is by no means negligible. There can be no doubt that **regional and local authorities** have a particular role to play in this area by setting up mechanisms for promoting local forms of partnership in the area of continuing training and the retraining of workers.

The **fiscal instruments** available to Member States (the lowering of social contributions for businesses which organize training measures etc.) should also be used, since they place fewer restrictions on public budgets than does direct funding. **Systems of compensation for unemployment should be modified** and formulas developed for **reallocating part of this funding for training measures,** in particular for the long-term unemployed and for young people entering the labour market without skills.

It is important to set up **generalized and versatile systems of 'training credits' ('training vouchers')** which all young people would receive and could spend relatively freely throughout their working lives in order to obtain new knowledge and to update their skills. Such systems already exist in certain Member States, but are limited in their scope and target population. Formulas which are more ambitious and of broader scope should be examined and developed on the basis of the models which are best adapted to the various national cultures: statutory entitlement to 'training leave' with financial assistance from the State; incorporation of the right to training in collective agreements, etc. In this context, **possible ways of linking these formulas with measures for increasing flexibility in the conditions applicable to employment and for sharing working time** should be studied and tested.

On the basis of a partnership between universities, public authorities and businesses, systems of initial and continuing training should be set up in the areas corresponding to the technological and social skills required for developing functions and occupations (multidisciplinary types of training; training for work in an environment which makes intensive use of information technologies; compound, technical and management skills, etc.). One pivotal aspect should be the development of **training by the new technologies,** more particularly information technologies, with a view to enhancing the quality and diversity of basic education and training and introducing modular and interactive elements.

By extending and emulating the measures implemented in certain Member States, the countries of the Community should also adopt the provisions needed to **increase the flexibility of the various parts of education systems and the level of decentralization of management of education systems:** within certain limits, and account being taken of the risks of increasing inequalities in education and eroding its humanist and cultural vocation, it is also desirable to give greater choice to students and to stimulate competition between establishments of higher education.

(ii) Community action

The Community could and should take a certain number of specific steps to support and complement all these measures. These steps can be bracketed together in **three main groups.**

In an extension of existing programmes and regulations, and against the backdrop of the implementation of the guidelines for future education and training programmes, the first objective should be **to develop still further the European dimension of education:** to improve the quality of training and to foster innovation in education by increasing exchanges of experience and information on good practices and developing joint projects; to establish a genuine European area of — and market in — skills and training by increasing the transparency, and improving the mutual recognition, of qualifications and skills; to promote European-level mobility among teachers, students and other people undergoing training, that is to say physical mobility and the 'virtual' mobility made possible by the new technologies of communication; to develop common databases and knowledge on skills needs; to conduct comparative research on methodologies used and policies implemented; to improve the interoperability of systems of distance learning and to increase the level of standardization of the new decentralized multi-media training tools, etc.

In association with the measures taken at Community level in the areas of social and employment policy, and in concert with the Member States, the Community should *set in place a political framework for the medium and long-term measures for linking the systems of continuing training and training credits with measures for increasing flexibility and reducing working time.*

Generally speaking, the Community should **set firmly and clearly the essential requirements and the long-term objectives for measures and policies in this area** in order to make it easier to develop a new model for growth, competitiveness and employment in which education and training play a key role and to ensure essential equality of opportunity and the coherent development of the three dimensions of the European system of education and training (education, training and culture). One way of sending an important signal and creating added awareness in this area would be to announce and organise a 'European Year of Education' (perhaps in 1995).

Chapter 8

Turning growth into jobs

8.1. Introduction

The Community will need **both sustained economic growth** and a more **employment intensive** pattern of growth if it is to meet its employment and unemployment objectives.

This will require **changes in economic and social policies** and **changes in the employment environment** as expressed in the structure of labour market, taxation and social security **incentives.** This implies new relationships and new methods of participation between all those effecting, and affected by, the changes that are required.

Producing more jobs from whatever rates of economic growth the Community can achieve requires a **new solidarity** — between those with work and those without, as well as between those who earn their income from work and those who earn their income from investments.

At the same time, the Community needs to improve its **long-term competitiveness** and avoid overreacting to short-term changes in price competitiveness resulting from the vagaries of exchange-rate movements. It means both **investing in people** and developing an active policy of encouraging **new economic activity and employment growth** in domestic and internationally competitive sectors.

This chapter recognizes the need for **more efficient labour market** and associated policies. It also recognizes that the **market alone cannot solve** the employment, unemployment and associated social problems faced by the Community. There is a need to take full account of the **real costs of unemployment for both societies and economies** in developing fiscal as well as labour market and social policies.

This means significant changes, but it does not simply mean a deregulation of Europe's labour markets. Rather, it implies a **remodelled, rational and simplified system of regulation and incentives** which will promote

employment creation, without putting the burden of change on those already in a weak position in the labour market.

All Member States are suffering serious short-term unemployment problems. The scale of these problems should not divert the Community from the longer-term tasks, however. An end to recession will not bring an end to employment difficulties. Short-term concerns should be balanced against the **longer-term imperatives** of expanding employment opportunities and of ensuring that economic and social progress march in step.

The approach and proposals outlined in this chapter support the medium-term strategy of **'moving towards the 21st century'.** In order to achieve these objectives, and pursue the appropriate mix in terms of policy and delivery, it will be essential to engage the active participation of the widest possible range of economic and social actors at all levels. 'Bottom-up' initiatives need to be encouraged as much as possible. The social partners especially have a substantial responsibility and opportunity to **work together in new ways** to find new solutions, including at European level, through the machinery set up under the terms of the Social Protocol.

8.2. Member States' views

All the Member States agree in their contributions — albeit with certain nuances — on why unemployment is so high in the Community, their **diagnosis** being that unemployment and the inadequate level of job creation are due principally to **structural factors,** exacerbated by the effects of the current recession.

There is unanimous agreement on the fact that **labour markets do not work efficiently,** with a lack of flexibility — more particularly in terms of the organization of working time, pay and mobility — and an inadequate match of labour supply to the needs of the market, especially as regards workforce skills and qualifications. This rigidity is the root cause of what are relatively high labour costs, which have risen at a much greater rate in the Community than amoung our principal trading partners. As a result, firms are liable to make any necessary business adjustments by manipulating the labour factor, the tendency being for human labour to be substituted by more capital-intensive factors.

Social protection schemes have — in part at least — had a negative impact on employment in that they have, in the main, tended to protect people already in work, making their situation more secure and consolidating certain advantages. They have in effect proved to be an obstacle to the recruitment of job-seekers or of new entrants to the labour market. A number of Member States make reference here to a dual standard of treatment working to the detriment of the jobless.

Mention is also made of other factors which militate against jobs, such as the high level of non-wage costs, particularly in the form of statutory levies and charges, and insufficient motivation to work due to inappropriate social protection systems and employment services. Certain Member States also cite competition from low-wage countries as a contributory factor to the loss of jobs, particularly in labour-intensive or unskilled sectors.

Together with the broad agreement among the Member States on their diganosis of the situation, there is also a wide measure of agreement on what remedies should be adopted. There can certainly be no miracle cure, but there is a need for a **thoroughgoing reform of the labour market,** with the introduction of greater flexibility in the organization of work and the distribution of working time, reduced labour costs, a higher level of skills, and pro-active labour policies. There is also a good degree of convergence on the need to maintain social protection systems. Finally, reference is also made to giving priority to combating unemployment among young people and long-term unemployment, as well as social exclusion.

The introduction of more **flexibility** should centre on the way **work is organized,** for example by removing obstacles which make it more difficult or costly to employ part-time workers or workers on a fixed-dura-

tion contract, and gearing careers more closely to the individual, or facilitating forms of progressive retirement. As regards the **distribution of working time,** there are suggestions on calculating working time on an annual basis and on reducing working hours in a period of recession. Obstacles to mobility (whether sectoral, geographical or in-house) should also be eliminated. This increased flexibility should be reflected in collective bargaining rules and systems, to make them more appropriate to the specific situation of local markets and undertakings.

As regards ways of **reducing labour costs,** suggestions are made for gearing levels of pay to company performance and productivity as a way of encouraging the recruitment of young people, and as an alternative to laying people off in a period of recession. A number of Member States make a plea for pay restraint to reflect economic circumstances at a local, sectoral or more general level, as a means of enhancing competitiveness and containing inflation, and to boost jobs. However, some Member States caution that pay restraint should not result in demand contracting over-much.

Most of the **Member States** make reference to this subject in their contributions, suggesting various means of cutting social welfare contributions, more particularly by concentrating such cuts on unskilled jobs. Among the suggestions made for compensating for this loss of income, there are proposals for taxing polluting activities or products, energy or scarce natural resources, or encouraging private insurance schemes. The idea of introducing a 'green tax' receives a varied response, with some of the Member States having reservations about the effect of such taxes on international competitiveness.

To create more **jobs for young people,** there is a suggestion to introduce greater flexibility with regard to the minimum wage, reduced social welfare contributions or other contract terms, for example by introducing flexible forms of apprenticeship, training or practices.

The ideas put forward on **pro-active labour policies** centre on three main aspects. Some of the ideas concern the **employment services,** for example enhancing and refining the role of employment agencies and creating a better match between labour market supply and demand, by way of closer liaison with undertakings and with local markets, or by the establishment of private employment agencies. Most of the Member States believe that substantial employment prospects could be opened up by developing labour-intensive service activities (for instance, by introducing a greater degree of liberalization), and by introducing **new activities,** for example in the social and cultural fields, and in terms of health, the environment and the quality of life in general. Finally, many of the Member States call for an **examination of social protection systems** to ensure that they actually encourage people to work, for benefits to be more closely geared to the specific market situation, and for expenditure to be targeted more accurately to concentrate the effort on those in real need.

Many of the Member States suggest the introduction of a form of cost/benefit analysis for Community legislative proposals in the social field.

Finally, as regards the **instruments** needed to implement these major reforms, the Member States stress the need for social consensus and for a cooperative attitude on the part of all the parties concerned, with some of them proposing a search for consensus at Community level.

8.3. Scale and nature of the problem

(a) High recorded and hidden unemployment

Over the past three years, **recorded unemployment in the Community has risen sharply.** It now stands at almost 16 million people or around 10.5% of the registered workforce. **All Member States have been affected,** although levels of unemployment vary considerably between them.

It follows a period when unemployment had been falling with increased and stable economic growth. However, even after four to five years of steady economic growth at the end of the 1980s, when unemployment reached its lowest level for a decade, it was **still at 12 million or over 8% of the labour force,** and with only 60% of people of

working age in employment. One consequence was that, of the 10 million extra jobs created in this period, only three million were taken by the registered unemployed with the remainder taken by new entrants or re-entrants to the labour market.

(b) Low rate of employment

Europe's **employment rate** — the proportion of its population of working age that is in work — is the lowest of any industrialized part of the world. Moreover, it has fallen over the past two decades — from somewhat above 60% to somewhat below. In contrast, the employment rates in Japan and Scandinavia have remained consistently above 70%, and that of the United States of America — which started in 1970 at a similar level to the Community — has grown throughout two decades to reach its present level of 70%.

Divergences in employment-creation performance between the Community and other developed economies, and between Member States, are much greater than would be implied by differences in economic performance. Between 1970 and 1992, the US economy grew in real terms by 70% — somewhat less than Community growth of 81%. Yet employment in the USA rose by 49%, **compared with only 9% in the Community.** In Japan, where the economy grew by 173% from its 1970 level, employment grew by 25%.

In most European countries the proceeds of economic growth have mainly been **absorbed by those who remained in employment,** and there is a large pool of unemployed who have been excluded.

The Spanish economy is the most striking example. Between 1970 and 1992, the Spanish economy grew by 103%. But in 1992, employment was actually 0.3% less than it had been in 1970. Other EC economies also show **relatively low employment growth** compared with output. Over the 1970-92 period, the total growth in output and employment was, respectively: Germany, 70% and 11%; France, 77% and 6%; Italy, 85% and 18%; UK 51% and 3%.

While employment rates in the Community are broadly related to levels of development with southern States having rates of employment of around 50 to 55% — there is nevertheless a great deal of **variation between economies at similar levels of economic development.** Thus the Netherlands has a much higher rate of employment than Belgium, and Portugal a much higher rate than comparable southern economies.

(c) Changes in hours of work

When examining **changes in working hours,** and considering the potential of job creation in the Community, it is important to **draw a distinction** between the volume of work and the number of people in employment. A number of Member States have, to date, succeeded better than others in translating a given volume of work into jobs, both by reducing normal working hours by a variety of means and by increasing the number of part-time jobs.

The Netherlands has gone **much further** in this direction than other countries. In 1991, those in employment worked an average of only 33 hours a week as compared with 39 hours a week in the Community as a whole. In Denmark, the figure was **similarly low** at under 35 hours a week. In both cases, these figures reflect the relatively high proportion of people working part-time instead of full-time — 33% in the Netherlands and 23% in Denmark, higher than anywhere else in the Community.

Between 1983 and 1991, the longest period for which comparable data are available, the average hours worked per person per week declined by only 3% in the Community as a whole — by just over one hour. In the Netherlands, by contrast, the reduction was 13% — equivalent to each person working an average of five hours a week less in 1991 than only eight years earlier.

The reduction in hours worked in the Community over the 1980s is not substantial in most countries apart from the Netherlands. However, it seems that in northern Member States, except for the UK, it had an effect on the labour market over this period. The volume of work undertaken, in terms of the total number of hours worked, went up by only around 2% in Denmark and Belgium but, because of the reduction in average hours worked, the number of people in employment increased by 8%. In Germany,

the volume of work rose by 7% and the number of people employed by 12%. In the Netherlands, more than half of the rise in employment of 30% seems to be attributable to the fall in average working time.

Graph 1: **Contribution in hours worked to the growth of numbers employed 1983-91**

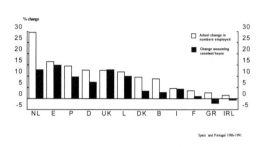

Spain and Portugal 1986-1991

The fact that average weekly hours of work fell between 1983 and 1991 in all Member States, except the UK, means that the available work was shared among more people.

The experience of the recent past is **very relevant** for future job-creation prospects and for the debate on distribution of work and income. In a real sense, such redistribution occurred over the 1980s in many Member States, though only in the Netherlands and perhaps Denmark was it a **deliberate part of labour market policy.** However, the issue is complex and job-creation potential is dependent on a number of social, fiscal and regulatory factors. Also, not all countries are well placed to do so, especially when their levels of income per head are lower — and therefore the income available to be shared along with work is correspondingly less.

(d) Difficulties facing particular groups

The unemployment rates of **young people** (those under 25) are double those of adults. They range, however, from less than 10% in Germany and Luxembourg to 20 to 30% in much of the South of the Community and in France and Ireland.

The incidence of **unemployment among women in the labour force** in the Community is significantly higher than among men. In May 1993, the unemployment rate for women averaged over 12% whereas for men it was around 9%.

Long-term unemployment has become endemic in the Community. Over half the unemployed have been unemployed for more than one year. It is a particular problem for young people in the South — where they account for 50% of the long-term unemployed. In the North, for men in particular, it is often more concentrated among unskilled middle-aged workers, who have lost their jobs through firm closures. In these areas, youth unemployment accounts for only 15 to 25% of the total.

8.4. Costs and causes of unemployment

The **economic and social costs of this unemployment** are enormous. They include not only the direct expenditure on providing social security support for the unemployed, but also the loss of tax revenue which the unemployed would pay out of income if they were working; the increased burden on social services; rising poverty, crime and ill-health; and the increasing levels of educational underachievement.

Graph 2 illustrates the **direct costs of unemployment** in each of the Member States. These costs comprise the amounts paid out in unemployment benefits and the income lost, i.e. the amounts that would be received from taxes and social contributions were those unemployed people in employment.

In Germany, for example, the figures suggest that unemployment will **cost the government** ECU 40 billion in 1993 — ECU 19 billion from benefit payments and ECU 21 billion from foregone income. The estimates suggest that unemployment throughout the Community will cost governments in excess of ECU 200 billion in 1993, which equates to the GDP of Belgium. These costs, it should be noted, do not take account of the wider social costs mentioned above.

Part of the present unemployment in the Community is a legacy of the **depressed rate of economic growth and rigidities in the labour market.**

Graph 2: **The cost of unemployment in the Member States**

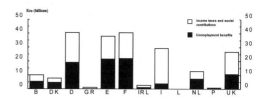

Expenditure on unemployment benefits and foregone revenue from income tax and social contributions is significant in most Member States. For the Community as a whole, the cost of the two elements is estimated at ECU 210 billion in 1993 — almost 4% of Community GDP. The true costs are even higher than this because of lower indirect taxes and all the social costs associated with unemployment.

Slow growth has not only meant low rates of employment creation, however. It has also **inhibited the process of structural economic adjustment.** Before 1973, the creation of new jobs in growth sectors was large enough to absorb those losing their jobs in agriculture and declining industries, and unemployment for the most part remained below 2 to 3%.

Since 1973, job creation in growth sectors has been much slower. The **shift in employment has been much more painful** due to the shortage of alternative employment opportunities, the limited possibilities for companies to shift labour from declining to expanding activities and the **significant impact of new technologies** in replacing labour, particularly in terms of manual and low-skill occupations.

Even if manufacturing employment began to increase again during the period of fast growth at the end of the 1980s, the secular tendency has been for employment in goods-producing industries, including agriculture, to decline. Employment in service-producing industries has increased, thereby **partially offsetting** losses elsewhere in the economy. There are signs that growth in service industries will no longer be possible on the levels previously achieved. To begin with, services now represent such a large share in all developed economies that income arising from productivity gains in goods-producing industries will not be sufficiently large to finance employment gains elsewhere in the economy. Further income gains will now largely have to come from productivity gains within the service sector itself. Such gains are indeed possible and are likely to arise from a combination of the **successful application of information technologies and new organizational methods,** and from competitive pressures on those service industries subject to international competition or those which represent a significant input to other firms.

A corollary to substantial restructuring in the service sector is that unemployment is also likely to affect those with a **higher level of educational attainment** and not just the poorly qualified, unskilled part of the labour force. In turn, this will create further challenges to containing unemployment.

At the same time, Member State economies and labour markets have been slow to cope with other structural changes. These have included the effects of the continued **industrialization of the less developed parts of the world** with the eventual relocation of activities. They also include the **effects of Community integration** with, on the one hand, the completion of the internal market leading to rationalization, restructuring and relocation and, on the other hand, the progressive convergence of richer and poorer Member States. All this means that the labour market too will have to adapt to changed circumstances.

The inflexibility of the regulatory framework is also an important factor. Labour markets are not flexible enough to ensure that optimum use is made of human resources. They are subject to restrictions affecting the organization of working time and part-time work and are hampered by barriers to mobility, be it geographical, structural or within a particular business.

The systems of — and rules governing — social protection and the protection of workers have protected primarily the existing labour force, in some cases making it more difficult for new entrants to obtain work. The result has been the creation of a dual labour market, which can be seen in particular in the high levels of unemployment. This duality is also present between temporary and permanent work and between part-time and full-time work.

Social and demographic changes have also been significant:

(i) the progressive **decline in the importance of traditional households** (husband, wife and children) as the main economic and social unit in society, and the increasing participation of women in the labour market;

(ii) **demographic changes** with declining birth-rates leading to an ageing population. While this has not, as yet, resulted in an ageing working population — since the effect is offset by the increasing participation of younger women — it will do so post-2000. Demographic changes are, however, bringing pressure on social security budgets;

(iii) a **shift in consumer and political preferences** away from the public provision of goods and services towards more private provision has brought a reduction in public sector activities, and hence employment, in many areas of the economy, including areas of potential employment growth.

8.5. The consequences of change

The overall effect of these various economic and social factors has been to:

(i) **increase the pace of change needed in economic and labour market structures** in order to maintain the Community's competitive economic performance, and thereby maintain employment and real income levels;

(ii) alter the composition of the Community's labour force in ways that require major **changes in labour market organization,** as well as in supporting activities — from training to childcare;

(iii) **limit the ability of governments to intervene** directly in the employment-creation process and oblige them to rely more on creating the right market conditions and providing appropriate incentives as a means of promoting employment.

8.6. The need for new policy responses

In the face of persistently high levels of unemployment in the Community, and clear evidence of its growing structural dimensions, some observers have advocated wholesale **labour market deregulation** — especially of employment protection legislation and wage determination — as the only way of bringing its labour markets into equilibrium.

Most Member States have gone somewhat in this direction — with an emphasis on encouraging wage moderation, increasing external labour market flexibility, and reducing the growth of social security expenditure. Many enterprises have followed the same route — with the emphasis on increasing internal flexibility and reducing fixed labour costs.

At the same time, government actions have reflected **wider concerns** — such as the need to maintain social and industrial peace, and to avoid creating further poverty among those groups already in the weakest position on the labour market.

The arguments are not just social or political. Evidence that **income distributions have worsened** in certain Member States provides grounds for caution. The Community cannot hope to address the consequences of the international relocation of many jobs through wage-price competition, and that many problems of price competitiveness are due more to the vagaries of exchange-rate movements. This argues for **long-term, strategic responses** rather than short-term ones.

However, where most of the Member States' responses have converged is that actions have generally been aimed more at reducing unemployment than at increasing employment. This has been reflected in the large number of employment and training schemes created for the unemployed, and in specific incentives to encourage the recruitment of target groups. Unfortunately, little has been done to **adapt the wider legal and financial environment and regimes** — which provide the main incentives in the labour market — to the new economic and social realities, or to **modify the institutional structures** which surround them.

In broad terms, the way in which taxes, and social contributions, are raised seems to take **little or no account of their potential effects on the level of employment**, still less of the potential effects they may have in, for example, discouraging firms from offering jobs to less skilled and lower paid workers.

Also, many **national fiscal systems are poorly adapted** to present and developing employment needs, and disincentives and administrative obstacles to flexible or variable patterns of work abound.

Attempts to reduce levels of job protection in order to introduce more flexibility into labour markets have often led to the **growth of two-tier labour markets** — those with secure permanent jobs and those with insecure temporary jobs.

Pressure to increase labour market flexibility without countervailing actions has moreover, often **reduced, rather than increased, the incentives for firms and individuals to invest in much needed training and retraining,** as has the lack of taxation encouragement to training.

Also, the range of special measures and incentives which help reintegrate the long-term unemployed, young people, women heads of household and returners, the disabled or disadvantaged groups in the labour market have become so numerous and complex that they overcomplicate the recruitment decisions of firms.

Failure to address these fundamental issues in developing responses is at the **heart of the Community's labour market difficulties.** It is important to find a better balance between combating unemployment and job creation, and to ensure we do not only rely on market forces to resolve the highly complex problems of achieving higher economic and employment performance. It is also important that we acknowledge that all of these factors together with the ineffective gearing of, and interaction between, labour market and other policies have inhibited the growth of more effective labour markets.

8.7. Proposals for action: Broad objectives

While the Commission considers that some further **reform of labour market regulation** is called for this has to be accompanied by **other tasks,** namely to:

(i) **raise levels of employment** and **not just lower levels of unemployment;**

(ii) **focus** not on the workings of the labour market, narrowly defined, but **on the broader employment environment,** paying particular attention to the effects of financial deterrents to employment creation embodied in taxation and related fiscal systems;

(iii) increase the Community's **investment in human resources,** on which long-term competitiveness ultimately depends.

That a **higher rate of employment** can be achieved for a given level of economic activity is amply demonstrated, not only by examples from outside the Community — USA, Japan and Scandinavia — but also by those within. Denmark has among the highest rates in the world.

The **diversity of results** demonstrates that there are multiple routes to follow. The challenge for the Community is to achieve **high employment** results in ways which are compatible with its general economic and social goals and criteria.

Fundamental **economic and social changes** are required, however, if income and employment opportunities are to be distributed more widely among those who wish or need to work. This is not based on a static vision of job and wealth creation. The objective must be continually to increase the stock of jobs and wealth by increasing competitiveness and value-added. However, the manner in which this process gets translated into new and additional employment opportunities is not preordained. Different societies **can and do make political and social choices which give different results.** If Europe is to set itself a goal of reducing unemployment, which in turn requires maximizing employment opportunities — due to the presence of hidden unemployment — then it will require a general **reform of the systems of incentives which affect employment in the labour market.** Indeed, there is no real alternative if a continued disenfranchisement of a significant minority of its citizens is to be avoided.

There will have to be four interdependent targets:

(i) to identify the changes which are taking place in the labour market, especially concerning part-time and flexible work and to achieve **a wider**

distribution of jobs and income. This includes changing the **pattern and level of working time** to reflect new work organization and job needs; **adapting the incidence of taxation** in ways that encourage more employment; and improving the **adaptability of the labour market** by adjusting the regulatory framework;

(ii) **to improve access to the labour market, especially in less developed regions and among disadvantaged social groups.** In particular, this means addressing **youth employment** problems; combating **long-term unemployment** and labour market **exclusion;** and promoting and improving our efforts towards **equal opportunities** between women and men. In this regard, public employment services, together with private agencies, would have a vital role to play in adopting a more proactive approach to job placement;

(iii) to **raise the stock of human capital** in ways that ensure that Community competitiveness is optimized. Particular attention is given to **continuous training and upgrading skills, basic and introductory training** and **new technology skills;**

(iv) to **anticipate and accelerate the development of new jobs and new activities,** particularly labour-intensive ones. This includes **exploiting the potential of SMEs and developing new jobs** in the environmental industries and services — notably, the care sector and the audiovisual, arts, cultural and tourism industries.

8.8. Specific actions

(a) Labour costs and job creation

There is evidence that there may be a mismatch between productivity and labour costs in the low skill part of the market.

Existing collective bargaining and related taxation and labour cost arrangements have the effect of causing gains from economic growth **to be absorbed mainly by those already in employment,** rather than creating more jobs. To change this would mean seeking political and social partner agreement on:

(i) keeping hourly wage increases below the growth of productivity;

(ii) accompanying measures to ensure, by a variety of different instruments, that economic growth is better translated into new jobs and a reduction of unemployment.

(b) Flexibility and job creation

Member States should seek to remove obstacles to **already changing** trends, preferences and demands of employees and employers regarding patterns and hours of working, which will **increase the number of jobs for given levels of output.** This cannot be pursued by a top-down, mandatory approach seeking to legislate for a shorter working week. It should rather be pursued by a range of appropriate means which could include:

(i) adjusting the legal framework so that those who are willing, and often keen, to **work shorter hours** do not suffer loss of social protection and poorer conditions of service;

(ii) negotiating the balance of social protection between part-time and full-time workers so as to **avoid major discontinuities,** and in order to make the decisions of both employees and employers about preferred working patterns more neutral;

(iii) minimizing **artificial financial incentives** for those of above-average incomes to work above-average hours;

(iv) encouraging the national cyclical trends towards a **shorter working week** per employee, where appropriate, while increasing utilization of capital equipment and ensuring competitiveness;

(v) developing measures which provide incentives to filling the new employment opportunities by people **from the unemployed register,** for example through types of job rotation schemes such as that initiated in Denmark;

(vi) **reductions** in annualized hours and a favourable examination of career, training, parental and sabbatical **leave breaks.**

(c) Taxation and incentives: Low-skill job creation

Member States should seek to address the present **disincentives to employing less skilled workers** by a range of possible measures, including:

(i) adjusting taxation systems as they affect employers, notably by making **non-wage employers' costs neutral or progressive,** rather than regressive as they generally are at the moment (see Graph 3), in order to encourage the provision of more jobs for the relatively less skilled by reducing their cost to employers (this approach concerns the adjustment and targeting of taxation incidence, not the level of revenue raised overall);

Graph 3: **Employer's social contributions at different wage levels**

Index (Contribution at average wage = 100)

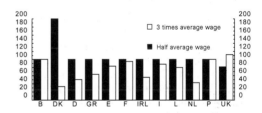

In most Member States, employers' social contributions are regressive — they are at a lower rate on high wages than on low wages. The only exceptions are Belgium and Portugal where the rate is the same at all wage levels and the UK where the rate increases as wages rise (but only slightly). In all other countries, apart from Denmark, although the rate is the same at half the average wage as at the average, it is lower for those on three times the average wage. In Denmark, contributions are highly regressive but the rate is very low (1% of wages as opposed to over 20% in most other Member States).

(ii) lowering the **relative cost of labour with respect to the other production factors** (capital, energy and non-energy inputs), for example by reducing the employers' social security contributions and increasing revenue through other means so as to neutralize the effects on the social protection of workers;

(iii) improving the prospects of labour market entry for the least competitive by restructuring national government income support schemes in ways which **enable income from work to be topped up with income from social**

147

security, **by developing integrated taxation and income support systems** with appropriate safeguards. The job generation potential of such measures might be maximized by their operation through a single government agency;

(iv) re-examining the ways in which the present interplay of taxation, regulation and related structures could be adapted to enable a **widening of the concept of work,** incorporating all forms of paid or partially paid work within a common framework encompassing the social economy, intermediate employment enterprises and the informal economy, thereby **enabling the re-entry into the formal labour market** of many citizens who have to work at the margins.

(d) SMEs, new activities and job creation

Member States should address **existing barriers to maximizing the job-creation potential** of SMEs and areas of new employment growth and activity by a range of measures aimed at anticipating and accelerating SME and new jobs growth.

(i) **In terms of SMEs,** these could include measures to:

- facilitate and maximize participation of SMEs in the common internal market by **strengthening their competitiveness** regarding such issues as their access to finance, to information sources, to the results of research and development, and to training, including support through the new European Social Fund Objective 4;

- identify and review those **financial, fiscal, administrative and legal constraints** which fall disproportionately on small and medium-sized firms in order to avoid such measures inhibiting the growth of employment. Small businesses are important as creators of new jobs but they have the **least capacity to pass on costs,** because they have little market power and the highest cost of coping with regulation, due to a lack of specialist staff;

- **an important part of SME development** and the generation of new jobs concerns the best uses and development of **women's work** in ways that improve job creation and fight inequality between women and men. Women's full integration in the labour market is expected to **create jobs in the provision of services and goods not yet integrated** in the market and currently being provided by either unpaid women's labour or paid informal women's labour;

(ii) In terms of **new jobs and activities** more generally, measures could include those which:

- **promote the development of new employment opportunities** through the use of public-private partnerships at all levels, and notably in potential growth areas such as environment, energy, transport, leisure, arts, sport and the care sector;

- encourage, while respecting existing competition policy, specific sectors, such as the **audiovisual industries,** which could have a strong impact in terms of inward investment, export revenue, and diverse types and levels of employment in a growing media/leisure market. **Pump-priming finance** can be important, particularly where high potential profit is balanced by high risk;

- exploit fully the employment potential represented by the environment sector. This covers not only the clean-up activity needed to deal with the legacies of the past, but the new monitoring, standard-setting and maintenance areas which now offer a challenge and opportunity to employment in science and technology. Public expenditure associated with EC programmes could **contribute strongly to job creation** related to supply of equipment, construction and contracting services, in particular in Objective 1 regions. This could average ECU 25 billion per annum 1993-2000, which by the end of the century could have created 100 000 permanent jobs and 200 000 jobs related to supply of equipment, construction and contracting services in these areas;

- encourage growth in the employment-intensive areas of the **care sector** and of the **provision of household services.** It is necessary to enhance the perceived value, and therefore encourage increased skills in such sectors;

- in support of all the above, **strengthen the role of local economic and employment development** through the decentralizing of public agency and government decision-making and expenditure, and support this by Community-wide inter-area cooperation designed to transfer know-how and experience;

- finally, progress on all of these fronts is dependent on ensuring that, at all levels, the social partners are encouraged to **develop new models of workplace relationships** in order to improve flexibility, and keep pace with the changing structures of production, in both large and small firms.

(e) Raising the stock of human capital

The **inadequacy of present education and training systems** in meeting the challenge of long-term competitiveness should be addressed by developing a range of measures, in the context of national structures, to:

(i) establish a **Community-wide guarantee** that no young persons can be unemployed under the age of 18: they should be guaranteed a place in the education and training system or in a linked work and training placement;

(ii) set progressive targets up to the year 2000 for the **elimination of basic illiteracy,** and lack of other basic skills, on the part of school-leavers;

(iii) raise the status of **initial vocational education and training,** and encourage the development of the entrepreneurial skills of young people and their

capacity to exploit the new technologies throughout appropriate work experience;

(iv) extend the **scope and range of existing apprenticeship schemes,** and/or other forms of linked work and training, in active cooperation with the social partners;

(v) improve the **coordinated provision of guidance and placement services,** notably at local level, to provide systematic advice to young people on career and job opportunities;

(vi) encourage universities and other higher education institutions to **collaborate more intensively with industry and commerce,** especially with a view to ensuring the transfer of innovation and technological breakthroughs through continuing training schemes to firms, especially small and medium-sized;

(vii) examine ways of **introducing tax incentives for firms and individuals** to invest in their continuing training, as an expression of public policy commitment to the development of life-long learning opportunities for adults;

(viii) the social partners should be encouraged to set up collective agreements, including at European level, **to extend access to, and participation in, continuing training** as an essential means of improving the motivation and quality of the workforce as a whole. The setting-up of company-based training plans, linked to company business plans, should be widely encouraged, drawing appropriately on the possibilities opened up by the new Objective 4 of the European Social Fund. A **strong emphasis should be placed on anticipative training** within companies so as to plan ahead for restructuring, and also new ways of mastering technological change. The dangers of an excessive

149

emphasis on automation producing a 'culture of no skills' and job displacement should be avoided, and experiments involving the development of human-centred technologies should be given priority and appropriate encouragement.

(f) Targeting specific groups

Member States have to ensure that additional jobs are most effectively made available to those in a **disadvantaged position in the labour market.** This was not achieved in the employment growth period of the second half of the 1980s, and the Community now faces the danger of **not only a dual labour market but also a dual society.** In order to address this threat to social cohesion, Member States are asked, firstly, to have regard to the reintegration potential of the proposals outlined earlier, in terms of the job-creation potential of changes in labour costs, flexibility, taxation and incentives, and, secondly, to consider improving specific integration and reintegration measures in ways which could include:

- **strengthening efforts to integrate or reintegrate the long-term unemployed and unemployed young people, by providing clearer stepping stones to the formal labour market,** and to find worthwhile alternatives to inactivity. This would include the introduction of minimum standards for Member States on those measures for which Community support is sought. Such standards could include:

  coherent links with the labour market;

  minimum training/qualification standards;

  independent counselling;

  adequate post-activity placement;

  equitable remuneration;

  full range of 'soft infrastructure' support (child-care, literacy, etc.);

- providing stronger support in terms of resources, devolved responsibilities, encouraging links to the private sector and employment services to the wide range of **intermediate labour market**

agencies (often voluntary sector, local and regional government) which have **demonstrated their ability** to play a strong role in providing effective stepping stones to the formal labour market;

- within this, examining ways in which the social economy can be encouraged, through tax exemptions, public/private partnerships, part work and part income support models, to **engage unemployed people, voluntarily, in actions** which close the gap between people **wishing to work and unmet social needs;**

- **strengthening equal opportunities policies for women and men in employment** by:

  (i) eliminating any potentially discriminatory fiscal and social protection policies which can discourage women's equal participation in the formal labour market;

  (ii) improving **existing career opportunities** for women, thereby generating demand for support and technical assistance services such as child-care and vocational training;

  (iii) ensuring that taxation and social security systems reflect the **fact that women and men may well act as individuals in seeking employment and reconciling family and working life.**

Within all the above efforts aimed at disadvantaged groups, it is important to strengthen and focus the **role of employment services.** Public employment services should be encouraged to **sharpen the guidance and placement services offered to the unemployed, targeting more effectively the individuals concerned at local level.** The provision of these services should be dovetailed with related but often separate vocational guidance units and monitored on a regular basis.

They should also be encouraged to establish **coordinated jobs needs audits at local level,** distilling the potential range of employment opportunities which exist but are unmet and making available such information in more imaginative ways. The results of these audits could be disseminated widely through appropriate national machinery as well as via EURES at European level.

Youthstart

In order to respond more effectively to the problems facing young people in the labour market, Member States will be invited to cooperate in establishing a voluntary **youth guarantee scheme throughout the Union,** to be known as Youthstart. Under this scheme, Member States should progressively take the necessary steps to ensure the availability of access to a recognized form of education or training, including apprenticeships or other forms of linked work and training, to all young people under the age of 18. Assistance to Member States to fulfil such an aim is available under the terms of **Objective 3 of the European Social Fund.** Special efforts should be targeted by Member States at those young people leaving school with **no diploma or basic qualifications.**

In the framework of Youthstart, opportunities should be provided to interested young people to take part in **voluntary transnational exchanges,** involving work experience and training in another Member State. Voluntary organizations and the social partners should be associated with such arrangements. Young people would be encouraged to develop their **vocational, personal, entrepreneurial and linguistic skills through gaining experience in projects involving environment protection, urban regeneration or restoration of the cultural heritage.** Support for innovative transnational action to underpin Youthstart will be provided under the 'Innovation' section of the European Social Fund, drawing also on the experience to date of the PETRA programme.

There is also a need to encourage **good practice** in temporary job agency activity. Empirical evidence suggests that **temporary work,** as actively operated in a number of Member States, can **lead to permanent job creation,** by helping to accumulate work experience and training or serve as a kind of probationary period. Also, many people wish to work under such arrangements. It is, however, essential that such instruments offer a path **towards permanent jobs rather than replacing them.**

8.9. Conclusions

Reducing unemployment necessarily requires **increased employment opportunities on an unprecedented scale.** Pro-active labour market policies will be central to such a strategy and will require a radical new look at the whole range of available instruments which can influence the employment environment, whether these be regulatory, fiscal or social security incentives. The vast bulk of these measures will be for individual Member States to decide upon in responding to their diverse national situations.

However, the Community can and must play an important supporting role by:

(i) providing a forum where **a common broad framework strategy** can be agreed, and by

(ii) underpinning national measures with **complementary Community action,** whether in the form of financial support through the European Social Fund (which represents 13% of all Member States' expenditure on active labour market policies at present) or through networking and other measures designed to **ensure the transfer of good practice and experience.**

The overall objective should be to encourage the development of national labour markets towards a **Community labour market.** This could produce a more skilled, flexible, mobile, linguistically able and culturally sophisticated workforce, able to exploit Europe's inherited advantages in the developing world markets.

Chapter 9

Statutory charges on labour

A coordinated Community strategy for rekindling growth and overcoming a structural crisis cannot disregard the weight and structure of statutory charges,[1] through which the equivalent of **40% of Community GDP** is channelled.

Between 1970 and 1991 statutory charges rose in the Community from 34 to 40% of GDP. Over the same period they remained stable in the United States of America, at slightly below 30%. In Japan, statutory charges have increased appreciably since 1980 but in 1991 stood at 31% of GDP, i.e. the same level as in the USA and a quarter lower than the average level recorded in the European Union.

Within the European Union there are variations between Member States. In a number of countries the overall level of statutory charges is close to, or in excess of, 45% of GDP. Such is the case in Denmark, the Netherlands, Belgium and France. The United Kingdom, by contrast, has stabilized its statutory charges since 1980 at a level that is markedly lower than the Community average.

The growing significance of statutory charges raises the question of whether such an increase, which is part the result of the slowdown in economic growth over the past 20 years compared with the previous period, is not itself becoming a cause of that slowdown in growth. This explains the determination of governments in most Member States to **stabilize or reduce statutory charges as a proportion of GDP.** But such policies for stabilizing statutory charges presuppose a long-term effort to control public expenditure and have frequently run foul of the priority need to reduce excessive public deficits.

It is also on account of **their structure** that statutory charges **have an impact on growth,** **competitiveness and employment.** For a firm, this structure partly determines recruitment and investment decisions because it alters the costs of the factors of production (labour, capital, energy, other scarce resources). Particularly where demand is hesitant, statutory charges which immediately increase production costs are felt more keenly than those imposed on products sold or on profits.

Table 1: **Changes in statutory charges**

(as % of GDP)

Country	1970	1980	1991
B	36.1	43.6	43.7
DK	40.5	44.8	47.1
D	35.7	40.7	40.5
GR	n.a.	30.7	39.7
E	n.a.	25.8	34.4 [1]
F	35.1	41.1	42.8
IRL	31.6	33.7	36.4
I	25.8	29.9	39.0
L	30.8	45.4	47.1
NL	37.4	44.3	46.3
P	n.a.	29.7	35.6
UK	37.2	34.8	34.4
EUR 10	34.4	37.3	39.6 [2]
EUR 12			39.6 [2]
USA	29.2	29.3	29.8
JAP	19.7	25.4	30.9

[1] 1990.
[2] Task Force estimates.
Source: OECD.

An analysis must therefore be made of whether the structures of the tax systems, which vary very widely from one Member State to another, could not gradually be adapted to make them less prejudicial to labour. This would involve **reducing non-wage labour costs,** i.e. the statutory charges (taxes and social security contributions of employers and employees) imposed on labour. To be more effective, this reduc-

[1] The sum of taxes and obligatory social secury contributions.

tion in the statutory charges which are pushing up the cost of labour would have to be coordinated with active employment policies. It could form part of efforts to rekindle growth by restoring confidence (revival of demand), by stepping up investment — particularly non-physical investment (training, research) — and by improving the use of equipment through a rearrangement of working hours.

In order to maintain a high level of social protection and to meet the need to reduce budget deficits, the **easing of statutory charges, which would amount to 1% to 2% of GDP,** would largely be offset by a rise in other charges. These would consist particularly of charges on scarce natural resources and on energy — in order to reinforce environmental protection — and, where appropriate, of taxes on consumption and investment income.

Both for alleviating the charges on labour and for offsetting that through other tax bases, each Member State would adopt measures that would be appropriate to its own situation and consistent with the smooth functioning of the single market.

9.1. Views of the Member States

Most Member States refer to this topic in their contributions. They advocate a reduction in social security contributions, which would be achieved in various ways but particularly by concentrating those reductions on unskilled jobs. The suggestions put forward for offsetting the loss of revenue include the possibility of taxing polluting activities or products, energy or scarce natural resources, and promoting private insurance schemes. The possible introduction of 'green taxes' is not viewed uniformly, however, since some Member States have reservations about the impact of such taxes on international competitiveness.

9.2. Current structures and impact on employment

(a) Charges on labour

Charges directly imposed on labour are equivalent to 23.5% of Community GDP, i.e. **more than half the figure for statutory**

charges as a whole. Since 1970 these charges on labour have increased in the Community by 40% in real terms, twice as rapidly as in the USA.

In a number of Member States charges on labour are equivalent to more than 25% and, in some cases, almost 30% of GDP (the Netherlands, Belgium, Denmark, Germany and France).

Table 2: **Statutory charges on labour (approximation used: personal income taxes + social security contributions)**

(as % of GDP)

Country	1970	1991	Change 1970-91
B	19.6	29.5	9.9
DK	21.2	27.3	6.1
D	18.8	25.9	7.1
GR	10.1	16.5	6.4
E	8.2	20.4	12.2
F	16.9	25.4	8.5
IRL	8.3	17.8	9.5
I	12.7	23.6	10.9
L	16.2	25.0	8.8
NL	22.7	29.7	7.0
P	n.a.	16.0	n.a.
UK	16.7	16.7	0.0
EUR 12	16.6	23.5	6.9
USA	15.9	19.4	3.5
JAP	8.6	17.6	9.0

Source: OECD.

In the United Kingdom charges on labour have stabilized since 1980 at a level appreciably lower than the Community average and comparable with the current level in Japan.

If these tax and social security charges are expressed as a proportion not of GDP but of total labour costs, they account on average for **more than 40% of overall labour costs in the Community.** This level is much higher than in Japan (20%) and the USA (30%).

(b) Diversity of charges

In some Member States, the charges on labour consist primarily of income tax, with social security contributions playing only a minor or very minor role: such is the case in Denmark, the United Kingdom and Ireland.

Other Member States, by contrast, have very high social security contributions and a relatively low level of income tax. This is particularly the case in France and Greece.

Finally, on average in the Community, two thirds of compulsory social security contributions are borne by employers and one third by employees. In some Member States, however, such as Belgium and France, the employers' share is higher, accounting for some three quarters of total social security contributions; in the Netherlands, by contrast, employers' social security contributions account for less than half of total social security contributions.

Table 3: **Structure of statutory charges by major category (1991)**

(as % of GDP)

Country	Indirect	Direct [1]	Social security	Total
B	11	17	16	44
DK	17	29	1	47
D	11	13	16	40
GR	19	8	12	39
E	10	12	12	34
F	14	10	19	43
IRL	16	15	6	37
I	11	15	13	39
L	16	17	14	47
NL	11	17	18	46
P	15	11	10	36
UK	13	14	7	34
EUR 12	12	14	14	40
USA	5	16	9	30
JAP	5	17	9	31

Task Force estimates.
[1] Includes capital taxes.
Source: Eurostat and OECD.

(c) Impact on employment

The high level of non-wage labour costs is prejudicial to employment, exerting a dissuasive influence: it encourages the substitution of capital for labour and promotes the parallel economy; it particularly affects employment in SMEs; finally, it leads to relocation of investment or activities.

Faced with inadequate demand, firms attempt first and foremost to reduce their costs by laying off workers, labour being the adjustment variable. The rise in unemployment pushes up contributions and reduces the number of contributors; labour costs increase, and so forth; and a kind of vicious circle is established. A firm which, by laying off workers, reduces its own costs also passes on the cost of unemployment to other firms in industries which cannot lay off workers as easily, and they too see their situation deteriorate.

Highly labour-intensive firms, whose labour costs and social security budgets are relatively high, are then in turn compelled to lay off workers, to relocate or to resort to the underground economy, either directly or through subcontracting.

The size of the underground economy varies from country to country and according to the methods used to estimate it, but is probably equivalent to between 5% and over 20% of GNP. If the real figure were 10%, this would represent a loss of the order of 5% of GDP in statutory charges. In terms of jobs, the loss is even greater since, to the extent that these activities are carried out by those falsely registered as unemployed, they are an obstacle to bringing down unemployment.

A reduction in the charges on labour, accompanied by tighter controls against fraud, would be likely, if not to reincorporate some of those activities into the normal economy, at least to slow their growth.

(d) Special case of SMEs

Although 70% of private sector jobs are created in SMEs, it is these firms which are worst affected by administrative complexity and the high level of charges on labour: firstly, it would seem that, in the case of small firms, it is the high level of charges rather than net wages that triggers a psychological reaction against the idea of recruiting labour; secondly, however justified they may be, controls, forms and checks have to be multiplied by the number of administrative departments involved and are viewed as an additional labour cost. This extra burden seems all the more onerous when it has to be borne by someone not familiar with such matters and when it relates to only a small number of jobs.

Several types of tax measure could, therefore, assist SMEs:

— administrative tasks could be simplified: the creation, for all statutory charges, of a single department with which to correspond would be an improvement;

— SMEs that were not limited companies could opt for taxation at the relevant rate of corporation tax and not, as now, in accordance with income-tax scales;

— external financing could be promoted by eliminating double taxation of venture-capital companies;

— the survival of SMEs could be assured by preventing taxes levied on transfers of businesses — particularly cross-fronter transfers — from jeopardizing their existence.

9.3 Guidelines for reducing labour costs

(a) Objective

In order to help maintain employment and create new jobs without reducing wage levels, therefore, steps must be taken to reduce non-wage costs, particularly for less skilled labour. Unemployment is particularly high among unskilled workers. Furthermore, in most Member States non-wage costs bear relatively more heavily on those in low-paid employment.

The Member States should set themselves **the target of reducing non-wage labour costs by an amount equivalent to 1% to 2% of GDP;** this figure could vary according to the tax structures in the Member States.

(b) Implementation

The objective being to reduce labour costs, the reduction could differ from one Member State to another depending on the extent to which it is applied to employers' social security contributions and/or to employees' social security contributions and/or to taxes levied directly on wages.

Social security contributions themselves are sometimes divided up according to the various objectives involved: family, health, old age, unemployment.

In these cases, the reduction could relate primarily to contributions which finance expenditure normally pertaining to national solidarity: family allowances, the minimum old-age pension, serious illnesses, or long-term unemployment. In the case of schemes in which the benefits are more directly related to the contributions (e.g. retirement pensions), it is for each Member State to determine the respective proportions of compulsory and voluntary contributions to be paid under insurance schemes or savings arrangements.

Furthermore, the reduction of statutory charges on labour should apply as a priority to the **lowest earnings.** This would make it possible to limit the budgetary cost of the measure per job saved or created while responding to the scale of unemployment among the least skilled workers.

The flexibility of work should also be encouraged

Experience in some Member States suggests that more flexible organization of work would stimulate job creation. The promotion of more flexible working arrangements could be backed up by reductions in the statutory charges currently imposed on such arrangements.

With regard to services, whether market services or otherwise, which are in contact with the public, an adjustment of working time accompanied by tax incentives would make it possible to increase employment, use equipment more intensively (longer opening hours), and meet a demand (more practical opening hours, longer free time).

The reductions could also be specially targeted on the **creation of new jobs** and the **recruitment of young people.**

But it is clear that if measures to bring down statutory charges substantially are to be effective, **they must be simple.** While it may appear desirable to make certain tax advantages conditional upon the taking of action consistent with the objectives of active employment policies, it is important to avoid schemes which cannot work well because of their complexity.

(c) Effect on employment

The results of several econometric models (see annexed table) confirm that reductions in social security charges offset by an increase in other charges produce a significant positive effect on employment. The most favourable results are observed when the reduction in employers' social security contributions is targeted on categories of workers with a low level of skills and if a tax on CO_2 energy is introduced rather than VAT being increased. On a favourable hypothesis, these models show that if employers' social security contributions are reduced by 1% of GDP, **the unemployment rate falls by 2.5% over four years.**

9.4. Possible compensatory measures

In view of the need to keep budget deficits as small as possible, compensatory measures should be introduced to offset the reductions in statutory charges designed to reduce labour costs.

The reduction in social security contributions could be partly financed by the contributions of persons for which jobs had been created, by the reduction in unemployment benefits resulting from an increase in employment, and by tighter control of public expenditure to make it more efficient.

But in most cases, **compensatory measures in the form of taxation** will be necessary to ensure the tax neutrality of the reductions made. From the various possibilities, measures should be chosen which do not have an adverse effect on the competitiveness of Community industry.

Of course, a detailed study should be made of the effects and the combination of these different possibilities.

(a) Environmental taxes

Environmental taxes, charged for example on the use of limited natural resources and energy, may be envisaged.

The CO_2/energy tax proposed by the Commission in 1992 could raise an amount of revenue equivalent to some 1% of GDP; the other possibilities include taxes on polluting or energy-intensive equipment, some of which would have the advantage of internalizing costs for the environment. In all these cases, predictability and tax neutrality should be assured so as not to handicap industries exposed to international competition, and appropriate **tax incentives** should be studied.

An increase in excise duties on energy products may also form part of a policy of environmental protection enjoying fairly broad popular support. One option to be set alongside the introduction of a tax on CO_2 would be to extend the existing excise duties charged on mineral oils to other energy products (natural gas, coal, electricity), which are also responsible for environmental damage.

According to various studies, carried out both by the Commission departments and in a number of Member States, a transfer of social security charges worth some 1% of GDP to a CO_2/energy tax in the region of USD 10 a barrel would have beneficial effects not only on the environment but also on the use of CO_2.

(b) Taxes on consumption

An increase in excise duties on tobacco and alcohol provides a source of additional budget revenue and a means of preventing widespread social problems, and can help the social security budgets to make savings (by reducing the need to treat cancer and alcoholism).

Since VAT has very little influence on international competitiveness (it can be deducted on exportation) the idea of a social VAT has been mooted.

It is considered in some quarters that **VAT** could be raised to offset the reduction in social security charges. In theory, the increase in VAT accompanied by a reduction in social security charges could enhance business competitiveness in the Community. Moreover, the system of minimum rates in force in the Community authorizes Member States to raise their rates of VAT. Nevertheless, any increase in VAT and therefore in prices is bound to inhibit consumption and may have economic drawbacks. The question therefore deserves thorough examination in each case. In addition, within the Community, it would be necessary to ensure that disorderly increases in VAT, in particular in the countries where the standard rate of VAT is already high, did not create distortions of competition or call into question the approximation of rates carried out for the entry into force of the single market. If the Member States wish VAT to be increased, it would be better to consider making the change at Community level, in particular by raising the common minimum rate of 15%. For, if the approximation of rates embarked upon in recent years in the Community were to be abandoned, the establishment in 1997 of the definitive VAT arrangements (payment of VAT in the country of origin) would be threatened.

(c) Other taxes

Of the other possibilities, it is necessary to mention measures concerning the taxation of capital.

Without standing in the way of investment, this would mean altering the structure of statutory charges on the different factors of production (labour, capital, scarce natural resources) so as to favour employment instead of discouraging it.

A tax on the income from financial capital which the Commission has been advocating since 1989 would also have the advantage of making it more attractive to channel savings into productive investment and the creation of businesses.

9.5. Conclusion

A substantial reduction in non-wage labour costs (between 1 and 2 percentage points of GDP), particularly for the least-skilled workers, would play a key part in effectively combating unemployment and promoting job creation.

This easing of the burden of statutory charges, which would be introduced as part of active employment policies, would have to be offset by tax measures so as not to swell budget deficits.

Given the diversity of tax systems (taxes and social security contributions) in the European Union, it is impossible to identify a single method for shifting some of the statutory charges on labour onto other factors of production or onto consumption. However, possible compensatory tax measures include environmental taxes (taxation of CO_2 and excise duties on energy), excise duties on consumer products that are damaging to health, taxation of interest income applicable to all Community residents and, where appropriate and subject to certain conditions, an increase in VAT.

In order to ensure that these changes to the structures of statutory charges lead to a coordinated recovery of the European economies, the Member States must be aware of the importance of joint consultations and cooperation in this field.

157

Table 4: **General hypothesis: Reduction in employers' social security contributions with compensation via other statutory charges**

Models used			
(A) Elements of the model			
	Quest	Mimic	Hermes
Countries concerned: Period: Hypotheses:	EUR as a whole 7 years Generalized reduction (1% of GDP) (average reduction in rate of 10%). Reduction (1% of GDP) targeted on low wages (average reduction in rate of 40%)	Netherlands 10 years Generalized reduction (0.6% of GDP) Reduction limited to low wages (0.6% of GDP)	B, D, F, I, NL, UK 9 years Generalized reduction of 0.33% in 1993 to 1% in 2001
Compensatory measures	Increase in VAT Increase in income tax CO_2/energy tax of USD 10 per barrel	Energy tax based mainly on consumption	CO_2/energy tax

(B) Results of simulations in employment terms

Extent of new job creation: Percentage difference relative to reference situation at the end of the simulation period.

	Quest	Mimic	Hermes
Reduction in social security contributions and increase in VAT	0.0	—	—
Reduction in social security contributions and increase in income tax	0.7 [1]	—	—
Reduction in social security contributions and introduction of CO_2 tax	1.0 [1]	0.6 [3]	0.6
Differentiated reduction in social security contributions and introduction of CO_2 tax	2.2 [1,2]	1.0 [3]	—

Table revised on 15 December 1993 for the second edition of the White Paper.

NB: The variations in terms of the unemployment rate are not fully comparable between models because of the different ways in which the supply of labour is modelled.

[1] In terms of the fall in the unemployment rate, these figures correspond to − 0.7, − 0.9 and − 0.2 percentage points respectively.

[2] Assuming that the net budgetary resources generated by economic growth are re-invested in job creation, this figure would be 3% (or − 2.7 percentage points of unemployment).

[3] In terms of the fall in the unemployment rate, these figures correspond to − 0.3 and − 0.6 percentage points respectively.

IV — TOWARDS A NEW DEVELOPMENT MODEL

Chapter 10

Thoughts on a new development model for the Community

10.1. The structural links between environment and employment

(a) The inefficient use of resources in the Community

The current development model in the Community is leading to a sub-optimal combination of two of its main resources, i.e. labour and nature. The model is characterized by an insufficient use of labour resources and an excessive use of natural resources, and results in a deterioration of the quality of life. The Community needs to analyse in which ways economic growth can be promoted in a sustainable way which contributes to higher intensity of employment and lower intensity of energy and natural resources consumption.

(i) The 'underuse' of labour resources

The use of labour resources has been persistently discouraged for several decades Although the growth in labour productivity has been a major element contributing to a continued increase in net income per head, a critical point seems to have been reached.

On the one hand, the substitution of labour by capital has been accompanied by a continued increase in the use of energy and raw material, leading to an over-exploitation of environmental resources.

On the other hand, business strategies are being driven by labour-saving considerations to an extent, where the productivity gain at the business level seems to be increasingly neutralized by an increase of costs in the sector. One of the clearest examples is unemployment, whereby labour is pushed out of business but at the expense of an increase in unemployment benefits.

The financial requirements of those social security arrangements increase the indirect labour costs further, intensifying the tendency towards labour saving. This mechanism has in addition led to a considerable loss in competitiveness on external markets as sophisticated technology is increasingly being installed in low-wage countries.

Many countries have tried to manage the problem through a reduction in social security provisions, however with limited success. The resulting increase in poverty and income disparities has led to social tensions and a decay of the quality of life in many urban centres.

The 'underuse' of labour resources has apparently not only a quantitative but also a qualitative nature. The organization of work in a standardized way, frequently in huge production units, has distanced the individual from the results of his work. The resulting loss in motivation and creativity, compared to what can be observed in small businesses and farms, is therefore likely also to have had an impact on the economic output as well as on the enjoyability of many jobs. Some businesses have successfully managed to recuperate the lost human capital by combining small, more or less independent production units in an efficient and flexible way.

(ii) The 'overuse' of environmental resources

The 'underuse' of labour is combined with an 'overuse' of environmental and natural resources. During the last two decades, and in particular since 1973, it has become increasingly clear that the latter resources are not available in unlimited amounts. Because the market prices do not incorporate sufficiently the limited availability of those natural resources and the environmental scarcities related to their consumption, their overuse has become systematic. This situation cannot be maintained any longer for different reasons:

(i) the clean-up of past damage requires mounting costs (e.g. polluted sites);

(ii) the reduced availability and quality of natural and environmental resources represents a burden to future genera-

161

tions and a reduced capacity for long term economic prosperity;

(iii) extrapolating current industrial consumption and production patterns to the entire world would require about 10 times the existing resources, which illustrates the scope for possible distribution tensions at global level if current tendencies are not curbed;

(iv) some forms of pollution are threatening not only local ecological systems but also the natural balance of the entire planet, e.g. climate change, ozone layer, bio-diversity.

These inefficiencies represent significant but hidden welfare losses. As current economic accounting does not reflect unpriced resources such as the environment, only partial estimates are available. It is, for example, generally recognized that the external cost of current transportation systems alone amount to at least 3 to 4% of GDP (environmental pollution, accidents, traffic jams). The more research intensifies, and the more is known about these hidden costs which someone ultimately has to bear, the more those estimates become a cause of concern.

Another inefficiency of the current development model concerns the external effects related to the use of fossil and nuclear energy. Although intensified technological progress is able to solve many problems, it is also true that energy can no longer be seen as an unlimited resource, particularly not if the external costs related to climate change, acidification, health risks, nuclear waste and risk are concerned. The relative position of energy in the new development model is therefore a key element to be considered.

A more attentive look at the way the Community uses its labour and environmental resources leads to some fundamental weaknesses in the incentive structure of the EC's economy as a result of public intervention (e.g. fiscal treatment of labour costs, transport infrastructure) as well as of market forces (environmental externalities). As a consequence, it is open to question whether an increasing part of the measured economic growth figures does not deal with illusionary instead of real economic progress

and whether many traditional economic concepts (e.g. GDP as traditionally conceived) may be losing their relevance for future policy design.

(b) The request for a new 'sustainable development' model

The inadequate use of available resources — too little labour, too much use of environmental resources — is clearly not in line with the preferences of society as they are revealed through the democratic system: people expect for themselves and for their children on the one hand more jobs and a stable income, but on the other also a higher quality of life. The latter element is reflected through an increasing demand for enjoyable jobs and environmentally-friendly products and public goods.

Any new policy will have to contain substantive answers on how to reduce pollution and how to improve the quality of life in a broad sense. The former element concerns the reversing of the currently negative relationship between 'classical' economic growth and more pollution. People no longer see why the use of more packaging or the presence of more printed advertising material in their mail boxes contributes to higher economic growth figures, as is officially registered.

Improving the quality of life, on the other hand, not only concerns habitats and nature protection, but also the amenity of the landscape, better integration of new buildings and transport infrastructure into historical urban centres, or the availability of parks and other green zones in urban areas. In such a way, the quality of life of millions of people can be substantially improved.

A more adequate policy should therefore be able to offer society a better quality of life with a lower consumption intensity and as a consequence with a reduced stress on environmental resources. In this same context, the creation of more challenging jobs is to be situated, as well as the valorization of human capital in local networks, fostering individual responsibility and social participation. The new development model for the Community therefore has to address the inefficient use of available resources in a wide perspective, i.e. taking into consideration the overall quality of life of the citizen.

Some of these questions have a Community dimension. Indeed, the transition phase towards a more optimal economic model is easier to realize if several countries act together, as this minimizes costs and maximises results. Furthermore, many measures implicitly or explicitly concern sectoral policies as well as the steering of market forces within the internal market. This potential new role for the Community is now explicitly recognized by the Treaty as sustainable development has been incorporated as an overall Community objective.

(c) Clean technology is a key

A major element of the new development model will be to decouple future economic prosperity from environmental pollution and even to make the economic-ecological relationship a positive instead of a negative one. The key for doing this will ultimately lie in the creation of a new 'clean technology' base.

There are already important examples which show that bringing the environmental resources explicitly into the production function is able to make such a decoupling possible. The German and Japanese economic growth figures for the last two decades although being the most successful ones in the industrial world, were brought about with a negligible increase in energy consumption somewhile before a linear relationship was considered to be common sense. The driving force behind this basic change has been a high energy price which, also contrary to the usual expectations, did not hinder but rather encouraged economic growth.

Although economic models tend to see technological achievements as exogenous, it should be recognized that these are essentially the result of fundamental incentives originating from the public and private sectors. Moreover, it should be clearly stated that any technology is made by man and that in that respect continued investment in human capital is critical. Solving the current environmental problems is a major challenge in the coming years.

The new integrated technology, of which very likely only the tip of the iceberg has been seen, should result in a reduced need for new environmental resources through:

(i) improved 'nature productivity' of products: e.g. increased energy efficiency, less raw material-intensive products (lighter cars, etc.);

(ii) a longer product lifetime: making repair and control services more attractive, which are labour-intensive activities *par excellence;*

(iii) more reuse and recycling: use the same raw materials or spare parts far more frequently;

(iv) improved process technology: the production processes (and not the final consumers) generate the largest quantities of waste water, solid waste, etc.

The gradual implementation of the new clean technology will generate a continuous renewal of the capital stock of the Community and will need particular training requirements for the newly-qualified engineers and managers. The resulting integration of clean technologies by industry will become far more important than the current clean-up activities such as waste and waste water treatment, however important they are for the immediate future. The relative, and even the absolute, importance of those activities is expected to decline the more society comes closer to the sustainable development model.

The new clean technology is likely also to generate, apart from a substantially improved environment, considerable secondary benefits for the Community:

(i) in competitiveness terms, in a double perspective: the Community would improve the overall strength of the economy through optimal use of its resources and the prevention of costly clean-up operations, while a first-mover advantage can be exploited; the latter element is not to be underestimated as the new technology is not only a necessity in the industrial world but also in the NICs and LDCs;

(ii) in strategic terms: the enormous dependence of the Community on the rest of the world for its imports of energy and raw materials would be reduced and better managed; the savings made through avoided imports could be used to encourage sustainable development, in particular by transferring clean technology to LDCs;

(iii) the Community would show internationally how sustainable development can be translated into practice, would diminish its excessive use of primary resources, and would thereby soften considerably future distribution problems for scarce environmental and natural resources at global level.

10.2. Ways to facilitate the structural change

(a) The need for a strategic microeconomic policy

The decoupling of economic prosperity from environmental deterioration through the creation of a new clean technology base is unlikely to happen without an active and imaginative policy support. To that end, **existing policy instruments will have to be reoriented in so far as they encourage the inefficient use of resources in the Community.** Particular attention will have to be given to many regulations which have been gradually developed during the last few decades but which no longer serve objectives which belong to the new sustainable development model. On top of that, **market prices will have to internalize systematically all the external costs that they generate to society.** Such a review should end up in a set of clear signals and incentives to all economic agents and decision-makers.

The first key element of a strategic microeconomic policy concerns a significant reorientation and encouragement of basic research in areas of particular relevance to the model of sustainable development (renewable energy, recycling and new materials, biotechnology, etc.). This reorientation also concerns economic science and in particular the so-called area of green accounting, which is basically a systematic analysis and estimation of all external effects. In combining scientific and econ-

omic information, a better understanding of the problems and solutions concerning the use of natural resources and their relative importance will be obtained.

The second key element concerns the speeding up of the implementation of basic research results into marketable innovations. To that end, a consistent set of pragmatic incentives is to be developed to economic agents considering investments related to the new products and production processes, including new and innovative forms of work organization. This should create a 'virtuous' circle of confidence with consumers and investors concerning the societal project of a sustainable economic future.

(b) Policy instruments at macro-economic level

The set of incentives envisaged above concerns a gradual and systematic review of many policy instruments, of which several have a Community dimension. In this context, the following instruments merit particular attention:

(i) **Indirect taxes** on pollution are a powerful way to address hidden subsidies in so far as external costs are generated at the expense of the society as a whole. Therefore, market prices may have to be corrected to cover the environmental damage related to the use of particular products, e.g. energy sources according to their CO_2 content.

(ii) **Fiscal regulations,** and in particular tax deduction schemes, are a powerful way of encouraging sustainable economic activities (e.g. pre–market research on green innovations) but are currently having, in many cases, a negative environmental impact (e.g. generous tax deduction schemes for the use of private cars, real estate taxation favouring suburban development, etc.).

(iii) **The dynamics of the internal market** can be steered to generate optimal resource use in the Community: firstly, sound competition on a level playing field gives a higher chance of generating the necessary technological changes and renewal of capital stock; secondly, public procurement regulation could be explicitly curbed towards sustainable objectives; thirdly, the internal relocation of economic activities wil contribute to the most efficient exploitation of environmental resources inside the Community as well as to a reduction of the far too-high environmental pressure in some areas. The same argument applies, of course, to the enlargement of the Community.

(iv) **International trade and cooperation policy:** as environmental problems frequently have transfrontier and global aspects, they lead to more intensive international cooperation. In many cases, the involvement of Community ressources for dealing with foreign environmental problems are shown to be a cost-effective solution for environmental problems inside the Community (acidification, pollution of rivers, reduction of CO_2). This is equally true for structural problems in the area of growth and employment. In both cases, real and sustainable solutions have to take into consideration this international dimension, in particular concerning regions close to the Community, e.g. Central and Eastern Europe, the CIS and the Mediterranean basin.

(c) Policy instruments at sectoral level

Apart from the instruments which are to be situated at the macroeconomic level, the Community also disposes to some extent of instruments in particular sectoral areas, the importance of which is likely to grow the more the Community strives at the above-mentioned new economic model. The following sectors merit particular attention and have been explicitly addressed in the fifth environmental action programme:

(i) **Energy:** the way energy is consumed is at the centre of the new development model. In parallel to the liberalization of the internal energy market for electricity and gas, the Community will have to make strategic choices which until now have been sole Member State responsibilities. Those options in particular concern a vigorous development of demand-side management as

well as a diversification of supply towards environmentally-friendly energy sources. Important tools have been used in the past (e.g. Euratom) and need reorientation and strengthening.

(ii) **Transport:** the huge welfare losses mentioned in the previous section will have to be eliminated thorough revision of investment and planning in transport infrastructure (in particular in urban areas). Tax and subsidy instruments commonly used in the past could be substantially revised as well as zoning and urban planning conceptions.

(iii) **Agriculture:** the current review of the CAP reform leads to a reduction of the general price support which is compensated for by direct financial support for farmers and accompanied by other measures allowing for the remuneration of agricultural practices, favourable to the environment as well as by a fair remuneration of activities safeguarding hydro-geological balances (quality of drinking water, avoidance of soil erosion, etc.) or improving the amenity of the landscape. This tendency should be reinforced gradually in the years to come. In such a way, the current imbalances in environmental terms will increasingly be eliminated, while a new basis is being laid for sustainable activities and an improved quality of life in rural areas. In this respect, it is also important to evaluate, economically as well as environmentally, pilot projects being undertaken in several Member States, concerning the production of biofuels (biomasse, diester, bioethanol) particularly with a view to reaching environmentally-friendly energy scenarios.

(iv) **Industry:** a new set of business-minded environmental instruments is to be exploited and a start has already been made through eco-auditing, eco-labelling, voluntary agreements, liability schemes, etc. Some of those instruments will create new job opportunities, particularly in environmental services

(d) Short-term policy recommendations

If it is recognized that the current recession has a dimension beyond the business cycle, preparation for the long-term project needs to start now. This implies not only a systematic reorientation of public policy according to the lines sketched out above, but also the design of anti-cyclical policy measures which could at the same time contribute to the objectives of the sustainable development model.

A basic recommendation concerns the prevention of further environmental degradation through the creation of an 'environmental infrastructure'. Notwithstanding the gradual development of clean technology, in the short and medium term clean-up activities are likely to remain significant, and should even substantially grow in the immediate future. It concerns a considerable backlog of investments in waste recycling equipment (compare over-supply of waste paper), in waste incinerators (incorporating best available technology standards), in waste water treatment equipment.

Many of these activities concern construction activities and are likely to mobilize a significant number of jobs in the short term, while the financing should be provided for by levies and charges in conformity with the 'polluter pays' principle foreseen in the Treaty. The public expenditure and the employment generating capacity can be the more important insofar as the basic infrastructure is still to be built, for example, water sewerage networks.

The same employment-generating possibility applies to the build-up of a higher capacity in the field of collective transportation systems, which is capable of improving substantially the quality of life of millions of people living in urban agglomerations.

Queries also reveal that a considerable demand and an explicit willingness to pay exists for the creation of enjoyable and environmentally friendly projects at the local level, including the creation of parks, walking or jogging and cycling circuits.

The field of energy use has been indicated several times as one of the key areas of the new economic development model. In particular in households, efficiency standards in energy use can be substantially improved — indicators frequently indicate 40 to 50% — provided appropriate investments are being undertaken in the area of housing (double/triple glazing, roof insulation, best available technologies (BAT) boilers). A considerable amount of jobs can be created in this context, provided sufficient incentives are being developed.

Finally, if the double challenge of unemployment/environmental pollution is to be addressed, a swap can be envisaged between reducing labour costs through increased pollution charges. One particular concrete Commission proposal, which fits completely with the perspective of long term structural change, concerns the carbon/energy tax: external costs related to energy use are being addressed, while the substantial revenue (approximately 1% of GDP) can be used as a first step to accommodate high wage costs by employers.

An important dimension of the proposal concerns the widely advocated shift towards a more intensive use of indirect taxation, as well as a widening and balancing of the tax base on energy products. In the Community these proposals enjoy popular support: about 60 % of European citizens are in favour of such a tax.

10.3. Conclusions

The nature of the structural change the Community is going through needs to be recognized and adressed. It is important to develop a societal project for a higher quality of life in the Community, which can motivate people and hence can generate the required human energy:

(a) The serious economic and social problems the Community currently faces are the result of some fundamental inefficiencies: an 'underuse' of the quality and quantity of the labour force, combined with an 'overuse' of natural and environmental resources. Both elements are at the heart of the economic development model followed by the Community during the past few decades.

(d) The basic challenge of a new economic development model is to reverse the currently negative relationship between environmental conditions and the quality of life in general on the one hand, and economic prosperity on the other. In this respect, a widespread implementation of clean technology is a key aspect. It is to be stressed that much scientific knowledge is already available but is waiting for insertion into the economic system.

(c) The transition towards a new 'sustainable development' model requires the development of a consistent set of market incentives. The basic task will consist of a systematic review of existent macro and sectoral policies with as a basic guideline that market prices have to incorporate all external effects. Indeed, many policy decisions in the field of taxation, subsidization, competition, infrastructure, labour

organization, land use, urban planning, etc., were developed in a gradual way and on an *ad hoc* basis, or in view of long-term considerations which no longer fit the goal of sustainable development. The same applies even more to policies in the field of energy, transport, industry and agriculture, where several choices, made in the 1950s and 1960s, should be the subject of a review.

(d) Any short-term policy recommendation to overcome the current recession should make a first step in the policy reorientation mentioned above. Moreover, in the same long-term perspective, considerable employment opportunities can be created in environmental infrastructure, energy efficiency improvements, the creation of enjoyable natural areas and the clean-up of polluted zones.

European Commission

Growth, competitiveness, employment — The challenges and ways forward into the 21st century (White Paper)

Luxembourg: Office for Official Publications of the European Communities

1994 — 167 pp. — 17.6 × 25.0 cm

ISBN 92-826-7423-1 (Parts A + B)

ISBN 92-826-7071-6 (Part C)

Price (excluding VAT) in Luxembourg: ECU 14 (Parts A + B)

ECU 10 (Part C)